THE TROUBLED, TRIUMPHANT CHURCH

[signature]

1 Cor. 9:22

THE TROUBLED, TRIUMPHANT CHURCH

*An Exposition
of First Corinthians*

Paige Patterson

Thomas Nelson Publishers
Nashville • Camden • New York

Published in Nashville, Tennessee, by Thomas Nelson, Inc. and distributed in Canada by Lawson Falle, Ltd., Cambridge, Ontario.

Printed in the United States of America.

Scripture references are from the Criswell Study Bible, King James Version of the Bible.

Library of Congress Cataloging in Publication Data

Patterson, Paige.
  The troubled, triumphant church.

  Bibliography: p. 323
  1. Bible. N.T. Corinthians, 1st—Commentaries.
I. Title.
BS2675.3.P35   1983   227'.207   83-21968
ISBN 0-8407-5867-7

Presiding over one of the great churches of Christendom, influencing the course of a multimillion-member denomination, and extending the influence of Christian truth to international audiences—all from the hallowed sanctuary of a Dallas pulpit—Dr. W. A. Criswell, who is beginning his fortieth year as the pastor of the First Baptist Church in Dallas, has demonstrated repeatedly the truth of the Scriptures in essence and in action. In a spirit and an oratorical splendor like Chrysostom, the golden-mouthed preacher of Antioch, Dr. Criswell has faithfully proclaimed the unsearchable riches of Christ for over fifty years. To this prophet of God, my own pastor and the Chancellor of the Criswell Center for Biblical Studies, I gratefully dedicate this volume.

CONTENTS

P R E F A C E

The Ephesian epistle declares that Jesus "loved the church and gave himself for it"(5:25). The church is the only organization that bears the imprimatur of the Lord. No reflection is intended upon the multitude of excellent parachurch organizations which are so influential in our society. Nevertheless, the truth remains that the church is still the entity that our Lord instituted and commissioned to do the work of Christ until He returns. Furthermore, in those most agonizing moments of life when decisions requiring godly counsel must be made, when death, disease, and other turmoil must be faced, it is the local church that must stand by to minister. Though gratitude to God is in order for the wonderful freedoms we enjoy for ministry through media channels, the local church above all remains essential in the midst of the trauma of life.

The church of the modern era is faced with imminent dangers. Recurring word of defections from ministerial ranks alerts the careful observer to strategic difficulties in local church leadership. The frequency of church divisions, the lack of unity and brotherhood in many congregations, and the apparent inability of thousands of local churches to grasp the opportunity of the moment and be faithful to the spiritual vision—all point to the perplexities and dangers which are a part of modern church life.

In light of both the importance and the dangers associated with the ministry of the local church today, 1 Corinthians is an ecclesiastical handbook for a modern era, offering priceless insights into the building of great lighthouses for the dissemination of the gospel. Although not every modern problem is addressed by Paul in this epistle, the principles necessary for the handling of every issue are embodied in the book. In many respects 1 Corinthians is a book more essential for the life of the church today than it was in its own era. Because of its relevance to the present distress, I have made an attempt to provide an exegesis of its message with particular emphasis upon its applicability to the present church milieu.

Those who have labored with me to make this monograph possible are many more than can here be recounted. Nevertheless, I wish to acknowledge especially my spouse, Dorothy, God's gift to me, who has provided the spirit and encouragement to continue the writing task, to say nothing of hours and hours of careful proofing of the manuscript. My fourteen-year-old son, Armour, has been my constant companion in athletic endeavor, thus providing diversion from the task when needed, and a wonderful fellowship of father and son, while Carmen, my daughter, has faithfully brought me hot tea and never ceased to encourage me with sweet notes left on desks at both home and office. Martha Seaton, my executive assistant, has painstakingly typed the manuscript, almost miraculously deciphering my hieroglyphics. My appreciation should also be extended to Dr. George B. Davis, dean of the undergraduate school of the Criswell Center for Biblical Studies, for his helpful insights on church discipline. Keith Ninomiya, Mike Komatsu, and Mark Taber have been my faithful student interns who have labored with the minutia of organization and administration to give me time to work on the book. Editor Larry Stone and President Sam Moore of Thomas Nelson have graciously encouraged me in more ways than I can say in this ministry of writing. To all of the above I express a special word of appreciation, reminding them that in a real sense the book is as much theirs as it is mine.

Paige Patterson
President's Office
Criswell Center for Biblical Studies
May, 1983

In the first Christian century the increasingly decadent Roman state found itself enamored with the mystique, wealth, and ostentation of the East. While Roman legions guaranteed safe passage on the handily constructed Roman roads and increasing maritime commercial routes, the hand of land jutting from the European continent out into the midst of the Mediterranean and dividing the Ionian from the Aegean Seas was destined to play an increasingly important role as the crossroads of the world where East and West met together. This isthmus of land incorporating Macedonia and Achaia had provided the intellectual stimulus for several generations in the ancient world. The Roman system of jurisprudence and the efficiency of the Roman legions had carved out a colonial empire unmatched heretofore even by Phillip of Macedon and his gifted, handsome son Alexander.

To the southwest of Athens, long the intellectual capital of Greece, there lay a narrow neck of land about ten kilometers in width separating the Gulf of Corinth from the Saronic Gulf. Immediately to the south of that land bridge, two kilometers from the Port of Lechaeum on the Gulf of Corinth and eight kilometers east of Cenchreae on the Saronic Gulf, lay the city of Corinth. In antiquity it was sometimes referred to as Corinthus Bimaris or Corinth Between the Seas. The fingers of land which represented southern Achaia were also called the Peloponnesus. Maritime traffic was always reluctant to brave the more open waters to the south of the Peloponnesus, especially at certain seasons of the year.

The cargoes, and eventually the sailing vessels themselves, were first transferred across the ten kilometers from one gulf to the other through the rigging of an elaborate contraption and later through a permanent canal. The canal was originally the dream of Demetrios, a ruler of Macedon at the beginning of the third century before Christ. Later Nero actually began the project but abandoned it. The dragway or *diolkos* saved two hundred miles of difficult sailing for mariners crossing from the Aegean to the Ionian Sea.

Corinth, the thriving capital of Achaia, presided in a watchful posture over this commerce. Originally a Greek city, Corinth had been destroyed by the marauding Romans under Mummius

Achaicus in 146 B.C. The city lay virtually in ruins, largely deserted until Julius Caesar founded it anew in 44 B.C.—a little over a century later. He called it Colonia Julia Corinthus. In 27 B.C. the city became the seat of the governor for the province of Achaia, and in A.D. 44 it was designated a Roman senatorial province.

The ancient Greek city of Corinth was noted more for its licentiousness than for its learning. It was sometimes called the City of Aphrodite. Aristophanes coined the word *korinthiazes-thai* to express a reprehensible form of behavior characterized by lust and debauchery. The historian Strabo told of a thousand temple prostitutes inhabiting the temple of Aphrodite on the Acrocorinth. That the city was the playground for the multifarious groups of sailors and other travelers who entered its gates is indicated by Hegesippius, who called it "the lounge of Greece," and by Aristeides, who referred to it as "a palace of Poseidon." The luxury, splendor, and lavish wealth of the city only increased its evil and further circulated its reputation as a city of vice. Corinth as Paul knew it was Roman Corinth, a cosmopolitan melting pot populated by Greeks, Asians, and Italians, the latter of whom constituted the ruling class.

The city of Corinth had founded the colony of Syracuse and also a major colony on the island of Corfu. Tradition recorded this seafaring location as the place from which the "Argo," Jason's famous ship in Greek lore, had embarked on its voyage to seek the Golden Fleece in the recesses of the Black Sea. Corinth of Paul's day was the site of the Isthmian games, which were second only to the Olympic games. Even if some modern commentators are correct in their avowal that the debauchery of the city was much less during the days of its Roman rule than in the days of its Greek jurisdiction, it is nonetheless true that the vices of the city were still characterized by rather extensive degradation despite the fact that the Temple of Aphrodite, located on the top of the 2,000-foot outcrop of rock which formed the Acropolis of Corinth, was no longer the scandalous center of licentiousness it had once been.

To this city the apostle Paul came, as is recorded in Acts 18. Upon arriving in the city, the apostle discovered Aquila and Priscilla, who had left Rome because of the edict of Claudius. Being of the same craft, they worked together, and Paul preached in the synagogue every Sabbath (Acts 18:4). Silas and Timothy joined the evangelistic effort shortly thereafter (Acts 18:5), and about the same time the Jews refused to allow Paul to teach any more in the synagogue—hence, he entered into Justus' house, which was joined to the synagogue (Acts 18:7).

Crispus, who was the chief ruler of the synagogue in Corinth, was saved, and Paul continued for a year and a half with his ministry in Corinth (Acts 16:8,11). While there a potentially serious incident occurred in which the matter of the freedom of the apostle to preach was brought before Gallio, the governor of Achaia and the brother of the famous Roman statesman and philosopher Seneca. Noted for kindness and gentleness, Gallio refused to make any judgment about Paul, since he maintained that Paul had been involved in no matter of wrong or lewdness. The incident concluded with the rambunctious Greeks' attacking Sosthenes (who became the chief ruler of the synagogue after Crispus had become a believer) before the *bema* or judgment seat. Shortly thereafter Paul departed for Ephesus (Acts 18:19). All indications pointed to a fruitful and effective ministry in Corinth.

Authorship

Unlike so many of the epistles of the New Testament, the authorship of 1 Corinthians has never been seriously questioned. Even the most liberal scholarship regards 1 Corinthians as clearly the work of the apostle Paul. Not only is the language and style Pauline, but also the theology conforms to that of the other epistles which may clearly be attributed to him. 1 and 2 Corinthians are both critically important to an understanding of the apostle Paul himself. No other writings of the apostle are so intimately personal, revealing the apostle's emotions, feelings, and personal encounters, as are the two Corinthian letters. Paul's extensive stay in Corinth, coupled with the intensity of love that he felt for the people of Achaia, provide a pathos in the Corinthian letters which marks them with distinction.

Recipients

The destination of 1 Corinthians was obviously Corinth, and the recipients of the letter were members of a largely Gentile church. Some were members of the local aristocracy, such as Crispus, a former ruler of the synagogue, and some were commercially adroit individuals, such as Stephanas and the apparently prosperous woman Chloe. In addition, Justus apparently was wealthy enough to own a home large enough to provide room for the Christian meetings next to the synagogue (Acts 18:7). However, for the most part the membership of the church was composed of those who were not "wise men after the flesh," nor were there many who were mighty or noble in the assembly (1:26).

Furthermore, some of the Corinthian congregation had belonged to the listing of the overtly rebellious and immoral enumerated in 1 Corinthians 6:9–10. Though formerly fornicators, idolators, adulterers, effeminate, abusers of themselves with mankind, thieves, covetous, drunkards, revilers, and extortioners, they had been washed, cleansed, and sanctified. In short, the constitution of the Corinthian congregation reflected the city itself in what was largely a classless church with a wide racial mixture, including people of varied moral and spiritual histories.

Date and Place

1 Corinthians was written from Ephesus. In order to establish the time of Paul's residency in Ephesus and thereby pinpoint the time of the writing of the epistle, it will be well to give a brief chronology of the approximately twenty years of Paul's ministry up to the time of the writing of 1 Corinthians:

The conversion of Saul of Tarsus—A.D. 35 or 36

First visit to Jerusalem—A.D. 39 (Gal. 1:18)

First missionary journey of Paul to Cyprus and Asia Minor—A.D. 46-47

Return to Antioch in fall of A.D. 48

Second visit to Jerusalem 14 years after his conversion— A.D. 49 (Gal. 2:1)

First visit to Corinth where Paul remained for a ministry of eighteen months' duration—A.D. 50

Third visit to Jerusalem by Pentecost—A.D. 52

Three-year ministry in Ephesus from December, A.D. 52, until Pentecost of A.D. 55

Return to Corinth for three months—A.D. 55
Arrest in Jerusalem—A.D. 56

The general success of Paul's ministry in Corinth apparently is surpassed only by his work in Ephesus. This may be deduced by a comparison of the relative amounts of time spent in various places during his missionary activities. In some respects, however, the visits to Corinth—particularly the three-month visit in A.D. 55—may have reflected the problematic nature of that congregation more than the success of Paul's mission. It does seem possible to conclude, based on the historical references to the various rulers provided by Luke in Acts, that Paul was in Ephesus from A.D. 52 until Pentecost of A.D. 55. Sometime during this period 1 Corinthians was written.

According to 2 Corinthians 13:1, Paul made a second brief visit to Corinth sometime before Pentecost, A.D. 55. This was an exceedingly painful experience involving the disciplinary matter (2 Cor. 2:1-6). Afterwards he wrote to the Corinthians a sorrowful letter (2 Cor. 2:4) which has not survived. Titus was the courier who carried this letter to Corinth and then returned with encouraging news from Macedonia. In relief, Paul then wrote 2 Corinthians sometime immediately prior to Pentecost, A.D. 55. If this reckoning is accurate, then it appears that 1 Corinthians must have been written sometime before Pentecost of A.D. 55. Enough time must be allowed for the writing of two more letters, the travel of Titus to Corinth, and his return to Ephesus. Probably 1 Corinthians was written in the summer of A.D. 54; whereas 2 Corinthians was not written until shortly before Pentecost, A.D. 55.

Authenticity, Style, and Language

The Pauline authorship of 1 Corinthians is almost universally accepted. Although modern critical scholars have a tendency to dissect the letters and expurgate certain segments as non-Pauline, the fact remains that there is no reason to question 1 Corinthians as to its genuineness.

In the Muratorian Canon, 1 and 2 Corinthians stand first, and 2 Corinthians is quoted in the writings of the early church fathers, such as Clement of Rome, Barnabas, *The Didache*, Ignatius, and Polycarp. Irenaeus was especially fond of the epistle, quoting from it some 60 times, while Clement of Alexander referred to it 130 times, and Tertullian saw fit to make reference to 1 Corinthians more than 400 times.

The language of the epistle is described significantly by Hans Conzelmann who writes, "The epistle displays the well-known characteristics of the language of Paul. Elements of the higher *koinē* (and the classical language) stand side by side with elements of colloquial speech. On the average we have (elevated) *koinē* combined with elements of the LXX."[1]

In fact, of thirty quotations of Old Testament sources, twenty-five are taken from the Septuagint, although some of these quotes show some marked alterations in the direction of conformity to the Hebrew text. The Old Testament is quoted more often in 1 Corinthians than in any other books except Romans and Hebrews, and only in Romans did Paul quote from more Old Testament books. In 1 Corinthians multiple quotes are taken from Isaiah, the Psalms, Deuteronomy, Genesis, and Exodus; whereas Numbers, Zechariah, Job, Jeremiah, Hosea, and Malachi are also represented.

The text of 1 Corinthians is retained in hundreds of sources, the best of which are p⁴⁶, the Chester Beaty papyrus which contains the entire epistle and dates easily to the late second or early third century, and a somewhat later papyrus, p¹¹, which probably is from the seventh century. In addition, the uncial texts, Sinaiticus and Vaticanus, both fourth century texts, contain 1 Corinthians and provide strong textual authentication.

Issues Addressed

Perhaps the most remarkable feature of 1 Corinthians is its timelessness. An epistle written in the middle of the first century might remain true theologically and yet be so far removed historically from conditions existing twenty centuries later as to make it historically interesting and theologically crucial, yet with very little applicability to present-day problems. A perusal of the epistle and the particular problems addressed demonstrates exactly the opposite. In fact, the contemporaneity of the epistle is startling. Nine major subjects are discussed.

---

[1]Hans Conzelmann, *A Commentary on the First Epistle to the Corinthians*, p. 5.

(1) Divisiveness in the church and undue elevation of popular leaders (chs. 1–4,9),

(2) Church discipline and Christian moral behavior (ch. 5),

(3) The litigious spirit as an indication of Corinthian carnality (ch. 6),

(4) The privileges and limitations of Christian liberty (chs. 8,10),

(5) Domestic circumstances such as marriage, divorce, and the gift of celibacy (ch. 7),

(6) The involvement of women in the life of the church (chs. 11,14),

(7) The proper approach to the Lord's Supper (ch. 11),

(8) The constructive use of spiritual gifts (chs. 12–14),

(9) The doctrine of the resurrection (ch. 15).

These subjects are uniquely applicable to the present era, even in those cases where the specific matter which engendered the discussion may belong more to history than to the present. An example of this is the discussion of Christian liberty (chs. 8 and 10), that focuses on the propriety of Corinthian Christians' eating meat that had been sacrificed to idols. The precise questions have altered across the centuries, but the basic principles involved in Paul's discussion are applicable to every similar situation in which liberty may be so easily changed into hurtful license.

Sporadically throughout Christian history the issue of spiritual gifts has divided churches and demanded explanations from its adherents. However, the modern Charismatic Movement has once again raised the old questions with new intensity and thus has returned the epistle of 1 Corinthians to center stage. The same could be said of the question of participation of women in the life of the church. Are there limitations to capacities in which women may serve? If so, were these limitations applicable only to churches in the first century, or are they still to be observed today?

At first, broaching the subject of church discipline, especially as it relates to an exemplary morality, may seem unimportant to the present circumstance. However, it is generally agreed that any legitimate spiritual renewal must be accompanied by a meaningful church membership. Exactly how such could even be contemplated without some reinstatement of the discipline demanded by the New Testament documents is almost impossible to say. Consequently, chapter 5, which has been in most commentaries relegated to a position of relative unimportance, assumes a renewed significance for today.

In every era leaders with abundant charisma and dedicated constituencies become the occasion for divisions within the body of Christ. Sometimes these divisions revolve also around the presence of heresies. One such heresy which periodically suggests itself is that of questioning any anticipated resurrection of the physical body in a future life. As a result, the discussions of Christian leadership, divisiveness within the body of Christ, and the resurrection of the dead are problems of modernity just as much as they were of antiquity. Consequently, the whole epistle of 1 Corinthians has increasing impact upon the constructive thinking of the church today.

Outline[2]

Introduction (1:1-9).
  I. Disorders Reported to Paul (1:10—6:20).
    A. Division at Corinth (1:10—4:21).
    B. Church Discipline (5:1-13).
    C. Judicial Entanglements (6:1-8).
    D. Immorality (6:9-20).
  II. Problems Raised by the Corinthians (7:1—10:33).
    A. Marriage (7:1-40).
    B. Meat Offered to Idols (8:1—10:33).
  III. More Disorders Reported to Paul (11:1—15:58).
    A. The Woman's Position and Covering (11:1-16).
    B. The Lord's Supper (11:17-34).
    C. Spiritual Gifts (12:1—14:40).
    D. Resurrection (15:1-58).
  IV. The Offering (16:1-9).

Conclusion (16:10-24).

---

[2]*Criswell Study Bible*, p. 1344.

The Foolishness
of God

1. Confirmation of the Called (1:1-9)
2. Contention in the Church (1:10-17)
3. Confidence in the Cross (1:18-25)
4. Coronation for the Christ (1:26-31)

The *response* to trouble, and not trouble itself, largely determines both the degree of satisfaction and the extent of conquest which may be experienced. Although Paul knew that the general tone of this epistle would be threatening and somber, the apostle was equally cognizant that the troublesome circumstances at Corinth might easily become stepping stones to revival. Consequently this missionary statesman embarked upon his epistolary journey by expressing general confidence in the genuineness of the Corinthian Christians. While he was aware of the contentions in the church, he also had total confidence in the message of the cross, especially if the Corinthians would recognize the lordship of Christ in their lives and congregation.

1. Confirmation of the Called (1:1-9)

The salutation divides itself naturally into an address to the Corinthians (vv. 1-3), thanksgiving for the Corinthians (vv. 4-

7), and an expression of confidence in the Corinthians (vv. 8–9).

1:1 The origin and legitimacy of Paul's apostleship was under attack at Corinth. The authenticity of that apostleship was defended in two ways. First, Paul wrote that he was called to apostleship and, second, that this call to be an apostle of Jesus had its genesis in the will of God. Two distinct words are frequently employed in the New Testament to convey the idea of "sent." One of these is a general term *pempō*. The other word, *apostellō*, from which "apostle" derives, employs the preposition *apo* (from), which suggests the importance of the sender and the reason for the sending of a legate.

Paul's call to this apostolate was a special calling to an exalted office. The idea of a call is used in at least two distinct senses in the New Testament. In Romans 8:28–30 the calling is obviously the wooing of the Holy Spirit in the heart of the lost, a call to salvation. But in Acts 13:2, the call of God to Paul and Barnabas is to a specific work. The call to apostleship, though doubtless a third kind of call, is in type similar to the call to a particular work Paul and Barnabas experienced in Antioch.

This call to special ministry will always be associated with the saving work of Christ Jesus as Paul here indicated. It will be accompanied by that same enduring perception that one is called according to the will of God. Never will this call constitute in any sense a contradiction of the word of God as revealed in Scripture. Through the ministry of God's Spirit, all believers may be led or directed to occupational endeavor, but there remains a unique sense in which God calls men for distinct ministries, just as He did Paul.

There is no good reason to assume that this "brother" Sosthenes was other than the Sosthenes of Acts 18:17, although no evidence exists to prove or disprove this identity. His role in Acts 18 was obviously not that of friend. Nevertheless, the prominence of one by this name as the ruler of the synagogue of the Jews in Corinth and a person with Paul in Ephesus whose identity would be of interest to the Corinthians suggests the obvious. While it is mere speculation, the Christian community may have ministered lovingly to the needs of Sosthenes after he was ill-treated by the Greeks in Corinth. Perhaps out of that display of love in the face of harassment, Sosthenes was converted.

In any case, he was called "the brother." This is another instance of the use of domestic metaphors which abound in the Bible. In the Old Testament, Jehovah is the husband of His wife Israel. God is our Father. We are children of God individually and the bride of Christ corporately. Therefore, we are brothers and sisters in Christ. While the term does not imply an actual biological relationship, it was employed to stress the commitments encompassed in spiritual relationships. That designation is particularly important for a church engaged in a feud.

1:2 The addressee is, in the first place, the church of God existing in Corinth. The use of the word "church" to denote a local assembly is especially strong here, not only because of the geographical designation "at Corinth," but also because the church in its universal expression is clearly denoted by the concluding phrase in the verse. Thus the concept of a universal, invisible church consisting of all true believers is certainly scriptural. Equally certain is the fact that the term "church" is used more that 90 percent of the time to refer to the local assembly.

"Church" (*ekklēsia*, Greek, from *kaleō*, meaning "call," and *ek*, meaning "out") is a word the New Testament writers adapted to their own purposes. In secular Greek it meant an "assembly duly summoned."[1] As such, the concept served the early Christians, ideally emphasizing the "assembly" of believers (Heb. 10:25) as well as the authority for such assemblies, which were literally the "called out" of God.

Not only were the Corinthians summoned by God, they were also "sanctified in Christ Jesus" and therefore "called saints." "Sanctified" is a perfect participle. The Greek perfect tense portrays a past act, the consequences of which continue. Thus the Corinthians were, at some previous date, sanctified, the result of which continued even to the present.

"Sanctified" (*hēgiasmenē*) and "saint" (*hagios*) have a common etymology. The basic meaning of both is "separation." When one is saved, he is immediately placed in Christ Jesus and hence "set

---

[1]Henry Liddell and Robert Scott, *A Greek-English Lexicon*, p. 509.

apart" or "separated" from the common, unregenerate population of the world. He is also qualified to be called a "saint" or "holy one," not on the basis of any native righteousness but based on his new position "in" Christ.

Secondarily, the epistle is addressed to all who call upon the name of Jesus in every place. Some commentators, such as Leon Morris, reject the idea that this designation anticipates a wider audience than that of the Corinthian church.[2] These commentators see the expression as an extended definition of "saints." Perhaps, Conzelmann is right, however, when he suggests that "we cannot argue that Paul surely could not write a greeting to all Christians. He is using a full-hearted expression in the sense of the idea of the universal church."[3]

If Conzelmann is correct, the inescapable conclusion is that Paul realized that the letter he was writing, though specific and pointed, would be of value to the churches wherever it was read.

To call upon the name of the Lord is an indication of two related truths. First, the early Christian community must have developed a confession of faith which epitomized their distinctive faith. This first Christian confession was simply, "Jesus is Lord" (*Iēsous kurios*). Those two brief words declared at once the persuasion that Jesus was very God and, further, that the confessors were acknowledging His authority in their own lives. Second, the phrase constituted the one essential of the faith wherever it was found: Jesus is Lord!

The phrase "both theirs and ours" has been the subject of numerous ingenious attempts to assign some meaning other than the obvious. Frederic Godet assesses these and finds them wanting, concluding that the two pronouns "depend on the word Lord" meant that Jesus was their Lord (of the Corinthians) and our Lord (of Paul and Sosthenes).[4]

1:3 The order of the greeting here is constant in the epistles.

[2]Leon Morris, *The First Epistle of Paul to the Corinthians*, p. 35.

[3]Conzelmann, *First Corinthians*, p. 23.

[4]Fredrich Godet, *Commentary on First Corinthians*, p. 47.

Grace must precede peace. The usual definition of grace as "unmerited favor" is only partially adequate. Though no definition can capture the full significance of the concept, let me suggest a more inclusive definition: God's grace includes His undeserved, gracious acts whereby He has chosen to provide existence, with all its benefits, and access to God, with all its blessings, to those who are the objects of His purpose.

Peace is not the absence of strife because peace is not relegated to the heavenly state, the locus of its ultimate manifestation. Rather peace (*eirēnē*) is the confidence of God's favor, even in the midst of the conflict. The source of both grace and peace is not left to the reader's imagination. There is neither grace nor peace except that which emanates from God and from the Lord Jesus Christ.

1:4 The general salutation having been offered, Paul moved next to a warm, personal word of thanksgiving for the Corinthian believers. An insight into Paul's prayer life is discernible here. Apparently, the expression of thanksgiving to God for the Corinthians was frequently voiced, as the word "always" would indicate. Specifically, the apostle was grateful for the grace of God which had been given to the Corinthian church in Christ.

Almost certainly there is a connection between the grace (*charis*) given to the Corinthians and the gifts (*charismata*) of verse 7, which they had in profusion. These gifts, which occupy a large segment of the discussion in 1 Corinthians, are "grace-gifts" as the word *charismati* indicates; i.e., they were not given on the basis of what was deserved but rather as a sovereign, gracious act of God. The particular expression of the grace of God for which Paul was so thankful apparently related to the rich spiritual gifts of the Corinthians.

1:5 That the Corinthians received especially gracious treatment from the Lord's hand is verified in verse 5. They are described as having been made rich. The verb is in the passive voice, showing that these were not native endowments but gifts which God had given.

Modern interest in spiritual gifts has led to numerous efforts to provide categories which ostensibly aid in analyzing these gifts. That more than one system emerges is not unfortunate, since Paul himself apparently grouped them several different ways. For example, the Corinthians are said to have been rich in all "utterance" and "knowledge." Perhaps Paul did not intend to place all of the grace gifts in these categories, but they do work nicely for many of the gifts. Under utterance (*logos*, "word"), for instance, would fall "discernment of spirits," "words of knowledge," "words of wisdom," and perhaps even "pastor."

1:6 The purpose of these gifts is now expressed. By their very presence the testimony of Christ was confirmed in the believers. "Confirmed" (*bebaioō*) means "to secure" or "to guarantee." These marvelous grace-gifts which were imparted to the Corinthian church were a testimony to the reality of their experience with Christ, gifts vouchsafed to them to serve as a guarantee of what God was doing among them.

1:7 The result of this richness of spiritual gifts among the Corinthian believers was that in exercising these gifts they "came behind" no one. Even though "come behind" is an accurate translation of the Greek *hustereō*, this rendering might suggest a comparison of relative gift-possessions among various churches. Since all the churches apparently are supplied adequately, a better translation might be "defective." In other words, the richness of the gifts in the church at Corinth left them defective in no gift.

These gifts were in use while the Corinthians were "waiting" for the "coming" of Christ. "Waiting" (*apodechomai*) literally means "to welcome" or "to receive." "Coming" (*apokalupsis*) is one of several terms with which the New Testament writers described the return of Christ at the end of the age. This one emphasizes the return of Christ as an unveiling. The Greek word *kaluptō* means "to veil, cover, hide or conceal," while the preposition *apo* indicates the removal of the covering. The proper Christian perspective is to exercise all the gifts God gives while living expectantly, ready to welcome the Lord Jesus at His revelation or unveiling.

1:8 A promise of God's continuing activity in behalf of the Corinthian church was the cause for Paul's confidence in the future. God who had confirmed them in the past (v. 6) would confirm them continually in the future. This He would do to the end that they would be blameless in day of Christ. "Blameless" trans-

lates *anenklētos*, which is actually a combination of two words—
kaleō, meaning "to call," and the preposition *en*, meaning "in."
The reference is to a charge or an accusation that is "called in."
Finally, an alpha privative (actually the prefix *an* in this case) is
added, which negates the whole idea. Therefore, the meaning is
"unchargeable" or "above accusation."

The day of Christ is a reference to the return of Christ in awesome judgment. At that time every true believer will be "unchargeable." This is not due to his character or behavior but to
his position in Christ.

1:9 As Paul articulated the blessings and assurances of God,
he was moved to the ascription of praise. He was reminded of
the faithfulness of God. God is predictable, always acting in accord with His consistent, inimitable nature. In the faithfulness
He called us to a fellowship (*koinōnia*) with His son Jesus Christ,
who is our Lord.

"Fellowship" is a word that refers to things held in common.
Koinē Greek was the common Greek of the *agora* or market
place. That we have been called to common ground with the Son
of God, who is our Lord, is one of the most phenomenal avowals in language. Man has little in common with God. He is holy;
man is sinful. He is infinite; man is finite. The possibility of common ground is established through the work of Christ in our behalf. Sinners receive His righteousness as their own.

2. Contention in the Church (1:10–17)

Having concluded the formal greeting, Paul then plunged into
the heart of the Corinthian problem, addressing himself first to
the nature of unity (v. 10), the report of division (vv. 11–12),
and the requisite for healing (vv. 13–17). In one sense, the first
problem thus addressed was not the most serious dilemma for
the congregation. Other doctrinal problems were equally harmful. Perhaps the problem with divisions in the church was first
addressed due to its potential for rending the church of God.

1:10 First, a strong exhortation to achieve three goals was presented by the apostle, beginning with the word translated "be-
seech" (*parakalō*, meaning literally "to call to one's side"). In John

14:16 the Holy Spirit is referred to as a *paraklēton*, the one called to the side of the believer as his counselor. This is Paul's invitation to the Corinthian Christians to stand with him in these three matters, and the basis of his exhortation is none other than the name and the authority associated with the Lord Jesus Christ.

The three matters which concerned Paul were (1) that the Corinthian Christians would speak the same thing, (2) that there would be no divisions among them, and (3) that they would be perfectly joined together in the same mind and the same judgment. These three goals provide a striking picture of the nature of genuine Christian unity.

As surely as Peter's speech betrayed his Galilean origins (Matt. 26:73), so the speech of a church betrays its unity or the lack thereof. Paul's demand that the church of Corinth "speak the same thing" was a request that they agree among themselves concerning the basic rudiments that constituted the heart of the gospel. Having agreed upon the nature of those elements, the church should desist from the public debate of peripheral matters. Furthermore, Paul urged that there be no divisions (*schismata*). This word etymologically gives rise to the later ecclesiastical word "schism," which, as it eventually evolved, came to mean a total division. Apparently this was not yet the case in Corinth. Consequently, the word "division" here should be understood in terms of disagreements and divided loyalties which, nevertheless, possessed within them the seeds of dissolution.

Paul's desire was to have the Corinthian Christians perfectly joined together in the same mind and in the same judgment. "Perfectly joined" (*katērtismenoi*) is a medical term used by Galen to describe the setting of a broken bone or the fitting together of joints.[5] The church was to mend itself together in such a way that it had the same thinking and the same judgment resulting from its thought.

1:11 The reason for the exhortation becomes apparent. The

---

[5]Archibald Robertson and Alfred Plummer, *The International Critical Commentary: A Critical and Exegetical Commentary on the First Epistle of St. Paul to the Corinthians*, p. 10.

people of Chloe had related to Paul that contentions existed among the Corinthians. The precise identification of Chloe is not possible. The text is not explicit whether "those of Chloe" were children or household servants. In a sense, either would be unusual since only the woman is mentioned. This suggests that she was a widow, perhaps one of considerable wealth. Neither is it clear whether she lived in Ephesus, from which Paul wrote, or in Corinth, where observation of the church would have been easily possible. Whatever the case, people related closely to her had come to Ephesus and reported to Paul the presence of contentions.

"Contentions" (*eris*), meaning "a sharp challenge," includes the concepts of "wordy wrangling," "quarreling," or "strife."[6] Interestingly, from this term Emil Brunner has fashioned the word "eristics" to describe the task of Christian apologetics.

1:12 The precise nature of the contentions in Corinth is revealed. There were apparently four different groups that existed in the church, each clamoring for ascendency over the others. One group honored Paul, the founder of the church in Corinth. A second group paid homage to Apollos, the eloquent young orator of the faith; while a third group especially reverenced Cephas or Peter, one of the Lord's original twelve apostles. There is dispute about the nature of the fourth group. Some Christian commentators believe that there were actually only three parties within the church and take the last statement, "and I of Christ," to be Pauline sarcasm designed to illustrate the futility of the positions being taken by the other three parties. Others have suggested that Paul is saying that rather than belonging to either of the three parties named after mortal men, all should be of Christ. However, the tenor of the whole verse would seem to suggest that there was actually a Christ party in the church, perhaps one that had developed in reaction to the other three.

Still another question that has exercised the minds of expositors for most of Christian history has been the nature of the divisions. Various suggestions have been made to explain why these

---

[6]Liddell and Scott, *Lexicon*, p. 687.

particular people should have had their names associated with the development of division in the church. It is especially strange to find the name of Cephas in the group, since it is almost certain that the fisherman had not visited Corinth, nor, as far as is known, engaged in correspondence with anyone west of the Bosporus. In the final analysis, it is impossible to say what the various parties represented. Perhaps it was nothing more than what is so often repeated in any era of church history. At various crucial junctions in our lives, God uses certain individuals in a very profound way. Although we recognize this is the work of God, we cannot help but be grateful for the individuals who so profoundly moved us at a pivotal time. This certainly could be the case of the Corinthian church's earliest converts, who could be expected to relate principally to the ministry of Paul, the founder of the church in Corinth. It may also explain a younger contingency in the church identifying with the eloquence and wisdom of Apollos. With Jews moving into Corinth from the East, some associated with the work of Simon Peter could have easily found residence in Corinth and become a part of the church there. Then, perhaps, a well-meaning but not so successful response was the rise of the fourth party that claimed to be of Christ. Whatever the nature of the division, its presence was a clearly intolerable malignancy within the assembly.

1:13 Three rhetorical questions were then posed by Paul: (1) Is Christ divided? (2) Was Paul crucified for you? (3) Were you baptized in the name of Paul? While the answers are obvious, the questions themselves constitute poignant reminders of the basic nature of the Christian faith. Though formulated as questions, they nevertheless affirm the unity that is in Christ Jesus. Jesus is Lord and there is no other. Furthermore, even if the apostle himself had wished to die in behalf of the Corinthians, it would have been a fruitless endeavor. For crucifixion to transfer merit required perfection on the part of the one being crucified. This was something that Paul could not boast. Furthermore, baptism was an act of public identification. Even were one to be baptized by Paul himself, that public identification would have been with Christ and not with Paul. Therefore, they were baptized in Jesus' name.

1:14 Next, Paul expressed the gratitude of his heart to God that he had baptized none of the Corinthians with the exception of Crispus and Gaius. This verse always provides the deepest chagrin for those who are advocates of baptismal regeneration. Paul's major concern in his ministry was certainly the salvation of the lost, and yet he expressed joy that he baptized none of the Corinthians but Crispus and Gaius. This is a strange position indeed if baptism is essential to salvation. Joseph Beet argues that Paul personally baptized Crispus and Gaius because of the importance of these men in Corinth. Crispus, according to Acts 18:6–8, was the ruler of the synagogue who was converted, while Romans 16:23 suggests that Gaius was the wealthy entrepreneur in whose home the Corinthian congregation eventually met.[7] However, such an explanation would be contrary to the whole spirit of Paul. It also would fail to explain the "household of Stephanas" in verse 16. A better explanation would simply be that Crispus and Gaius and the household of Stephanas doubtless belonged to a small group of early converts in Corinth. If so, there would have been little other possibility but that Paul would have baptized them himself.

1:15 The reason for Paul's thanksgiving is now stated. Had he baptized many, the party spirit within the church might have indeed been heightened. Some might even have averred that he baptized in his own name.

1:16 The apostle then remembered that he baptized also the household of Stephanas. However, besides these, he did not remember whether there were any others. There are two interesting aspects of this verse. First, those who advocate the baptism of infants frequently appeal to the household baptisms of Stephanas, mentioned here, and of the Philippian jailor, mentioned in Acts 16. Again, Hans Conzelmann has laid the whole matter to rest: "In regard to the question whether in such a case children were also baptized, the term leads us nowhere."[8] In other words, Conzelmann knows that it is impossible to build a

---

[7]Joseph A. Beet, *A Commentary on St. Paul's Epistles to the Corinthians*, p. 31.
[8]Conzelmann, *First Corinthians*, p. 30.

case for the baptism of infants based on such shaky evidence. As a matter of fact, the testimony of Scripture regarding baptism is that only believers with a clear perception of the things of God were baptized.

The second issue concerns the doctrine of inspiration of Paul's inability to know whether there were others whom he himself baptized. If, as evangelicals claim, the Scripture writers wrote inerrantly and infallibly, how does one explain this inability on the part of the apostle Paul to remember if there were others baptized at his own hand? Charles Hodge answers perceptively:

> The nature of inspiration is to be learnt from the declarations of the Scripture and from the fact therein recorded. From these sources we learn that it was an influence that rendered its recipients infallible but it did not render them omniscient. They were preserved from asserting error but they were not enabled either to know or to remember all things.[9]

1:17 The case for the nature of Paul's ministry is now made even more explicit than it was in verse 14. Here Paul clearly distinguished between the preaching of the gospel and the act of baptism. He did not in any sense of the word wish to de-emphasize the meaning or importance of baptism. On the other hand, Paul did relegate baptism to a position of secondary importance, according primary billing to the preaching of the gospel. It is probably no accident that the verb "sent," which Paul here employed, is *apostellō*. In verse 1, Paul called himself an apostle. Examination of the English word "apostle" and this Greek verb *apostellō* establishes the common origin of the two. Paul was affirming that his role as an apostle was that of having been sent to preach the good news. Even this task was not to be done with the wisdom of words, lest the cross of Christ should be made of no effect. The phrase "not with wisdom of words" does not constitute special pleading based on any lack of eloquence on the part of Paul. It is rather an anticipation of the argument to follow in

---

[9]Charles Hodge, *Corinthians I and II*, p. 16.

which the apostle contrasted the paltry wisdom of the the most knowledgeable men with the ineffable wisdom of God. Paul meant only that he did not present his case with artful, philosophical sophistry because that would have obscured that astonishing message of the significance of the cross of Christ.

The phrase "should be made of none effect" is actually just one word in Greek (*kenoō*), meaning "to empty." He would do nothing in his presentation of the gospel message that would empty the message of the cross of its wisdom and power.

3. Confidence in the Cross (1:18–25)

In verse 17, Paul clarified the nature of his mission—namely, to preach the gospel. In the next section, he proceeded to identify the central feature of the preaching of the gospel—namely, the cross of Christ. First he spoke of the power of the saved (vv. 18–19), then of the province of God (vv. 20–21), and finally of a preview of failure (vv. 22–25).

1:18 Numerous unusual insights greet the careful reader here. In verse 17, Paul spoke of preaching the gospel (*euangelizō*). The word "preaching" occurs again in this verse. However, this time it is a very different word, different even from a third word for preaching (*kerussō*), which occurs in verse 23. The word here is *logos*. The distinctions present in these words are basically as follows: *kerussō* emphasizes the act of public proclamation; *euangelizō* specifies the content of the message proclaimed, indicating that it is, in fact, the best of news. But when Paul spoke of the *logos* of the cross (v. 18), he chose to use a word with a rich, philosophical heritage. As one can easily discern, the word *logos* provides us with the English word "logic." In a sense, this is precisely what is intended in the term, although the concept is more profound than just logic. In Greek philosophical investigation, *logos* carried the sense of logic and understanding. The New Testament writers, however, filled it with new meaning without subtracting the idea of "logic." John used the word *logos* to mean unique communication. Jesus is the *Logos* of God. He communicates to us who God is and what He is like. Although the word itself was not employed, the same thought pattern was certainly used by the author of Hebrews, who stated that in these last days God has "spoken unto us by his Son" (Heb. 1:2).

Therefore, it may be observed that when Paul spoke of the *logos* of the cross, he was speaking not only of a divine wisdom but also of a divine communication. The cross was at once both God's wisdom for the salvation of the race and the communication of such diverse attributes as His just holiness in reaction to sin and His love for the sinner. It is worth noting with R. St. John Parry that only Paul used the word "cross" to summarize the whole aspect of suffering in the life and work of Christ. As Parry writes, "It describes the death of Christ in its most profound humiliation and its most direct contradiction of men's ordinary thoughts."[10] Therefore, when Paul wrote of the word of the cross, he intended the reader to understand the full doctrine of the atoning death of Jesus.

However, this word of the cross is to those who are perishing foolishness. Two issues must be addressed here. First, "those who are perishing" is a present participle indicating continual action. In other words, the act of perishing has already begun and will continue unbroken unless there is repentance toward God and faith in Jesus Christ. The second thing to note is the word "perishing" itself. It is the Greek verb *apollumi*, which derives in turn from the verb *luō*, "to loose," and the preposition *apo*, which means "from" or "away from." Careful study of the word reveals no concept of annihilation. The fact that the process is already pictured as having begun should be ample indication that annihilation is not the idea of this word. Rather, the best insight to its meaning is simply to understand the most basic meanings already suggested. The word means literally "to loose from something." Those who are lost are being continually loosed from any relationship to God—even from temporal and physical blessings. Only as men are properly related to God does life have meaning and significance. Otherwise, it soon degenerates to mere existence—frustrating and meaningless existence at that. The process of perishing has already begun and will con-

---

[10] R. St. John Parry, *The First Epistle of Paul the Apostle to the Corinthians*, p. 11.

tinue infinitely into the future, ultimately culminating in eternal punishment.

To those who are thus perishing, the word of the cross is foolishness. The word "foolishness" *(mōria)* gives us our word "moron." It is a strong Greek term which, strictly speaking, means "absurdity." In other words, those who are in the process of perishing are so far removed from godly wisdom that the *logos* of the cross seems to be an absurdity. It is the antithesis of everything men are taught to believe. In this world men rise to position and prominence either by strength or cunnning or both. That anything significant should be accomplished through the ignominious death of a carpenter of Nazareth was sheer absurdity to the Greek mind.

However, for those who "are being saved" (another present participle) the word of the cross is the dynamic of God. "Being saved" is a present passive participle, indicating once again the inability of those who are being saved to accomplish that end in their own strength. It is God who is acting to save them through His own power *(dunamis)*.

1:19 This affirmation of the *logos* of the cross reminded the apostle Paul of Isaiah 29:14, which he then quoted. The King James Version text, "it is written," does not do full justice to the perfect tense verb employed there. The word *gegraptai* may be better translated "it stands permanently written." The promise of Isaiah 29:14 is that God will destroy the wisdom of the wise and abrogate or annul the understanding of those who are prudent. The verse simply affirms that when man has achieved his greatest mastery in areas of his intellectual pursuit, God ultimately so overshadows that earthly wisdom as to bring it to nothing.

1:20 This leads in turn to some penetrating questions. Where is the wise man? Where is the scribe? Where is the debater of the present age? The fact is that God has already reduced the wisdom of this world to foolishness. Though the groupings are doubtless of a general nature, there are three discernible kinds of accomplishment mentioned in this verse. "The wise" may well refer to the Greek philosophers who attempted in every way possible to ascertain the ultimate makeup of the world. The scribes, on the other hand, originally were the copiers of the important documents in Judaism, especially of the Torah. Because of their familiarity with the literature being preserved, they also became its principal interpreters. In these first two groups, one may then discern those who were on the cutting edge of the theoretical thinking of Paul's day and those who were the best interpreters of the wisdom recorded by the sages of the past.

One other segment is now featured—the debater (*suzētētēs*). Prowess in debate was greatly admired among the Greeks and Romans alike. A man who could think well on his feet and who could cleverly direct the progress of a discussion was considered a man of great wisdom. In the King James Version text, the word "world" appears twice, once when the text speaks of the "disputer of this world" and a second time when the text speaks of "the wisdom of this world." However, the two words are different. The first word is *aiōn* or age. The second word is *kosmos*, a word which encompasses much more. The debater of the age in which Paul lived flourished, but God had reduced to foolishness all three kinds of wisdom. The theoretical wisdom of the philosopher, the interpretive wisdom of the scribe, and the reasoned cleverness of the debater had all been brought to nothing as a result of what God had done in Christ.

1:21 The reduction of all the above to foolishness by virtue of the death of Christ is now explained. Since, according to the wisdom of God, the world by its own wisdom did not know God, it was pleasing to God to save those who would believe by the foolishness of preaching. Three important factors must be observed in this verse. First, as a part of His eternal wisdom, God decreed that men would not discover Him through the use of their own wisdom. Rather, God in His grace makes Himself known to us.

The second important factor concerns the method by which God has chosen to save those who believe. This method is the foolishness of preaching. As Spiros Zodhiates points out, "The objection of the natural man is not to preaching, per se, but to the preaching of the cross, which involves an acknowledgment of man's lost condition."[11] In other words, it is not just the fool-

---

[11]Spiros Zodhiates, *A Richer Life for You in Christ*, p. 343.

ishness of the method of preaching but the apparent foolishness of the message being preached which God has employed to awaken hearts to repentance. The third important factor to note in the verse is that the whole process is described as being pleasing to God. God apparently delights in taking what is insignificant to us and making it most significant. His delight resides in the wisdom of turning defeat into victory, as He did at the cross.

1:22 Examples of the nature of the wisdom that the world is seeking are now provided. The Jews required a sign, whereas the Greeks sought after wisdom. Although the importance of faith is continually emphasized in the Old Testament, it is noteworthy that the Jews of Jesus' day continually sought some sign of His Messiahship. The word "sign" (*sēmeia*) indicates "miraculous sign." On the other hand, the Greeks gave themselves to philosophical speculation and endless theorizing, a process which may be observed particularly in the writings of Plato or the Stoics.

1:23 The contrast with these approaches is the proclamation of Christ and His atonement. To the Jews the proclamation was a stumbling block. *Skandolon* ("stumbling block") gives us our English word "scandal." To the Jews the preaching of the cross was scandalous. It is not difficult to comprehend why the Jews so reacted. The constant pressure of the political entities in generation after generation have caused the Jews to long for the intervention of Messiah. Unfortunately, their desires for the coming of the Messiah were prompted more by the desire to throw off the yoke of bondage than to receive the holiness of God. The Messiah they expected and for whom they longed would be a conquering Son of David who would lead them to emancipation. That the Messiah would have come only to be crucified would mean that His mission had failed and that there was no hope for the future.

Nor was the Greek mind any more at home with such a concept. The tendency to view all materiality as evil made it very difficult for the Greeks to conceive of God's coming in human flesh. Furthermore, the idea that the suffering of one man could in some way lead to the holiness and happiness of other men was as distant to the Greek mind as the lands of the New World. So while the Jews were scandalized by the preaching of the cross, the Greeks' reaction tended to be what Luke described as the majority of opinion in Athens, "And when they heard of the resurrection of the dead, some mocked: and others said, We will hear thee again of this matter" (Acts 17:32).

1:24 The above analysis was not intended to indicate that there were no Jews or Greeks who responded. For both Jews and Greeks who were called to salvation, Christ was the power and the wisdom of God. The emphasis is upon the demonstration of the superior wisdom of God through the work of Christ and on the operational power of God in salvation.

1:25 The conclusion is inescapable. The foolishness of God is wiser than men, even these who have accumulated superior amounts of wordly wisdom. By the same token, the weakness of God is far stronger than even the mightiest of men. Paul did not here affirm that God is foolish or that He is weak. The argument was rather that the most elementary things of God are inscrutable to man. Furthermore, the most minute example of the power of God is totally overwhelming to man.

The most complicated algebraic equation is elementary to a God who designed the wonderful complexities of the human neurological system. By the same token, men with the production of their mightiest arms are not able to produce the cataclysmic and powerful upheaval of a great earthquake or volcanic eruption. Yet those matters are the smallest of the manifestations of the power of God.

4. Coronation for the Christ (1:26–31)

Moving from the emphasis on the word of the cross to a solution for the petty strife that existed in the church at Corinth, the missionary statesman Paul concluded the initial phase of his argument by an appeal to the Corinthians to recognize what God has actually done in Christ. In that recognition there should be an enthronement of Christ as Lord, which would come naturally once the Corinthians understood the lowliness of the called (v. 26), the rationale of God (vv. 27–29), and the glory of the Lord (vv. 30–31).

1:26 The Corinthians were asked first of all to examine their own ranks. Apparently the clientele in the church at Corinth was similar to what one would have found in most of the early Christian communities. Three notable class absences are featured. As the Corinthians examined their calling, they were asked to note that not many of those who were considered wise according to men in the flesh were a part of their assembly. In the second place, there were few who had risen to positions of prestige and prominence in the community so that they could be called "mighty men." In fact, men such as Crispus and Sosthenes probably found themselves suffering considerable social loss once they became followers of Christ. Even the noted Gaius may have faced considerable danger ultimately when the empire began to confiscate the possessions of believers. Furthermore, the vast majority of those in the early congregations were not noble as to birth. The word "employed" *(eugenēs)* literally means "well born." It is not that there were no such people who were followers of Christ. Certainly Joseph of Arimathea, in whose tomb the Lord's body was laid, was well born. And there were others. Paul's point is rather that God in His own wisdom has chosen to demonstrate His saving grace through those who would not be counted important in the estimate of the powerful and noble of this world.

1:27 God has in fact chosen the foolish things of this world, i.e., those things that the world would count foolish, to confound the wise. The word "confound" *(kataischunō)* literally means "to reduce to shame or disgrace" or "to cause to blush." Paul affirmed that the things the world views as foolish have been employed by God to cause the wise to blush. Furthermore, He has chosen the weak things *(asthenē)*, a word often used for the weakness associated with illness, to put to shame the things which are mighty.

1:28 The description continues by indicating that God has chosen the base and despised things of the world. Earlier, the word *eugenēs*, "well-born," was used. Here the word *agenēs*, which simply means "not of significant birth," is used. Those of no significance in this world by virtue of their birth and those things which the world views with contempt or scorn are the very things that God has chosen to use for the purposes of the demonstration of His own wisdom and power. The final clause of the verse, "things which are not, in order to make powerless or empty the things which are," seems to be a summary of all that has gone before. "Things which are not" does not seem to indicate lack of existence but rather unimportance in the eyes of men. By the same token, the "things which are" is an indication of those items which men view as critical. Paul's conclusion was that the Lord has used the very insights which man views condescendingly to render useless the pride of men.

1:29 The further rationale for this activity of God is found in the prohibition against any flesh seeking glory before God. The word "glory" is not the anticipated *doxazō* but rather *kauchaomai*. This word refers to an attitude of boastfulness. The subjunctive mood is employed, indicating potentiality. The indicative mood is used to indicate reality. However, the whole purpose of God's action is to render it impossible for any man to boast, and, therefore, the subjunctive mood of potentiality is employed. The propensity on the part of fallen man is always to boast in his accomplishments, even if that pride is contained in the heart alone. But God's plan of redemption resides totally in the grace of God. Man's inability to save himself or even to comprehend fully the wisdom of God leaves him no opportunity for boasting. This is the same kind of point that Paul was making in Romans 3:27 when he said, "Where is boasting then? It is excluded. By what law? of works? Nay: but by the law of faith." One cannot boast of what another achieved for him.

1:30 There is, however, another option for boasting. God has made Christ Jesus wisdom, righteousness, sanctification, and redemption. Each of the four terms illuminate what has, in fact, happened in our salvation.

(1) Wisdom. Those who are in Christ Jesus have the mind of Christ. Through the indwelling ministry of the Holy Spirit, they are able to perceive and comprehend the plans and purposes of God which are hidden from the rest of the world.

(2) Righteousness. That which is so elusive to us that we can never apprehend it is made available to us in Christ. Our sinful-

ness is transferred to Him on the cross. We in turn are accorded His righteousness.

(3) Sanctification. The term "righteousness" *(dikaiosunē)* is forensic in nature, having to do with our legal standing before God. If our salvation, however, were limited to a right standing before God, then the effects of salvation would be primarily eschatological and of only relative consequence for the present. Such is not the case, since Christ is also made our sanctification. Those who are in Christ are thus set apart to God, becoming partakers of His holiness (Heb. 12:10).

(4) Redemption. The word "redemption" *(apolutrōsis)* means "to loose or to free by means of payment." There is a sense in which we are slaves to sin and desire (Titus 3:3). The cross of Jesus Christ not only provided for us the mind of Christ, right standing before God, and position in the holiness of God, but it also released us from the slavery and the penalty of our sin.

1:31 The conclusion is inevitable. If there is to be any boasting, it must be the lauding of the Lord, who alone was able to provide wisdom, righteousness, sanctification, and redemption. Once again, Paul alluded to an Old Testament text in quoting Jeremiah 9:23-24. There man is cautioned not to boast (Heb., *halal)* in his wisdom, might, or riches, but rather to boast in the fact that he understands and knows the Lord. Once the Corinthians had enough of the mind of Christ that they understood their humble estate and the grace of God, of which each was a recipient, the contentions and strifes which existed in the church would be laid quickly to rest in the repose of humility.

The Deeper Life

1. The Power of the Spirit (2:1–8)
2. The Perception of the Spirit (2:9–16)

Every genuine believer who loves Jesus has at least some desire to know the deep things of God and to experience a deeper life with Christ. So much has this been the case among some evangelicals that a quest known as the "deeper life movement" has developed. Too often this deeper life movement has suffered from the myopia of self-assessment to the degree of losing sight of the world it is supposed to win. Often it has simply delved more deeply but with insufficient breadth, making its impact upon the world negligible. Nevertheless, the desire for a deeper life and a more profound walk with God has been a legitimate one since the days of Enoch, who "walked with God: and he was not; for God took him" (Gen. 5:24). In order to achieve this deeper life, however, one must comprehend that its achievement resides in the appropriation of the power of the Spirit (vv. 1–8) and the perception of the Spirit (vv. 9–16).

1. The Power of the Spirit (2:1–8)

Appropriating the power of the Spirit for one's spiritual pilgrimage is bound up in three things: recognizing the weakness of the flesh (vv. 1–3), experiencing the wake of the message (vv. 4–5), and abiding in the wisdom of the Spirit (vv. 6–8).

2:1 The missionary apostle personalized his first-chapter dissertation by reminiscing about his own experience in Corinth. He reminded his readers that when he was declaring to them the mystery of God, his coming to Corinth was not with excellency of word or wisdom. Several important features must be observed in this verse. The word "speech" is once again the Greek word *logos*, which is probably best translated "logical communication." The word "excellency" (*huperochē*) is a combination of the verb *echō*, meaning "to have," and the preposition *huper*, meaning "above." For one to have something above others suggests his rising to a station of authority or preeminence. Paul maintained that his coming to the Corinthians was not with condescending logic or wisdom characteristic of the Greek philosophical thought patterns. He was obviously speaking of the one-and-a-half-year period when he first proclaimed the mystery of God.

A textual problem concerns whether or not Paul's autograph used the word "mystery" or the word "witness." The two words are very similar in Greek. "Mystery" (*mustērion*) and "witness" (*marturion*) are, in fact, so much alike that manuscript copyists could easily look at one word while accidentally writing another. In most such cases, however, the textual evidence so overwhelmingly favors one of the words that the few existing variants are inconsequential. This is a classic case, however, where the evidence is rather evenly divided. The translators of the King James Version chose to use the word "witness" or "testimony," indicating that Paul was declaring to the Corinthians the testimony of God. Perhaps the textual evidence slightly favors the translation "the mystery of God."

We have gone to the trouble to belabor this point to demonstrate a crucial matter in biblical studies. We desire to know whether Paul wrote the "mystery" of God or the "testimony" of God. But while we await some final piece of evidence that would establish one or the other reading with convincing probability, either reading would be theologically accurate and thoroughly in keeping with the truths revealed elsewhere in the Bible. The proclamation of Paul certainly was the testimony of God. It was equally the proclamation of the mystery of God. A mystery refers to information which God makes available to man through specific acts of revelation. This is information which would never have been discernible as a result of human investigation. Two factors in the context make the reading "mystery of God" more probable. First, the whole discussion in the first three chapters of 1 Corinthians concerns the wisdom of God, which is totally different from the cumulative wisdom amassed by the human family. Second, the word "mystery" occurs again in verse 7 where Paul wrote that he spoke the wisdom of God in a mystery. No significant textual variants occur there, making probable the word "mystery" in verse 1 also.

2:2 Continuing the thought of declaring the mystery of God, the apostle affirmed that he would know nothing among the Corinthians but Jesus Christ and Him crucified. Many commentators have imagined that this represents a new direction in the missionary ministry of Paul. In Acts 17, Paul preached his famous sermon to intellectuals at the Areopagus in Athens. Only limited success resulted, including the conversion of Dionysius the Areopagite and a woman named Damaris, along with a few others (Acts 17:34). However, according to many the paucity of response in Athens caused Paul to take a simplified and less philosophical approach when he arrived at Corinth.

Such speculation scarcely does justice to the apostle. A careful investigation of Paul's efforts prior to the Athenian and Corinthian ministries will demonstrate that the central message of his gospel never changed. As does every successful preacher, Paul knew that his presentation of the cross of Christ must always take into account both the people and the culture. At Athens it was true that the initial part of his message was couched in more philosophical terms, but there was nothing abstrusely philosophical about the clear indication of the significance of the death of Christ, His resurrection from the grave, and the demand for repentance.

It is possible, however, that increasingly the Spirit of God impressed upon the mind of Paul the centrality of the doctrine of

Christ and His sacrifice. This determined allegiance to the pre-eminence of the person of Christ and His atoning work should also set the tone for our own commitments.

This should not be taken as a denial of the significance of any other doctrine nor should it be viewed as a prohibition of the illucidation of other important doctrinal truths. Rather, it is intended to be an emphatic statement of the foundational doctrine upon which all other truths would be constructed.

2:3 In consideration of the absence of condescending logic and wisdom and in light of the rather harsh treatment which he received during previous stops at Thessalonica, Berea, and even Athens, one can understand why Paul spoke of his coming to Corinth as one characterized by weakness, fear, and much trembling. This confession on the part of the apostle, first of all, should be a matter of immense comfort and encouragement to every Christian who finds himself desiring to share his faith yet hesitant to do so due to weakness, fear, and much trembling. If the most aggressive and passionate missionary in all history knew these human emotions, it is not too much to suppose that we will know them also. By the same token, one must remember that verse 3 is written in sequence, following the statements of chapter 1 to the effect that God has chosen the weak things of this world to put to shame the things that are mighty. If God was able to do that with Paul, surely He can do it with any believer.

2:4 Not only must one recognize the weakness of the flesh, he must also do his work in the wake of the Spirit of God. Sitting on the end of the runway at a large international airport, I watched with amazement as a small private aircraft turned too quickly onto the runway behind a powerful 747. The wake of that jet's powerful engines simply plucked the small plane off the ground as though it were a toy and laid it upside down upon the runway. Fortunately, the pilot, though shaken, was not injured. One could not help but be impressed with the wake of that man-made mechanical apparatus. Though the wake of the Holy Spirit is far more powerful, to be caught in the Spirit's wake is productive rather than harmful. Therefore, Paul spoke of his logic and his proclamation as not being characterized by enticing words of human wisdom. The word translated "enticing" (*peithoi*, Greek) means "persuasive." Paul once again differentiated between his own speech and that of his cultured contemporaries who, by the persuasiveness of clever argumentation, sought to win converts to their positions. This was not Paul's approach. Instead, his preaching was in demonstration of the Spirit of God and of power. The word translated "demonstration" (*apodeixis*) derives from the Greek word *deixis* and means "a convincing proof or display." Interestingly, one of Liddell and Scott's defining words is "macho," a term popular in our present generation.[12]

Paul's claim is that what may have been lacking in terms of man's persuasiveness was more than equalled by the clear, powerful display of the Spirit of God and His power. Without doubt, the reference here must be to the life-changing effect of the salvation experience which always constitutes one of the most irrefutable proofs of the validity of Christianity.

2:5 This demonstration of the Spirit and of power was not something that just happened but was an essential feature of the gospel. If what transpired in a man's life was the product of the persuasiveness of gifted men, then when a still more gifted orator would arise, pleading for a position diametrically opposed to what had been espoused by the hearer, his faith might be shaken. He would find himself in the same position which is characteristic of people in every age who simply listen to the clamor of varied voices with their conflicting and unverifiable claims. One never has the feeling that he can stand firmly and knowledgeably. Since, however, Paul's preaching and logic was in demonstration of the Spirit and power, the result was that the Corinthians' faith was not anchored in human wisdom but rather in the power of God. It was as impossible to deny the effects of the regenerating influence of the Holy Spirit within as it was to deny their own physical existence.

2:6 That Paul did not speak with the condescending wisdom of the world did not imply that his speech was void of wisdom. To the contrary, the supra-wisdom Paul employed was an insight which those who were being perfected recognized immediately

---

[12]Liddell and Scott, *Lexicon*, p. 375.

as divine wisdom. It was a wisdom that only they would recognize, since the princes and leaders of the world could not comprehend it for reasons stated in verse 14 of this same chapter. In fact, the basic distinction between Paul's wisdom and the wisdom of the philosophers was that the wisdom of the latter came to naught while Paul's wisdom led to God.

2:7 A further delineation of the nature of divine wisdom is that it does belong to the mystery of God. Again, the word "mystery" implies that which is hidden from the view of men until such time as God, by special revelation, makes it known. In fact, this is the precise definition Paul provided in speaking of it as wisdom which has been "hidden" (*apokruptō*, meaning "to conceal"). The perfect passive participial form indicates that though God had kept this wisdom hidden, He had appointed or determined that He would reveal it for the benefit of our own glory. The word "ordained" (*proōrizō*) simply means "to appoint" or "to determine." Once again, instead of "world," as the King James Version reads, *aiōn* is better translated "the ages." Consequently, before the ages of man's history even began, God had ordained or determined that He would reveal the mystery of His wisdom to man.

2:8 The inability of the princes of this world to understand the wisdom of God is demonstrated by one significant event. Had they known anything of the wisdom of God, they certainly would not have crucified the Lord of glory. Although the crucifixion of Christ is viewed by Paul as an absolute necessity for redemption, it is nonetheless true that the genuine people of God would never have crucified the Son of God. The abysmal failure of the philosophies and perceptions of mankind are epitomized in this incredible deed, the crucifixion of a Man who never harmed anyone and whose total concerns were those of compassion and love.

2. The Perception of the Spirit (2:9–16)

Once one has appropriated the power of the Holy Spirit in his life, he is also able to begin to understand the things the Spirit of God teaches. He will begin comprehending the depths of the

Spirit (vv. 9–11), comparing the truths of God (vv. 12–13), and cultivating the mind of Christ (vv. 14–16).

2:9 The familiar formula "stands written" precedes a one-line quotation from Isaiah 64:4. The thought placed before us has three aspects to it. First, the incomprehensible goodness of God has never been told to or previewed for man. Furthermore, it has never even entered his heart to conceptualize the things which God has prepared for him. Nevertheless, as verse 10 will indicate, he may know many of these riches ahead of time via the ministry of the Holy Spirit. In verse 11 the Holy Spirit has access to these things precisely because He is God—God dwelling in man. The saints of the Old Testament certainly had access to insight and information which were the product of direct revelation. They "saw" through the intervention of God in history and through the visions of their prophets such as Daniel. They "heard" through the messages of the prophets and the statutes of the law. For all of this, however, in the passage Paul quoted Isaiah confessed that it never entered the heart of man to understand the breadth of things that God had prepared for those who love Him. Two other factors are important. First, the Scripture is plain that God has made special preparation for man. In the second place, that preparation is limited to those who love Him. Certainly this is a passage which forever excludes any universalist ideas.

2:10 However, the deep things of God may be known after all. This is a result of the revealing activity of the Holy Spirit. "Revealed" (*apokaluptō*) is the same word from which we get Apocalypse, another name for the book of Revelation. Of the many ministries of the Holy Spirit documented in the Scriptures, none is more critically important than this ministry of revelation. The Spirit is the agent in revelation because He is able to search out the deep things of God. Two notations are important. First, the text does not actually indicate the "deep things of God," only the "depths." Furthermore, as Robertson and Plummer note, "the word does not here mean 'searcheth in order to know' any more than it means this when it is said that God searches the heart of men (Rom. 8:27; Rev. 2:23; and Ps. 139:1)."[13] In other words, because the Spirit of God knows the depths of God, He, therefore, is able to reveal these things to those who love God.

2:11 The reason for this ability on the part of the Holy Spirit is here specified in one of the Bible's important verses for establishing the full deity of the Holy Spirit. There has always been a tendency, even among some who recognize the deity of Christ, to treat the Holy Spirit as though He were some impersonal power or at least not God in the same sense that the Father is God and the Son is God. However, this verse points out that only a man himself knows the things that belong to his own private thoughts. There are aspects of the emotions, feelings, will, and even intellect of a man that remain unshared, even with his closest human confidant. Only the man himself can adequately know the kind of an individual he really is. By the same token, the deep things of God are open to no man. Only the Spirit of God is able to plumb the depths. The spirit of a man is the indispensable entity in his existence. Just as the man would not be a man without his own spirit, so God would be less than God without the Holy Spirit. The Spirit is God just as surely as the Father is God and the Son is God. He is, therefore, able to reveal those things He knows in depth (John 14:26; 16:13).

2:12 As a result of this ministry of the Spirit of God, believers have not received the world's spirit, which is so often in error and inevitably incomplete. Instead, the believer has received the Spirit of God so that he might know the things that God freely gives to all the elect. *Charisthenta*, meaning "gracious bestowal" and translated "the things given to us," is very similar to the word *charismata* or "spiritual gifts." Apparently Paul had already returned to the theme of spiritual gifts in this passage, specifying that the knowledge of the gifts that God has given to us is obtained through the ministry of the Spirit of God.

2:13 Interpreters sharply differ over the interpretation of this verse, especially the concluding phrase. The apostle followed his usual approach of first stating the matter negatively—what he

---

[13]Robertson and Plummer, *First Corinthians*, p. 43.

was not doing—and then presenting positively what he was doing. Paul declared that he was not speaking in the taught words of human wisdom. Though there are many matters that may be successfully communicated based on human knowledge, the spiritual truth of revelation does not fall in that category. Instead Paul positively wrote that he was speaking in taught words of the Holy Spirit. Here again is a clear claim for the full inspiration of the Scripture. In fact, it is interesting to note that the word *didaktos* clearly modifies the noun *logoi* ("words") in the text. Here, then, we have not only a claim for inspiration of the Scripture but also a declaration of verbal inspiration—i.e., the very words of the Scriptures were taught to the writers by the Spirit of God.

The next phrase has been the subject of considerable difference of opinion, basically revolving around two possibilities. Did Paul mean (1) that he interpreted spiritual things to spiritual men, or did he mean (2) that he compared spiritual truths with other spiritual truths? Representative of the interpreters maintaining the first view would be Arthur Penrhyn Stanley, who takes the position that *sunkrinontes* should be translated "interpreting" or "explaining" as it is in the Septuagint (Gen. 40:8,16; Dan. 5:12,15,26). Therefore, he also accepts *pneumatikoi*, which may be neuter or masculine, as being masculine in this case, and he argues that the verse means that Paul is interpreting or explaining spiritual truths to spiritual men.[14]

Thomas Charles Edwards would be representative of the alternative view which would insist that *sunkrinontes* means "interpretation" only when it is associated with dreams. Consequently, it should in this case have its usual interpretation of bringing together two things for comparison. *Pneumatikoi* would then be seen as neuter and the sense of the verse would be that Paul was comparing spiritual truths with other spiritual truths in the writing of Scripture.[15]

Happily, neither interpretation would do violence to the consistency of the theology of the New Testament. On the other hand, perhaps the matter can be resolved in the following way.

---

[14]Arthur Penrhyn Stanley, *Epistles of Paul to the Corinthians*, p. 57.

[15]Thomas Charles Edwards, *Commentary on First Corinthians*, p. 62.

Verse 14 seems to provide the contrast Paul was here anticipating, "the natural man understandeth not the things of the Spirit of God." One may thus see in the text a contrast between spiritual men (*pneumatikoi*) of verse 13 and natural men (*psuchikoi*) of verse 14. If that contrast is accurate, it probably settles the question of the gender of *pneumatikoi* in verse 13 as being masculine, referring to men who are spiritual by virtue of the indwelling Spirit of God.

There remains only the question of the proper interpretation of *sunkrinontes*. Should we render it "comparing," as the King James Version suggests, or "interpreting," thus depending upon a secondary meaning of the word? The question cannot be resolved with any certainty; but based on the conclusion that *pneumatikoi* means "spiritual men," it seems more natural to assume that Paul was here using the word *sunkrinontes* to refer to an "explanation" or "interpretation." Hence, the text would finally read, "We are not speaking words taught by human wisdom, but we are speaking words taught by the Holy Spirit, interpreting spiritual truths to spiritual men." Thus, two features are emphasized. First, the spiritual origin of the words and truths of Scripture, and second, the necessity of spiritual regeneration before the deep things of God may be ascertained.

2:14 The contrast is now placed clearly before us. The natural (*psuchikos*) or foolish man is not able to receive the things of the Spirit of God for two reasons. First, the things of God are simply foolishness, nonsensical absurdities which must be jettisoned because they fail the test of human logic. Second, even if the natural man did not immediately relegate the things of the Spirit to the world of the absurd, he would still find himself unable to understand merely because the things of the Spirit are spiritually adjudicated. The word translated "discerned" (*anakrino*) in the King James Version simply means "to judge again" or "to judge carefully"—hence, to discern. Spiritual men, then, are able to discern spiritual teaching through the capacity given them in the new birth. That capacity is not present in the natural man, who is unable to grasp these spiritual truths.

2:15 By contrast to the natural man, the spiritual man is able to interpret or discern all things, though he himself is not discerned

cerned or appreciated properly by those who are natural men. Once again, it is apparent that *pneumatikoi* refers to spiritual men who are made sensitive to the things of the Spirit via regeneration. The ability ascribed to these spiritual men to discern or judge all things is similar to John's expression in 1 John, where he remarks that we have no need that anyone should teach us due to the "unction" (*chrisma*) that is given to each believer (2:20,27). However, even in the midst of this exercise of spiritual insight, the spiritual man does not need to expect natural men to understand or applaud him in his spiritual endeavors.

2:16 The natural man fails to understand either the commitment of the spiritual man in particular or spiritual truths in general because no man has known the mind of the Lord, nor has anyone become His instructor (see Is. 40:13, which in itself constitutes a reminder of the superiority of the knowledge of God). However, Paul affirmed that "we have the mind of Christ." Elsewhere, the same possibility was asserted when Paul wrote, "Let this mind be in you, which was also in Christ Jesus" (Phil. 2:5). Through the ministry of the Holy Spirit it is possible to know the mind of Christ and inculcate that in the lives of true believers.

The Judgment Seat of Christ

1. The Increase of the Father (3:1–9)
2. The Incisiveness of the Son (3:10–15)
3. The Indwelling of the Spirit (3:16–23)

Chapter 3 continues the discussion of the situation that existed in the church in Corinth—the lack of growth of the believers in Corinth, the certainty of impending judgment, and the awesomeness of Corinthian responsibility. For our purposes, the following outline will show the development of the passage: the increase of the Father (vv. 1–9), the incisiveness of the Son (vv. 10–15), and the indwelling of the Spirit (vv. 16–23).

1. The Increase of the Father (3:1–9)

This initial section discusses carnal men (vv. 1–4), caring ministers (vv. 5–6), and a cultivating master (vv. 7–9).

3:1 The apostle began this discussion with an astonishing turn in light of the closing verse in chapter 2. Having just discussed the natural man's inability to receive the things of the Spirit of God, while confirming that the Corinthian believers had the mind of Christ, he, nevertheless, was forced to say that while the Corinthians enjoyed this decided spiritual advantage, they had not availed themselves of all its potentials. As a matter of fact, when Paul attempted to speak to them as to spiritual men, he was not able to do so, but instead had to address them as carnal or fleshly men. To change the metaphor slightly, he suggested another model. They had to be addressed as infants in Christ. Paul used three descriptive terms to describe the relationship of men to spiritual truths. They may be described as (1) natural (*psuchikos*), (2) fleshly or carnal (*sarkinos*), or (3) spiritual (*pneumatikos*). Of these three groups, though both the carnal and the spiritual represent those who have been genuinely forgiven and redeemed, the former group—the *sarkinos* or carnal group—behaves in many respects just as the *psuchikos* or natural group. This is a tragedy in any church. The criteria for determining into which category a believer falls follows in successive verses.

3:2 The first test is growth in spiritual perception. Because the Corinthians were mere babes (*nēpios*, meaning "one so small that he is not yet able to speak"), Paul found that he had to feed them with milk and not with meat. The Corinthians were simply not able to assimilate a heavier diet of spiritual truth. Furthermore, at the time of the writing of this epistle they had progressed no further. This second mark of carnality, or lack of progress in spiritual matters, is a sure index to hindrance of growth. One must not conclude that it is an unacceptable condition to feed upon the milk of the word. In 1 Peter 2:2, Peter instructed his readers to be like newborn babes desiring "the sincere milk of the word that ye may grow thereby." But surely it would be tragic for a newborn never to reach a state in which he could handle a more substantial diet. The same is true in the church. Therefore, a lack of interest in the word of God and the absence of progress in spiritual growth are the first two indications of carnality.

3:3 A third index to the fact of carnality is carnal behavior. Paul indicated that the Corinthians were still carnal since there existed among them envy, strife, and division—all of which indicated that they not only were carnal but also were walking about continually as mere men. Whereas in the case of the Corinthians, the particular behavior patterns that indicated their carnality were jealousy or envy, strife, and division, other behavior patterns could indicate the same carnality. In fact, as the epistle progressed, the apostle alluded to additional factors, such as preoccupation with spiritual gifts and tolerance of grievous sexual sin within the church membership. In some of the more dependable manuscripts, the word "division" does not occur in this verse. Whether it was originally in Paul's letter is not of consequence, since surely the result of envy and strife would naturally be such divisiveness.

3:4 More specifically, Paul returned to the propensity of the people to align themselves with certain gifted leaders as a signal of their basic carnality. While one associated himself with Paul and another with Apollos, etc., the association which ought to have been cherished was the individual's relationship to Christ.

3:5 A portion of the problem existing at Corinth was due to the tendency to think more highly of leadership than ought to be the case. There is a continuing tendency toward this in modern-day Christianity. In a sense, the tendency to identify more strongly with Christian leaders than with Jesus, the founder of Christianity, is another sure insight into one's stature as a babe in Christ. So then, it became important to identify properly Paul, Apollos, and others. The apostle proceeded to identify them as merely ministers through whom one believed. There are three important points to notice here.

(1) The apostle referred to himself and to Apollos as "ministers" (*diakonoi*). This word gives us our English loan-word "deacon." It is used in two different respects in the Scriptures. The generic use of the term in Greek is one of the words descriptive of a servant. In the case of *diakonia*, the reference is to the service of a table waiter. Its technical use is found in 1 Timothy 3, where there are specific qualifications provided for those who aspire to the office of a deacon, which in the early church was an official assignment related to the exercise of service to the needy of a congregation. It is almost certain that Paul did not use the term for Apollos or himself in this technical sense. The generic sense was intended. These great leaders, the learned Paul and the eloquent Apollos, were actually table waiters.

(2) Their responsibility was to present Christ just as a waiter would present a tasty meal to his customer. In other words, the task of Paul and Apollos was not to rule but to serve as the wait-

ers who brought Christ to the people.

(3) This was to be construed as a common experience that God gave to all. In everyone's life, some other individual or individuals have served as the *diakonoi* who brought the word of God to them. Consequently, Paul affirmed that there was nothing special about himself or Apollos. They had simply served in a role that many others had also assumed.

3:6 This is not to indicate that there is no difference of function. In the case of the Corinthians, Paul planted, Apollos came later to water, but it was God who ultimately gave the increase. Paul accomplished his purpose through an excellent agricultural metaphor. The faithful farmer may plant at the most opportune season. Others may come behind and provide irrigation; but having done all that they can do, they can never actually produce the plant. The mystery of the growth of the oak from the acorn or the wheat from the grain is bound up forever in the counsels of God. God alone makes the plant to grow, and God alone turns the hearts of men and regenerates them.

3:7 The conclusion to be drawn from the above assessment is that those who plant and water amount to very little. This is not meant to be a statement of "conspicuous humility" or unnecessary denegration of the importance of the messenger. It is rather a comparative statement. Contrasted with God, who gives the increase, His ministers amount to very little. They are able to carry out the assignment that God has given them, but ultimately it is God alone who can provide the effective increase.

3:8 A second consequence of the above assessment is that actually those who plant and those who water are one. Why should divisions relating to the personalities of its leaders exist in the church? Their commitment is to one end—the planting, watering, and successful growth of the vineyard of the Lord. Accordingly, each will receive his own reward according to his labor. The mention of reward *(misthos)* alerts us at once to the fact that while it would be quite sufficient for God's mercies toward us to be exhausted in salvation, there is more in terms of reward. This reward, which shall be discussed further in the succeeding verses, is directly tied to our "works" *(kopos*, which gives us our word "copious" and refers to diligent, strenuous, and extensive labor). Generally speaking, classical Greek employed the word *misthos* to describe the wages of a hired hand. Gradually, however, the word also picked up a secondary meaning of "reward." Precisely which idea is intended in the text is open to some question. Based on the agricultural metaphor Paul was developing in verses 4-9, the logical understanding of *misthos* would be "wages." On the other hand, the word is once again employed in verse 14 in a context where it almost certainly implies "reward." Perhaps both concepts were in some sense present in Paul's use of the word.

The importance of works as a part of the Christian faith is central to this passage. A frequent accusation against those who, like Paul, champion salvation by grace alone, appropriated by faith and in no sense attained by human works, is that such a position relegates works to a position of unimportance. Nothing could be further from the truth. Evangelical Christians simply affirm that works are the logical result of salvation and not the producing agent of salvation. Once we are saved, then we will want to labor extensively and copiously as the Lord has given us assignment.

3:9 This assignment of works is specified again in verse 9 in three separate metaphors—a general one, followed by an agricultural one, and culminating in an architectural model. First, we are "workers together" (*sunergoi*) with God. The King James Version states that we are "laborers together with God." The "with" is certainly not theologically wrong, but the genitive case employed suggests that we are God's employees. That idea is furthered by the two additional models. First, the agricultural model—you are God's "husbandry" (*geōrgion*, combining *ergon*, the same word used in combination with the preposition *sun* in the phrase "workers together," and *gē* which means "earth"). Literally, the reference is to workers in the earth, or farmers. Changing the model to get still another idea, one which lends itself more adequately to the turn of the discussion he will next pursue, Paul further stated that we are God's building (*oikodomē*, a builder or architect). A better translation might be, "you are God's builders." Now the three metaphors are all before us. The Christian is a laborer, a farmer, and a builder. He is, therefore, a diligent worker, one who is concerned with growth and productivity and one who is involved in the building of permanent structures.

2. The Incisiveness of the Son (3:10–15)

The discussion of Christians as builders provides the matrix for the following discussion in which Paul examined the foundation (vv. 10–11), the framing (v. 12), and the firing (vv. 13–15) of Christian labor.

3:10 Paul's immediate assignment, based on the grace of God given unto him, was to be a wise master builder. The word for "master builder" is *architektos*. One can quickly spot the English word "architect" in this Greek term. Literally, it means "chief carpenter." Interestingly, Paul also used the adjective *sophos* ("wise") to describe his architectural skills. Earlier he tended to depreciate the *sophia* of the world, but this *sophia* was a God-given wisdom. Paul insisted that he had laid the foundation upon which others had built, but he also reminded every man to give special attention to exactly how he built upon that foundation. Paul's reference to himself as the master builder would not be applicable to every church, but it was certainly applicable to the church at Corinth, as becomes apparent in his description of himself as the father of the Corinthians in terms of their own Christian experience; i.e., he was the one who laid the foundation of the church at Corinth (4:15). Since that time, others, including Apollos and the Corinthians themselves, had been constructing a superstructure on that foundation.

3:11 The nature of the foundation for every church is Christ Himself. It was Paul's insistence that Jesus alone was the foundation of the church. That avowal provides light for the passage in which Jesus said "upon this rock I will build my church" (Matt. 16:18). Some have felt that the foundation stone (*petra*) in the Matthew passage was intended to symbolize the confession of Simon Peter. While no theological tenet would be violated in that understanding, it does seem that this verse (2:11), as well as 1 Peter 2:4–8, point to Jesus Himself as the foundation.

3:12 The kinds of materials with which one builds the superstructure of his Christian life are of great importance. It may well be that the precious stones mentioned here by the apostle were not to be understood as diamonds and sapphires but as various kinds of marble which, together with the ornamentation of gold and silver, would produce a handsome edifice if constructed by a wise architect. On the other hand, wood, hay, and stubble—building materials of less pretentious housing—were typical of some areas of the country. Wood would be used for the rafters, the doors, and the windows, while hay (*chortos*) refers to dried grass, which, if mixed with mud, would provide the walls, and straw (*kalamē*) would be used for the roof. This roofing material, typical of the poorer homes in the ancient Near East, was obviously used in the home to which the four men brought their crippled friend, disassembling the roof of the house in order to lower him before Jesus (Mark 2).

The two types of building materials described are noteworthy contrasts in two respects. First, gold, silver, and precious stones are rare and therefore of great value. Wood, hay, and stubble are common and consequently of little value or consequence. The second notable contrast is in regard to the effect of fire. When subject to intense heat, gold, silver, and precious stones survive and do so in a purer form. Wood, hay, and stubble, on the other hand, are quickly burned, and whatever value may have been there initially is lost.

Paul's point is that once the foundation of Jesus Christ has been laid in a man's life, he spends the remainder of his days, however long that may be, building a superstructure. Some build of noncombustible spiritual materials which are of lasting value, while others build the superstructure of their lives in a carnal fashion, oblivious to the values of spiritual materials. The exhortation in regard to this building is found in the last phrase of verse 10, "let every man take heed how he buildeth" upon this structure.

3:13 Having discussed the foundation upon which our lives in Christ are built, and having further discussed the framing of the superstructure, Paul then moved to the firing of the superstructure or the test by fire. The apostle declared that there was to be a day of testing when the nature of one's word would be revealed by fire. There are at least six different kinds of judgment clearly indicated in the New Testament.

(1) The judgment of the cross itself (Rom. 8:34)
(2) The judgment of angels (1 Cor. 6:3; 2 Pet. 2:4)
(3) The judgment of the church (1 Cor. 5:13)
(4) The judgment seat of Christ (Rom. 14:10; 2 Cor. 5:10)
(5) The Sheep and Goat judgment (Matt. 25:32–46)
(6) The Great White Throne judgment (Rev. 20:11–15)

The judgment which took place on the cross was a judgment of sin. Consequently, all who are in Christ Jesus have been judged already and, hence, have passed from death unto life. The judgment of angels, which, according to Peter, is future, and to which Paul alluded in chapter 6, is one which involves believers as judges. In addition, the church is responsible for exercising a judgment within its own fellowship (5:12).

Three decidedly futuristic judgments are also apparently delineated in the Scriptures. Some have sought to interpret them merely as different descriptions of the same judgment. Others have found at least two of the three to be synonymous. However, the only way that such conclusions are possible is for the interpreter to demonstrate an almost total disregard for the specific details in those passages.

For example, there is no mention of the presence of any believer at the Great White Throne Judgment (Rev. 20). Apparently, this is a judgment which occurs after the millennium at the end of the earth's history. It is a judgment in which all the lost are shown full justice in God's judgment against them. By the same token, the Sheep and Goat Judgment (Matt. 25) is so different in its description that it could scarcely be the same judgment. While this one is in some respects the most difficult of all to interpret, it is probably best understood as enacted at the judgment determining who will enter the millennial kingdom of the Lord at the end of the Great Tribulation.

In Romans 14:10 and in 2 Corinthians 5:10, we are told of the appearance of believers before the *bēma* or the judgment seat of Christ. Although the word *bēma*, which is mentioned in those two passages, is not mentioned in the verses before us at the present moment, there can be little doubt that the judgment herein described coincides in both purpose and time with the *bēma* of Christ. This is a judgment which the believers of the Church Age apparently face immediately upon their translation into heaven. Several important features of this judgment should be noticed. (1) No one will face this judgment except those who have laid an adequate foundation; i.e., they have had an experience of salvation in Christ. This rules out the presence of any unbeliever. (2) The judgment specifically has to do with an evaluation of the works of the believer following his salvation experience. (3) In a real sense, it is not so much a judgment as it is a determination of that which has lasting value and significance within the believer's spiritual pilgrimage. In a sense, it could be termed "the reward seat of Christ."

Approaching the ruins of the main thoroughfare of ancient New Testament Corinth, today one sees the *bēma*, a large raised platform some eight to ten feet in height. It was a place to which victorious returning warriors came to be rewarded for their heroism. It was also frequently the place for the crowning of winning athletes as well as for the distribution of various citizenship awards. There were times when it also served the purpose of judgment (Acts 18:12f), but as often as not, its purpose was reward.

The judgment every believer faces is not a judgment for his sin. As indicated previously, his sins have already been judged on the cross. Consequently, the purpose of this judgment is the determination of reward. In that day, every man's work will be made manifest. It is expressly said, "The day shall declare it." The day is apparently not just any day but specifically the day of Christ or the time of His return for His church. Furthermore, the nature of the testing of our works will be revelation precipitated by those fires which test every man's work in order to determine the permanent value of it.

3:14 The result of this testing will be both positive and negative. Positively, the portion of a believer's work which survives the test of fire will remain, and he will receive reward *(misthos)* for it. This, of course, raises the question of the nature of heavenly rewards. Does this indicate that some may have little or no reward while others receive great reward? Furthermore, how can happiness be experienced in heaven by one who has received little reward when he observes others receiving great reward? And, finally, what is the nature of heavenly reward? The answers to these questions are not provided with the specificity which satisfies our curiosities. However, some of the broad outlines are present. First, Scripture clearly teaches a distinction in the amount of reward provided. Not only is that the case in this particular passage, but it is also emphatically the teaching of our Lord in the parable of the talents when the Lord said to the man who had received five talents and delivered five more beside to this master, "Well done, thou good and faithful servant: thou hast been faithful over a few things, I will make thee ruler over many things: enter thou into the joy of thy lord" (Matt. 25:21). Clearly, there is distinction in what is done for the servants, and it is further evident that rulership is involved in heavenly reward.

In answer to the question, "How, then, in heaven can men be happy seeing others who have experienced greater reward than themselves?" one must remember that heavenly perception will be far better than our present limited vision. Those who are present with the Lord will have such clear insight into the nature of heaven and the nature of hell and precisely what it is that they have avoided in eternal punishment and what they have received in eternal bliss so that just to be present with the Lord will be total happiness. To ask which man would be happier would be like asking which of two men struggling for survival in a desert, bereft of access to water, is the happiest—the one staggering upon a trickle of fresh, cold water making a small pool adequate to slake his thirst or the one falling into an enormous waterfall. They are both equally happy to have survived and to have their thirst quenched, even though one has profusion of water and the other only a little.

In addition to the indication that rulership responsibilities may well be involved in the nature of heavenly rewards, the New Testament writers also speak of crowns that are to be given. Note the following:

(1) An incorruptible crown for mastery of the spiritual life (9:25),

(2) A crown of rejoicing given to faithful soulwinners (1 Thess. 2:19),

(3) A crown of life given to those who suffer great tribulation for the cause of Christ (James 1:12, Rev. 2:10),

(4) A crown of righteousness given to all those who love His appearing (2 Tim. 4:8),

(5) An unfading crown given to faithful shepherds (1 Pet. 5:4).

The precise nature of these crowns is not specified. They are clearly *stephanos* crowns—i.e., victors' crowns, rather than *diadēma* or kingly crowns. Furthermore, the recipients of those crowns obviously recognize that even the crown itself is actually a manifestation of the marvelous grace of God. It is, therefore, no wonder that we read of the twenty-four crowned elders, apparently representative of all the redeemed of all time, sitting around the throne of God with their *stephanos* crowns upon their heads, falling before the throne and casting their crowns at the feet of the Lamb and shouting, "Thou art worthy, O Lord, to receive glory and honor and power" (Rev. 4:11). Even the rewards given for our works are expressions of the manifold graces of God, but this does not change the truth that those works in the category of gold, silver, and precious stones, which abide the testing of fire, result in the receiving of great reward.

3:15 In contradistinction, those works characterized by wood, hay, and stubble, when subjected to fire, will be burned. The man therefore suffers loss though he himself is saved, yet so as by fire. In a frantic search to find some scriptural precedent for the doctrine of purgatory, the Roman Church has sometimes appealed to this passage, but there are no purgatorial fires here. This is not the purging of evil but the annihilation of what is worthless. As a matter of fact, in the parallel passage Paul wrote, "For we must all appear before the judgment seat of Christ; that every one may receive the things done in his body, according to that he hath done, whether it be good or bad" (2 Cor. 5:10). But the issue here is not between good (*agatha*) and moral evil, as we would expect with the word "bad" in the King James Version text. If the writer had intended "bad" in the sense of evil, he would probably have used *kakos* or *ponērōs*. However, the word "bad" (*phaulos*) simply means "worthless." We will stand before the judgment seat of Christ to receive the things done in our bodies, whether they are good or worthless. Those things which are worthless, such as wood, hay, or stubble, are simply annihilated and are of no further value at all.

If, however, the fire mentioned here is not purgatorial fire, and if it is not the fire of divine judgment as such, then what kind of flame is this? When John looked from his vantage point on Patmos at the wonderful, exalted, and glorified Jesus, he found that "his eyes were as a flame of fire" (Rev. 1:14). Again, our Lord identifies Himself to the church at Thyatira by saying, "These things saith the Son of God, who hath his eyes like unto a flame of fire" (Rev. 2:18). Although it is conjecture, one may conclude that when the believer stands for the first time before the glorified, exalted Jesus, the gaze of our Lord shall penetrate the very thoughts and motivations of his life. Every action, thought, or motive that is ignoble and unworthy of Him will be incinerated in the penetrating gaze of the Lord. But those things which are worthy of Him, through the grace of God, shall be preserved, and the believer will receive reward.

3. The Indwelling of the Spirit (3:16–23)

This information concerning the judgment seat of Christ prompted Paul to a discussion of the temple (vv. 16–17), the thoughts (vv. 18–20), and the temptations (vv. 21–23), which are all a part of man's present pilgrimage.

3:16 First, there is the startling information that the Corinthians were to consider themselves the very temple of God. There are two words for "temple" in the Greek New Testament. One is the word *hiera*, which encompassed the entire temple complex. The other is the word *naos*, which generally was used to describe only the Holy of Holies where God was uniquely to dwell. Interestingly, Paul did not speak of the Corinthians as the *hiera* but as the *naos*, the innermost dwelling place of the Lord. In fact, the Corinthian church could consider itself the Holy of Holies because God's Spirit was dwelling among them. Paul returned to this thought in 1 Corinthians 6:19 where he spoke very specifically of the body of the individual believer as being the *naos* of God. In chapter 3, however, he seems to have included the entire Corinthian congregation as the temple of God. Certainly this is based on the individual indwelling of the Holy Spirit, but the congregation here also was viewed corporately as the temple of God.

3:17 Understandably, this analysis of the nature of the Corinthian congregation resulted in awesome responsibility. Therefore, the apostle warned, "If any man defile the temple of God, him shall God destroy." The reason for this serious warning was that the temple of God was to be maintained in holiness. The words "defile" and "destroy" are the same in the Greek New Testament, except for the fact that the second use of *phtheirō* is in the future tense. The significance of this word is not annihilation. The idea is better served by the translation "spoil," "ruin," or "corrupt." Therefore, if any man spoils the temple of God, God will also spoil him. This gives a clear insight into the seriousness with which God views the continuing ministry of His churches.

3:18 Moving from the temple of God, Paul then examined the very thought life of men. No man was to deceive himself. If someone seemed to be wise in the present age, he was to become a fool so that he might be wise. There was no invitation here on the part of the apostle for a man to adopt strange and obnoxious behavior or to delight himself in ignorance. He was simply using the words "wise" and "foolish" in the way in which he utilized them in chapter 1. If someone seems to be wise, then he should demonstrate that perception by adopting the wisdom of God, even though it is foolishness to men.

3:19 That the above interpretation of becoming a fool is what the apostle had in mind is now verified in the statement that the wisdom of this world is foolishness to God. He then proceeded to quote Job 5:13 and in so doing utilized a word which occurs only one time, a *hapax legomena,* in the New Testament. *Drassomai* is a picturesque word which means "to put forth the hand and capture." God is said to capture the wise in their own devices or in their own craftiness. Craftiness *(panourgia)* is composed of the Greek adjective *pan,* meaning "all" or "every," and the word *ergon,* meaning "work." Therefore, God is pictured as capturing the wise in the midst of all their cunning and artful wisdom or works. The intent of the verse is to point out that when man has extended himself to the very limits of his thinking ability, he still finds it impossible to evade the Lord. Like Adam, modern man, hearing the voice of the Lord God in the cool of the day, finds that he can never hide from an omniscient, omnipresent God.

3:20 This inability of man to evade God has to do not merely with his actions but even with his thoughts. Paul quotes the psalmist, "The LORD knoweth the thought of man" (Ps. 94:11). The word "thoughts" (*dialogismos*, Greek) literally means "to think one's way logically though a circumstance." But the wisest of man's dialogues, upon examination, are found "empty" (*mataios*, meaning "groundless," "fruitless," "unprofitable," or even "erroneous"). These words could not possibly describe more accurately the wisest of the moralistic and spiritual thinkers who come to their conclusions without benefit of divine, special revelation.

3:21 In light of the above, a man faces some special temptations. The major temptation is to glory in men. This is exactly the mistake that the Corinthians were making. They gloried in their human leaders rather than in their Heavenly King. This temptation must be resisted in the future, since all things belonged to them. The intention in this statement is apparently to remind the Corinthians of what Paul had said earlier when he stated that it was the believer's prerogative to "know the things that are freely given to us of God" (2:12).

3:22 Not only are these spiritual matters a part of their possession, but Paul, Apollos, Cephas, the world itself, life, death, things present, and things that are coming—all belong to the believer. Two things astonish the reader who examines this listing. First of all, it is apparent that the very leaders of the Christian faith in that era are described as being the property of the believing church. The church does not belong to the leaders; the leaders belong to the church! That simple adjustment in thinking is critical to the success of the congregations of the Lord wherever they exist.

A second apparent oddity about the listing is the presence of the word "death." One is not surprised that the believers are to rejoice in the fact that Paul, Apollos, Cephas, the world, life, things present, and things to come belong to them, but are they to rejoice that death belongs to them? The answer is emphatically, "yes." God's view of death is very different from that of most men. He expresses this viewpoint through the psalmist: "Precious in the sight of the LORD is the death of his saints" (Ps. 116:15). In other words, physical death, while never to be sought by a believer, who is also charged to "work out your own salvation with fear and trembling" (Phil. 2:12), nonetheless is not something to be feared. As a matter of fact, it represents a final escape from the propensities toward evil which are still a part of his nature. In addition to that, it represents his homegoing to be with the Lord who bought him. Consequently, even death belongs as a prize to the believer.

3:23 Just as all things belong to the believer, the believer belongs to Christ, and Christ is of God. These concluding phrases are not merely an addendum to what Paul was stating. He has been developing his thought to this concluding and crowning moment. What is important is not that one belongs to the party of Paul or of Apollos or of Cephas. All that is important is that he belongs to Christ, because Christ, in a very unique sense, is of God. The extensive argument of the first three chapters concerning the party spirit in the church at Corinth has now culminated at this peak of insight, focusing upon the Messiah of God. It is as if the events of the transfiguration of Christ had once again been portrayed before the eyes of the Corinthians. Peter's suggestion that a tabernacle should be built for Moses, Elijah, and Jesus was met with a firm voice from heaven, "This is my beloved Son, in whom I am well pleased; hear ye him" (Matt. 17:5), and when the luminous cloud had passed over, it is also recorded that "they saw no man, save Jesus only" (Matt. 17:8). Paul seems to have been saying to the Corinthians: "Build no tabernacles for Paul, Apollos, or Cephas; hear Christ alone."

Revealing the Counsel of the Heart

1. Hidden Things of Darkness (4:1-7)
2. Harsh Trials of an Apostle (4:8-13)
3. Heartening Testimony of a Father (4:14-21)

1. Hidden Things of Darkness (4:1-7)

The fourth chapter brings to a conclusion the discussion of the divisions in the church at Corinth. The zenith in the discussion has been achieved in the closing verse of chapter 3. Now, in chapter 4, there are some natural conclusions that arise therefrom. Paul discussed the hidden things of darkness (vv. 1-7), the harsh trials of an apostle (vv. 8-13), and the heartening testimony of a father (vv. 14-21). In this discussion, he made two essential affirmations: (1) eventually even the thoughts and motivations of a man's life will become patently evident, and (2) Paul himself did to some degree occupy a position of superiority with reference to the Corinthians by virtue of the fact that he had begotten them in the Lord.

In the first section of chapter 4, Paul discussed the necessity of accepting the stewardship that God has given us (vv. 1-4), reserving the sentence about ourselves (v.5), and acknowledging the sovereignty of God in it all (vv. 6–7).

4:1 Two words which normally describe the work of slaves are employed. An enormous segment of the Roman Empire consisted of slaves, and it is to be expected that different words would become vehicles for expressing the status of those slaves. Ministers (*hupēretēs*) and stewards (*oikonomos*) are both used in this verse. Still a third term is employed in verse 15 where Paul used "instructor" (*paidagōgos*). Elsewhere in his epistles, of course the apostle also made use of the general words "slave" (*doulos*), "servant" (*diakonos*), and "household servant" (*oikētes*) to describe the various assignments of slaves.[16]

The two words employed in this particular verse link together one of the highest assignments with one of the most insignificant assignments in a Roman household. "Ministers" (*hupēretēs*), literally "underrower," referred to the galley slaves who provided the locomotion for the Roman brigs. On the other hand, if we are underrowers or galley slaves propelling forward the kingdom of our Lord, Christians also have an exalted office as stewards (*oikonamos*) of the mystery of God. The steward was the slave who had become so completely trusted that he had been given the assignment of manager over the entire house and, in some cases, over a whole estate. So at the same moment, believers are galley slaves and trusted managers of the mysteries of Christ.

The word "account" (*logizomai*) is a bookkeeping term. "Account" is a good translation, although in this particular case the words "calculate" or "reckon" might be more precise. In any case, the term suggests that men should reckon Paul, Apollos, and others, as both ministers of Christ and stewards of the mysteries of God. Household management of the mysteries of God does not imply full understanding of those mysteries, nor does it suggest ownership of them. It is merely recognition on the apostle's part that these mysteries of God (facts that should never have been ascertained by human reasoning) were vouchsafed through revelation to Paul and others to be presented and ex-

---

[16]For a full discussion of each of these terms, see my commentary *A Pilgrim Priesthood: An Exposition of First Peter*, p. 93.

plained to the Lord's people.

4:2 The conclusion, then, is not at all astonishing. It is required, or even "demanded," that a household manager be found faithful in the discharge of that responsibility. Paul recognized that the faithfulness of the steward and his master might not always be free of pain or confrontation. Certainly, in this instance the discharge of that responsibility was exceedingly painful. Nevertheless, he was bound to do as the Lord had asked him.

4:3 Faithfulness to the Lord was demanded even though there were those who would take issue with the apostle and, going beyond this, even judge his motivations. One of the most difficult things for any man to do is to remind himself that he may be a fruit inspector but not a root inspector. It is possible for us to disagree with the position enunciated by another individual, but it is never possible for us, as mortals, to know the motivations out of which certain actions or positions of another arise. Therefore, it is always exceedingly painful when others attempt what is clearly impossible in judging our motives. Paul had experienced that. How did he learn to deal with it? In verse 3, he simply wrote, "It is a very small thing that I should be judged of you." The word "small" (*elachistos*) is the superlative form of the Greek word *mikros*, which occurs in our English word "microscope." The word means infinitesimally small. Therefore, Paul literally said not that "it is a very small thing" but that "it is the most insignificant thing of all" that he might be judged (subjunctive mood indicates the possibility that it will happen) by the Corinthians.

Then there follows the phrase that is translated "or of man's judgment," literally, "or by a human day." This rather unusual expression has two notable features about it. First, it is a relatively rare use of the word "day" (*hēmera*), thus showing on the part of the apostle a rather remarkable grasp of the finer points of the Greek language. In the second place, it was apparently Paul's purpose here to contrast "man's day" with "the day" that shall try all men's works by fire (3:13), which is "the day of Christ." The apostle was simply saying that any day of judgment on the part of man is insignificant to him.

Paul then went one step further and wrote, "I do not even

judge myself." In this avowal, Paul did not mean that he never subjected his own spirit to careful scrutiny. Certainly he attempted to see to it that his motives as well as his actions were pleasing to God. On the other hand, he knew the depravity of his own mind and heart. After all, it was Paul who said, "For the good that I would I do not: but the evil which I would not, that I do" (Rom. 7:19). Consequently, he knew that there would be times when, if he were to judge himself, that judgment would not be sufficiently penetrating or harsh. There would be other occasions in which his judgment upon himself might be unduly critical. Therefore, he realized that the whole matter of the judgment of men's motives and thoughts must lie with the Lord. Thus far, then, the apostle had affirmed three things: (1) it was the least of all matters for him that the Corinthians might judge him, (2) no judgment day appointed by men held any fear for him, and (3) he even knew better than to attempt to judge himself.

4:4 The reason for this reticence to judge even himself lay in Paul's understanding that he was not omniscient. The great apostle affirmed that he did not know anything in and of himself. Only what was revealed by God in the spiritual realm was perfectly reliable. Therefore, his judgment is automatically shortcircuited in this regard. However, the apostle also recognized that this did not mean that all of his deeds, actions, and thoughts were thereby justified. While he was writing under the inspiration of the Holy Spirit of God, what he wrote was certainly true. Other times, he was a mere mortal, encompassed with all the frailties typical of the species. The fact that he did not know anything in and of himself did not justify his behavior or his thoughts. It just meant that ultimately the Lord was the one who judged him.

4:5 In light of the inability of men to judge even themselves, much less others, it is essential that sentence of any kind be reserved until the day of the Lord. Paul, therefore, cautioned the Corinthians to make no judgments about anything before that time. The word "time" is not *chronos*, from which we derive "chronology" and the standard we generally use for evaluating time as sequence of events, but rather *kairos*, a word almost always associated with the Lord's choice of times. The caution, therefore, is that men are to judge nothing before the Lord's choice of time. The expression "until the Lord come" is a still further delineation of "the day that shall declare it" (3:13). At that particular time two things will transpire. First, the hidden things, which are presently enshrouded in darkness, will be brought into the light. Second, the very counsels of the hearts of men will be revealed. The "counsels of the heart" is an expression that focuses on the motives which are present, underlying every act of a man. Thus we are appropriately reminded that even right actions may stem from inappropriate and ungodly motives. For example, a man may be a great soulwinner or a consistent student of the Scriptures for no other reason than attaining the praise of men.

Although the intents and actions of lost men will be judged at the Great White Throne judgment, this does not appear to be in view here. The concluding statement of the verse, "and then shall every man have praise of God," suggests that the bringing to light "the hidden things of darkness" and the revelation of "the counsels of hearts" is still a reference to the saints of God and to their appearance at the judgment seat of Christ. It is a terrifying moment when one stands before the penetrating gaze of the Lord's Christ with nothing hidden from his gaze. Our most depraved thoughts and the most precise nature of our motivations in the doing of the work of the Savior will also become apparent.

4:6 This section is concluded with a reaffirmation of the need to acknowledge the sovereignty of God in these things. First, Paul wrote that he had transferred all of these things to himself and to Apollos. The word "transfer" (*metaschēmatizō*) is made up of two words, one of which gives us our word "scheme" and means "a pattern of things." The prefix *meta* is a preposition indicating a change or exchange. The previous statements of Paul were, therefore, to be transferred to Apollos and to Paul in order that the Corinthians might be informed or taught not to think more highly of any man than is called for in the Scriptures. Were this to be the rule of thumb by which the Corinthians operated, then it would be impossible for a man to become inflated in his thinking concerning any of the spiritual leadership given to the church.

4:7 The section is concluded with a favorite device of the apostle—the use of three rhetorical questions. The first is simply, "Who makes you to differ?" The King James Version's "form another" is not in the original text. The implication here is that if, indeed, you differ from others, it is God who has prescribed the difference. The second question is, "What do you have or possess which was not given you by God?" The nature of this question was designed to remind the Corinthians that whatever their achievements may have been, they were really not the achievements of the flesh or the intellect but, again, the grace of God. In the third and final question, "Why then do you glory as if what you have had not been received as a gift from God?" the implication is that the Corinthians were at least in part guilty of receiving God's gifts and then treating them with arrogance of spirit as though these gifts were the result of personal achievement.

2. Harsh Trials of an Apostle (4:8–13)

The second section of chapter 4, first of all, is devoted to an assessment of Corinthian prosperity (v. 8), a further assessment of apostolic prospects (vv. 9–10), and finally, a realistic analysis of missionary privations (vv. 11–13). The contrast between the Corinthian prosperity and the apostolic and missionary tribulation is profound.

4:8 Many have suggested that his verse was stated tongue-in-cheek by Paul so that indulging in rather poignant irony, he painted the Corinthian mind as it perceived itself. There is reason to believe that this was taking place, since it would help Paul to establish the point he was about to make concerning the difficulties through which the apostles had walked and would continue to experience. On the other hand, it may be that this verse represents something of a realistic analysis of the Corinthian situation, especially in contrast to the apostolic mode of existence.

In any case, he speaks of the Corinthians as being "full" (*korennumi*). The word means to "satiate" or "satisfy." The reference here is apparently not so much to physical food as it is to the satisfying of all of their appetites. The condition of the Corinthians is further described as "rich," "reigning as kings" without the leadership of the church even present. It is particularly this last phrase that has raised the question as to whether or not Paul was indulging in irony. This is especially so since Paul added that he wished that they did reign as kings so that he, by his association with them, might reign also. The expression "would to God" is an exceedingly free translation of the Greek word *ophelon*. No Jew would be very comfortable with using the divine name so carelessly as this. Actually, this strong interjection might be better translated, "O that!" or "Would that!" so that the whole phrase is best rendered, "Would that you did reign as kings in order that we might be able to reign with you!" The implication is clearly that Paul did not conceive of himself as reigning at the moment, nor did he anticipate such a reign until the Lord established His kingdom. Consequently, he questioned whether or not the Corinthians really reigned.

4:9 Apostolic prospects are quite different from any possibility of treatment as royalty. Actually, Paul thought that God had set forth the apostles to have, as it were, a date with death. The vivid expression "appointed to death" implies that most of the apostles could anticipate rough treatment even to the point of martyrdom. What can be known historically of the lives of the apostles seems to verify this judgment on Paul's part. Not only, however, is it a matter of being appointed unto death, but they have also been made a spectacle (*theatron*) to the whole world, including both angels and men. Our word "theater" is derived from this picturesque word, which itself implies a production for public viewing. The lives, and even the deaths, of the apostles were made for public viewing.

The poignancy of this state of affairs can scarcely be overstated. Even for those whose lives are largely public matter, death at least is generally a private matter in which one's passage is shielded from the curious eyes of onlookers. Not so in the case of the apostles. In fact, it might be well said for all believers that their lives in Christ become a public spectacle, which should be free from the vices that would embarrass the rest of the world if such public display were made.

4:10 The assessment continues with a series of contrasts. Paul claimed that the apostles were fools for Christ. This represented a judgment of the world and Paul's acceptance of that judgment. By contrast, the Corinthians were wise in Christ. The word generally expected (*sophia*), however, is not here employed. The word is rather *phronimos*, which might be rendered "sagacious" or "wise" from the root meaning "to think."

Furthermore, the disciples were weak (*asthenēs*), a word frequently associated with the weakness engendered by grave illness, whereas by contrast the Corinthians were strong. Finally, the Corinthians are honorable, whereas the apostles are despised. The word "honorable" (*endoxos*) combines *doxa* (glory) and the Greek preposition *en* to mean honorable in the sense of being "in the glory"; whereas the apostles were *atimos*. *Timē*, the Greek word for "precious," is prefaced by the alpha privative, negating its significance and making it mean the very opposite of precious—i.e., "despised."

4:11 This state of affairs was not just one that existed in the past but one that continued as part of the missionary enterprise with no signs of abating. Consequently, Paul said that until "this present hour" the apostles experienced hunger, thirst, nakedness, and the blows of men, always without a certain place to dwell. Doubtless, all of these descriptions were intended to be understood relatively and not absolutely. The apostle indicated that he had no place that he could call his own home. His clothing was barely adequate and in winter seasons was probably inadequate. He often knew what it meant to experience a paucity of food and drink and was subject continually to the buffeting and bruising of the blows of men. Had Paul chosen to continue in the rabbinate, his learned teacher Gamaliel would doubtless have provided the best care for him in the discharge of his rabbinical duties. Even as a Christian, Paul certainly could have been adequately supplied and protected by his congregation. However, he was not herein complaining about his missionary enterprise, only stating the facts for the benefit of the Corinthians so that they might not be inflated in the estimate of their own labor.

4:12 The description of the work of the missionary continues. Paul indicated that he was laboring continually (*kopiaō*). Once again, this word, which gives us our word "copious," is an indication of the extent and degree of the labor to which the apostles gave themselves. Paul stressed, further, that they worked with their own hands. In the midst of such circumstances, they were reviled, a word which means "to speak evil against," and yet, in response, they delivered a eulogy (*eulogeō*), literally "to say a good word." In response to evil words said toward the apostles, they replied with good words. When persecuted, the apostles simply endured. The word (*anechomai*) derives from *echō*, "to have," and the preposition *ane*, "again." So to have it again and again is to endure patiently.

4:13 Not only are they persecuted with unkind things said, but they were also the subject of reproach. Yet when reproached, the response of the apostles was simply further exhortation or, as the King James Version translates, "we entreat." Finally, in two vivid metaphors, the apostle summed up the viewpoint of the world with regard to the apostles by stressing that they were made as the "filth" of the world and the "offscouring of all things until this very day." "Filth" is a translation of *perikatharma*. This word employs the Greek word *katharizō*, which means "to cleanse" or "to purify," with the preposition *peri* meaning "around." It refers to the filth surrounding some object which, when subject to a cleansing bath, is scraped away and left behind as the residue. The other word translated "offscouring" is similar. It, in turn, comes from two Greek words, *psaō*, which means "to rub or wipe away," and *peri*, which once again means "around." Anything that might be left in the cleansing bath would then be subject to vigorous wiping or rubbing to take away whatever defilement might remain. Paul chose these two terms to describe the perspective of the world with regard to the work of the apostles.

If the world so viewed the apostles, why is it that modern believers have a tendency to be unhappy and even jump the traces if others do not appreciate what they are doing in the work of the Lord?

3. Heartening Testimony of a Father (4:14–21)

The final section of chapter 4 becomes intensely personal. Having gone to great lengths to exhibit the superiority of Christ and to position the servants of the Lord as mere slaves, Paul concluded with a description of his own relationship to the Corinthians. He spoke first of the necessity of following Paul (vv. 14–16). He next featured Timothy (v. 17), and finally called upon the Corinthians to fear the Lord (vv. 18–21).

4:14 The necessity for the writing of all that had gone before was now brought to the attention of the Corinthians. None of these things had been written in order to shame the Corinthians but rather to "warn them." The word "shame" (*entrepō*) literally means "to turn inward," the act of one who finds himself suddenly put to shame. However, such was not what Paul desired. Rather, he had written to the Corinthians as to beloved sons (anticipating what he would next say about himself as father). His warning (*noutheteō*, literally, combining *tithēmi*, meaning "to place," with *nous*, indicating the "mind") was written to place these things in the minds of the Corinthians.

4:15 Following the suggestion of Corinthian sonship in verse 14, the apostle then moved to the uniqueness of his own position with the Corinthians. Many instructors (*paidagōgoi*) might come on the scene. This is the same word used by Paul in Galatians to describe the purpose of the law, which was "our schoolmaster to bring us unto Christ" (Gal. 3:24). The word "schoolmaster" is the same word that is here rendered "instructor," referring to a trusted slave who, in that position, occupied a place of greater esteem than any other slave in the household with the possible exception of the *oikonomos* or household manager. The *paidagōgos* was a slave placed in charge of the successful rearing of the children. He accompanied them to and from school to guarantee their safety, and most frequently labored with them as a tutor in the areas of their study. The term, then, is a favorable one, and Paul did not mean to reduce the instructors to a point of insignificance.

Yet the contrast follows strongly. Although there were many

instructors, there were not many fathers. Paul was apparently the first believer to arrive in Corinth, or at least the first to engage in missionary and evangelistic endeavor in that city. In so doing, it was he who fathered the church, winning those first converts. Thus, he had "begotten the Corinthians through the gospel."

4:16 Consequently, he has no hesitancy in exhorting the Corinthians to be followers of him. The word "follower" is *mimētēs* from which we get our English word "mimic." He called upon the Corinthians literally to "mimic" his doctrinal commitment and his lifestyle. Once again, this was not to depreciate at all what they might have imbibed constructively from other instructors, but it did call their attention to the importance of the leadership role of the one who first introduced them to Christ.

4:17 In order to assist them in getting these issues successfully resolved and clarified, Paul was going to send Timothy, whom he described as his own beloved son, faithful in the Lord. Of course, Timothy was not actually the biological offspring of Paul. He was the son of a Jewess, although his father was a Greek. Apparently he was a citizen of the city of Lystra. He had believed in the Lord, showed great potential, and was the immediate object of Paul's interest. Indeed, it seems probable that Paul took a greater personal interest in Timothy than in any other of the men with whom he labored (Acts. 16:1-4).

There is also indication that Timothy may not have been altogether successful in his ministry at Corinth. That problems still persisted at the time of the writing of 2 Corinthians is an indication that he was at best only partially successful. Nevertheless, the nature of his mission was to bring to their attention, literally "to make the Corinthians remember again," the ways of Christ as Paul had taught them everywhere in every church. Note once again the prominence of the local churches in the missionary work of Paul.

4:18 There is a final word of warning given by Paul. Some, he had heard, were puffed up or inflated in their own pride concerning whether or not Paul would come. Apparently they were spreading the word that while Paul threatened to come, he probably would not have the courage to show up and face the music.

4:19 Consequently, Paul pledged that he would come to them shortly, contingent only upon the express will of God. This expression is an important one for consideration in any era. There is no doubt that Paul's desire was to go to the Corinthians and personally straighten out the matter. Yet the very fact that he was sending Timothy (v.17) is an indication that apparently God did not will for him to go at the present time. As he would specify later, the work at Ephesus had proven a great open door, and he must stay as long as the Lord willed. Furthermore, it is apparent that Paul would not even do the thing that he most wanted to do unless he could be assured that it was God's will. For a Christian to distinguish between God's will and his own ardent desire to do a certain thing, though the thing in itself may be ever so noble, is one of the more difficult problems which believers face. Since our judgment may not be perfect, there ought always to be the effort to discern the mind of the Spirit.

In any case, when he did come to Corinth, Paul assured them that he would not know the speech of those who were puffed up, but rather he would speak to them in the power of God.

4:20 The reason for the speech of power would be because he spoke not out of the colloquia of men's wisdom but as a spokesman for the kingdom of God, and the kingdom of God was not a matter of word alone but was characterized by power. Consequently, when he came, his speech will be the speech of power.

4:21 There is a final urgent admonition provided. Almost plaintively, Paul raised the question as to the preference of the Corinthians. Did they want him to come with rod in hand, or did they prefer that he come in love and in a spirit of meekness? Very likely there was no intention that Paul would come with physical rod in hand, determined to administer corporal punishment, but the effect would be much the same if he were forced to use the rod of stringent verbiage.

Therefore, in effect, he urged an openness on the part of the Corinthians and a faithfulness in searching for the solution so that he might come in love and a spirit of meekness.

Renewing Church Discipline

1. Puffed-Up Pride (5:1-8)
2. Purified Participation (5:9-13)

Few facets of the modern life of the church have found themselves any further removed from New Testament Christianity than the subject of church discipline. Part of the problem has been a reaction against former doctrinal abuses, which sometimes resulted in the excommunication of individuals from the membership of the church for petty and insignificant offenses. On the other hand, much of the responsibility for the failure of the modern church in this area is due merely to our losing a concept of the holiness of God and of the importance of a pure church consisting of persons who are determined to do all that they can to keep the bride of Christ pure against the day of her presentation.

The two sections into which this chapter will be divided may be considered under the headings of the puffed-up pride of the Corinthians (vv. 1-8) and the purified participation of the Corinthians (vv. 9-13). The instructions given to the church at Corinth are applicable to our own day. At least a portion of the revival evangelical Christians anticipate must be associated with the restoration of church discipline with its corollaries of meaningful church membership and a purified church.

1. Puffed-Up Pride (5:1–8)

In examining the puffed-up pride of the Corinthians, note first the Corinthian crisis (v. 1), the corresponding critique (vv. 2–6), and the counter course recommended (vv. 7–8).

5:1 Paul opened the discussion by rehearsing for the Corinthians the information that he had been given. He began with the strong word *holōs*, meaning "actually." The statement follows that fornication had actually been heard to exist among them. The word *porneia* has been the subject of much recent discussion as to its precise meaning. The word itself is used in almost every conceivable connection in the Greek language with a range of meanings from prostitution, fornication, unchastity, harlotry, whoremonger, and, even in a slight variable as sodomite or homosexual. The general impression one receives from reading the New Testament literature is that the word *porneia* represents a general phrase encompassing every kind of sexual immorality. Whereas adultery is very specific and limited to sexual activities which are reprehensible within themselves but are made especially so by the violence they do to the sacredness of the home, *porneia* is a word which includes adultery but also covers every other form of sexual licentiousness. For example, in our own language, pornography is the writing or picturing of sexually explicit materials with one additional aspect attached. Normally, modern pornography is most frequently associated with the exchange of money. This will come as no surprise to a careful student of etymology, since, as Robert Gromacki points out, the noun *porneia* is derived from the Greek verb *pernemi*,[17] which had reference to the export of commodities for sale. Gradually the word became associated with the sale of bodies, often for sexual purposes, and also with bribery. The word *porneia*, then, apparently reflects involvement in sexual activities of any nature

---

[17]Robert G. Gromacki, *Called to be Saints*, p. 61.

other than those which are explicitly approved in the Scriptures. Often *porneia* had to do with purchased sexual experience.

In the case of the situation in Corinth, however, there apparently was no monetary exchange involved. On the other hand, the particular type of fornication which existed in the church at Corinth was repugnant even to most Gentiles, so much so that it was not even named among the Gentiles, further evidence of the multitude of offenses that can actually be covered by this word. In the case of the Corinthians, however, the statement is made that one of them apparently was sustaining relations on a regular basis with his father's wife. The strangeness of the language suggests that this incestuous relationship was not a man's entering sexual union with his own mother. Apparently the man's mother had either died or was divorced from his father. Therefore, the language indicates that the incest was with his father's wife.

5:2 The apostle Paul did not react so stridently against the existence of this problem in Corinth. Such occurrences were common in the decadent days of the Roman Empire, even as they are in our own day. While the apostle was disappointed that it had occurred, the nature of his real concern centered around the inactivity of the church at Corinth with reference to the deed perpetrated. He offered three criticisms concerning their actions. First, they were puffed up or inflated in their own estimate of themselves, and, hence, they had not acted. This word *phusioō*, which occurs repeatedly in the first four chapters, is now carried over into chapter 5 with a totally different subject. Yet the same pride and boastfulness which caused the party spirit was apparently also the cause of the inactivity of the Corinthians in recognizing and responding adequately to impurity within the church.

In the second place and as a logical corollary of the fact that the church in Corinth was puffed up with pride, the congregation had not mourned that the offender might be taken away. The act of mourning would have suggested the depth of sorrow present in the church over this impurity. The absence of mourning suggests that there was little sorrow present at all, even though the deed itself was common knowledge. Third and finally, the Corinthians had not taken action to enforce the ban in relation to this individual. He continued as an active member of the assembly, even though his lifestyle was clearly unacceptable in light of the teachings of Christ. In all three of these areas, the Corinthians had seriously offended.

5:3 Paul was not content simply to wait for the Corinthians to decide to do something about the situation. The apostle wrote so as to make it clear that he was going to force the issue, albeit for the good of the church as well as for the good of him who had thus sinned. Paul indicated that while he was absent in the body, he was nonetheless present with the Corinthians in spirit. There is a play on words here in the Greek text involving *apon* and *paron*. The former word derives from *apeimi*, which combines *eimi* with the preposition *apo*, meaning "to be away from." The latter word combines the same verb, meaning "to be," with the preposition *para*, which means "beside." In the play on words, he said, "Though I am not with you in the body, I am beside you in the spirit." This is the phrase which has given rise to the frequently repeated axiom usually utilized today to explain one's absence from the service of worship. The apostle further stated that though he was absent in the body, since he was present in the spirit, he had already judged, as though he really were present, concerning the man who had done this deed or involved himself in this practice.

5:4 Two important matters are observable in this verse. First, the action that Paul recommended was to be taken "in the name of our Lord Jesus Christ." What was being requested was not a reaction of wounded ego or feeling; rather it was an action based upon the authority of the Lord Jesus Christ. The authority to which Paul referred was, in all probability, that which our Lord delineated in Matthew 18:15–18. The method of discipline which Jesus advocated among His disciples is clear. In the event one discovers his brother in a trespass, he is to go to him alone and share the fault. If the brother still does not hear his compatriot, then the concerned brother is to take one or two others of the brotherhood with him, so that "in the mouth of two or three witnesses every word may be established." Should the erring brother be undaunted in his activity, then the whole matter is to be presented to the church. In the event that he fails to hear the church, then he is to be to them as "a heathen man and a publi-can." Such a program obviously is not designed to preclude any-one from the church. Church discipline always has restoration as the ultimate goal. Indeed, the whole process is so established as to make exclusion from the church or the exercise of the ban the last and most serious remedy—only to be used when all else has failed. Both of those observations are critical to the restora-tion of church discipline in our own day. If discipline is reinsti-tuted, this must be done with the goal in mind that the offending party would seek and find repentance and restoration to the lo-cal assembly. In fact, the program must be so formulated as hopefully to secure such repentance prior to the time when a brother would be excluded from the church.

The time for official action was stated as "when you are gath-ered together," with Paul's spirit being present among them, as he had already indicated in verse 3, and especially with the power of our Lord Jesus Christ resting upon them as their authority. Some have imagined that Paul referred to some special discipli-nary council of the church. The unlikelihood of that is lucidly stated by Beet in his commentary on 1 Corinthians: "It is re-markable that in this matter of discipline, and throughout these two epistles so full of church matters, Paul never refers to elders or bishops."[18] This is a significant omission. Although bishops and deacons doubtless existed in the churches, one is pressed to explain why they are not mentioned anywhere in this chapter on discipline. They are not mentioned because church discipline was never intended to be exercised by church officials but by the entire congregation (1 Tim. 5:20). The expression "when you are gathered together" may refer to any official assembly of the church. However, in view of the explicit instructions in verse 11 that the Corinthian Christians were not to eat with such a one, it is probable that the gathering to which Paul referred was for the memorial feast called the Lord's Supper. There is evidence to suggest that many of the churches celebrated the Lord's Supper

---

[18]Beet, *Epistles to the Corinthians*, p. 92.

every time they formally assembled. In any case, an assembly at which the fellowship feast of the church is to be observed is doubtless the most appropriate time for the action recommended.

5:5 The action the church was to take at that time was to deliver the offender to Satan for the "destruction of the flesh." Few verses have occasioned more discussion than this one. Two basic problems must be addressed. First, what did it mean to deliver the man to Satan, and second, to what did "the destruction of the flesh" refer? Three basic positions are advocated by commentators on the question of delivery to Satan.

(1) Leon Morris argues, "It is a very forcible expression of the loss of all Christian privileges."[19] R. C. H. Lenski suggests that the reason for the necessity of such action on the part of the church is that "... if no adequate measures are taken, the congregation itself becomes partaker of the sinner's guilt."[20] The latter point is an excellent one and certainly does constitute the grounds for the action being recommended.

Other verses in chapter 5 tend to verify the excommunication theory. Verse 7, for example, urges the Corinthians to "purge out the old leaven." Verse 11 stresses that the Corinthian Christians were "not to keep company" with such an offender. Verse 12 plainly says that the Corinthians had erred in not judging "them that are within," while verse 13 clearly reads "put away from among yourselves that wicked person." All this is substantial evidence that excommunication or the exercise of the ban is what Paul was recommending.

(2) Many believe that what is in view here is an apostolic judgment. The ban would hardly result in the destruction of the flesh, according to advocates of this second view. Perhaps Hans Conzelmann put it more strongly than anyone when he wrote, "The community merely constitutes the forum. It does not share in the action." Furthermore, Conzelmann concludes, "The destruction of the flesh can hardly mean anything else but death."[21]

---

[19]Morris, *First Corinthians*, p. 88.

[20]R. C. H. Lenski, *The Interpretation of First and Second Corinthians*, p. 216.

[21]Conzelmann, *First Corinthians*, p. 97.

In this he is faithfully following Deissmann in his advocacy of such a view. An impressive array of passages may be generated to support such a view. For example, when Ananias and Sapphira were untruthful with the church and with the Holy Spirit, apostolic judgment fell upon both of them, and one after the other they were carried out from the presence of Peter, who had confronted them, and were buried (Acts 5). It is no wonder Luke wrote, "And great fear came upon all the church, and upon as many as heard these things," and further, "And of the rest durst no man join himself to them" (Acts 5:11,13).

A similiar case may have been in progress in when Simon the Sorcerer attempted to purchase the power of the Holy Spirit from Peter. Peter replied, "Thy money perish with thee, because thou hast thought that the gift of God may be purchased with money. Thou has neither part nor lot in this matter: for thy heart is not right in the sight of God" (Acts 8:20–21). These words elicited this statement from Simon the Sorcerer, "Pray ye to the Lord for me, that none of these things which ye have spoken come upon me" (Acts 8:24). Apparently Simon felt that Peter's words had definite physical ramifications which he did not want to experience.

In another example, Paul spoke of some who had made shipwreck of their lives and then stated that Hymeneus and Alexander were in that category, " ... whom I have delivered unto Satan, that they may learn not to blaspheme" (1 Tim. 1:20). The expression "delivered unto Satan" may just be Paulinism, or it could be that it is an official apostolic judgment.

But surely Conzelmann is only partially right at best. His idea that the church was merely the forum rather than the body acting in this matter is an oversimplification. If there was, in fact, an overt apostolic judgment on this man, then certainly the church was only the forum in which that was taking place. On the other hand, if excommunication was in view, then the church must act also.

Furthermore, Conzelmann is unable to explain why it is that the apostolic judgment given was apparently not effective. The basis of his conclusion is Paul's argument for the restoration of the erring brother to the fellowship once he had become repentant. Apparently, at the time of the writing of 2 Corinthians, though the brother had been excluded from the church fellowship according to the mandate of Paul, he had since repented and yet had not been restored. In those critical verses of 2 Corinthians 2:6–8, Paul stated several things. (1) The punishment inflicted upon the man was sufficient to bring about repentance. (2) The punishment was inflicted by many, a clear indication of congregational action. (3) He ought to be forgiven. (4) He should be comforted lest he should be overcome with too much sorrow. (5) The Corinthians should confirm their love toward him.

Two things are apparent here. First, the man had not been physically affected, at least not to the point of death, by the so-called apostolic judgment, and second, what had been done to him had been by congregational action.

(3) A third viewpoint adopted by some commentators is that actually we are to understand a combination of these two positions. Robertson and Plummer argue, "There is no need to choose between the two interpretations which have been put upon this expression, for they are not mutually exclusive and both are true."[22] The church was to take definite action which would be accompanied by an apostolic judgment of rather decisive import. Charles Hodge argues similarly that there is a measure of truth in both views.[23]

The following conclusions are, therefore, defensible. (1) Conzelmann's view that only apostolic judgment is in view in the passage is clearly unacceptable. (2) The exercise of the ban or the withdrawal of fellowship from the erring brother is definitely in view in the passage. (3) It is possible that not only the ban but also the exercise of an apostolic judgment is present in the command. (4) Even if this latter conclusion is accurate, the absence of the apostles from modern church life precludes the applicability of the decisive apostolic judgment against anyone today. By the same token, the continuing responsibility of the church to

---

[22]Robertson and Plummer, *First Corinthians*, p. 85.
[23]Hodge, *Corinthians I and II*, p. 85.

exercise judgment in these matters and to attempt to preserve a pure church is mandatory today even as then.

The phrase "for the destruction of the flesh, that the spirit may be saved in the day of the Lord Jesus" has been subject to the same interpretive differences as the first phrase of the verse. The question is: To what does the word "flesh" *(sarx)* refer? Once again, three views meet us.

(1) *Sarx* refers to the carnal nature of the man and is to be distinguished in this regard from his body *(sōma)*. R. St. John Parry favors this view, stating, "Here the conception is that the removal of the man from the company of those who are under the protection of the Lord is to abandon him to Satan to do what he will with him with a final reservation."[24] Parry goes on to suggest that the verse primarily intends to tell us of the destruction of his fleshly nature in the ethical sense.

Favoring this view that the word "flesh" *(sarx)* is the very same word used in Paul's analysis of the three kinds of life in 1 Corinthians 2 and 3, one will recall that he wrote of a natural *(psuchikos)* man who was not able to receive the things of the spirit of God. He wrote of a *pneumatikos* man who demonstrated that spiritual nature by ferreting out constantly the things of the Spirit. But, in addition, there was a carnal *(sarkikos)* man who, though saved, demonstrated spiritual immaturity of an alarming variety. His actions were in some respects more like those of the understandable men of the world. It is, therefore, natural that Paul should use the word "flesh," not in terms of the physical body but in terms of the fleshly nature in verse 5. The idea, then, is that the delivery of the man to Satan (exercising the ban) would be the concluding event that hopefully would have the effect of awakening him from his spiritual slumber and causing him to destroy inordinate fleshly appetites to the end that the spirit would be saved in the day of the Lord Jesus.

(2) The second view argues that *sarx* does, in fact, refer to the physical body, since this would be the most natural meaning for the word "flesh." Consequently, what is anticipated in the apos-

---

[24]Parry, *First Corinthians*, p. 53.

tolic judgment is that Satan, who is the author of sin, suffering, and death, is provided his opportunity by the removal of heavenly sanctions protecting the brother from him. Satan is now free to advance just as he did in the Old Testament with Job once the Lord relaxed His protecting hand. The consequence of this will be physical disease and perhaps even the death of the body (11:30). Again, the case of Ananias and Sapphira and the near miss of Simon the Sorcerer might provide verification for this view.

(3) Once again, this view supposes that there is really a combination of possibilities. First, without a doubt, delivering one into the kingdom of Satan suggests that he is being excluded from the church of the Lord. However, not only is the exclusion taking place, but the apostolic judgment upon him means at least the probability of disease and the possibility of death.

When good evangelical commentators are so widely divided, there is indication that caution is in order and dogmatism is excluded. However, the following conclusions seem appropriate. (1) The purpose of whatever transpired with regard to the offending brother was to be certain that his spirit was saved in the day of the Lord Jesus. Paul seems to have been assuming here the possibility that the man's incestuous actions indicated that he might actually never have been saved at all. (2) In the event that the man was saved, the actions were still set in motion with a view to his restoration to the fellowship of the church. (3) It seems, therefore, highly unlikely that the words "destruction of the flesh" refer to death, although on occasion such apostolic judgments did occur. (4) The situation in the church of our own era demands the exclusion of unrepentant offenders through the exercise of church discipline, and, in that sense, the church is "delivering" unto Satan.

Olethros is not the general word that one would anticipate for "destruction." It may mean "to slay," "to destroy," "to be at the point of death," "to render useless or worthless," "to be undone," or simply "to be lost." An analysis of these possibilities may suggest that what is involved in the verse is not death or disease but rendering the fleshly nature of man powerless.

5:6 Paul's conclusion in his critique was that the glorying of the Corinthians in this matter was not good. Another rhetorical question was placed before them, "Know ye not that a little leaven leaveneth the whole lump?" Paul here borrowed a culinary metaphor, reminding the readers of the well known fact that a very small amount of yeast was capable of permeating the whole of the dough mixture in a relatively short period of time. It was not a matter of a small amount of yeast being present in the dough and thereby being relegated to a small portion of it. The permeating quality of the yeast soon would spread throughout the mixture. The nature of Paul's warning was that if the Corinthians did not do something about this particular problem, it would ultimately be the cause of the fermentation of the whole church.

5:7 A counter-course was then proposed for the Corinthian Christians. They were instructed to purge out the old leaven so that there could be a new lump, since they were in fact composed of unfermented substance—namely, the regenerate life. The command can hardly be interpreted in any other way than to suggest some kind of church action by which the church divested itself of one whose permeating influence would cause decadence in the assembly. Paul's Jewish background then asserted itself in the statement, "For even Christ our passover is sacrificed *or slain* for us." The reference to passover and to the slaying of the paschal lamb was engendered in the mind of the apostle by the mention of unleavened bread. At the time of the passover and in preparation for it, the people of Israel were to eat only unleavened bread. Immediately following the passover meal was the Feast of Unleavened Bread. For an entire week, the children of Israel would see to it that all leaven was excluded from their homes (Lev. 23:6). Since leaven is almost always a symbol of evil in the Bible, its absence indicated cleansing and the consecration of the total life of God.

The passover lamb that was slain prefigured the ultimate passover sacrifice, Jesus Christ. Since He died and brought about forgiveness of sin, the church of the Lord is under mandate to keep a perpetual Feast of Unleavened Bread, purging always from its presence any sin that might corrupt it.

5:8 The metaphor is continued with the instruction that the

feast was now to be kept, not with old leaven but with the un-leavened bread of sincerity and truth. The leaven that is specifi-cally mentioned in this verse is the leaven of "malice" (*kakos*, a general word for evil) and "wickedness" (*ponēria*, a general word for the most despicable forms of sinfulness). These two terms are general enough in nature to encompass just about every possible sin with which believers might become associated. By contrast the unleavened bread, which should be the staple of the church, is that of sincerity and truth. The word translated "sincerity" (*eilikrineia*) is a wonderfully picturesque term. It is derived from *krinō*, meaning "to judge," and *eile*, which is best translated "sun-shine." Therefore, the term literally means "to judge in the sun-shine" or "to judge in clear, penetrating light." Two virtues ought always to characterize the church. First, its openness to the scru-tiny of the light of God, with its corresponding openness to the scrutiny of the world, and second, its affinity for and commit-ment to the truth of God.

2. Purified Participation (5:9–13)

Specific information concerning a purified participation in the work of the church is now provided. Paul became very specific concerning eliciting sinners (vv. 9–10), excluding sinning saints (v. 11), and evaluating servants (vv. 11–13).

5:9 First of all, Paul made reference to a former letter he had written to the Corinthians. This letter has not been preserved. Though we do not know its precise contents, apparently it also dealt to some degree with ethical problems. The explicit instruc-tions in that letter, which are now repeated here, were that be-lievers were not to keep company with those who were fornicators. The Greek work *sunanamignumi*, translated here "to keep company," may also be rendered "to mix together," "to co-mingle," or "to have familiar intercourse with." The prohibition, as we shall see in the next verse, did not dictate total avoidance of such individuals, but rather the absence of intimate contacts with them.

5:10 The necessity of stressing that he did not mean total avoidance is apparent in Paul's delimitation of what was said in verse 9. He did not mean that Christians were to have no contact with the fornicators of this world, since, in order to avoid such contacts, one would find it necessary to depart from the world. Indeed, the absence of such contacts altogether would make evangelization of such sinners impossible. Furthermore, fornicators were not the only ones included. Also mentioned are the covetous, the extortioners, and the idolaters. The ancient world, just as our world today, was teeming with such people. It was not possible or even advisable to avoid contact with them. They all represented people for whom Christ died, and they were all objects of the love of God and His redemptive concern. However, close friendships or fellowships were not to be formed with these people. The apostle reiterated a similar charge, stressing that believers were not to be "unequally yoked together with unbelievers" (2 Cor. 6:14). This passage has often been used as a prohibition against marriage between a believer and an unbeliever. While the passage is certainly legitimately employed in this fashion, it refers to much more. It means that none of the more personal and intimate dealings in the life of a believer should be sustained with those whose commitment is to the darkness because "what fellowship has light with darkness?"

The other words describing the sinners of this world are as vivid as the word "fornicator." For example, "covetous" *(pleonektēs)* is derived from *echō,* meaning "to have," and the adjective *pleon,* meaning "more." The constant concern to have more can only be described as covetousness. The word translated "extortioner" *(harpax)* is derived from the word *harpazō,* which means "to seize," "to snatch," or "to take away forcefully." Interestingly, it is one of the words used to describe the taking away of the church when the Lord returns for His people. Generally, however, the word has a morally derogatory content.

5:11 If sinners are to be elicited for the kingdom, there comes a time when saints must be excluded. Having specified that he did not mean total avoidance of the sinners of this world, the apostle wrote that what he meant in his previous writing was that if any man being called a brother were to be found guilty of fornication, covetousness, idolatry, extortion, railing, or drunkenness, there was to be no fellowship with that individual. Interestingly, two additional words have been added to the list of unacceptable behavior patterns. One of those, "railer" *(loidoros)*, refers to one who feels a need to revile or slander others. Incredibly, such individuals do often exist in the church. Their intemperate language, focusing on others in their fellowship, is a sign that it is time for the church to take definite action regarding them. The other term, *methusos*, literally means "to be intoxicated or inebriated."

What is clearly present in the text is the presentation of six categories of behavior that are unacceptable for the saints of God. If persons in the church become participants in any of these six activities, it is time for the church to go through the disciplinary process, culminating, if necessary, in the exercise of the ban. Certainly we should not understand these six categories to be the only such categories which would call for church discipline, but at least there can be no doubt about these. Interestingly, all six of these categories would involve a believer in a kind of sinfulness that would soon become apparent to those observing the church from an external vantage point. Hence, the witness of the church would be greatly harmed. Furthermore, they are the kinds of iniquity that have a detrimental effect upon the life of the church and tend to pull others into their grasp.

The real question is, "How does the church express its determination not to have company with such individuals?" The answer Paul gave is in the concluding phrase of verse 11: "With such a one, no, not to eat." Some imagine that this verse prohibits the taking of a meal with a person who falls into any of the above mentioned categories. Some legitimate grounds for this may be observed in the ancient custom of sitting at meat only with those with whom one wished to develop a rather intimate fellowship. This kind of idea may be observed in the promise of Jesus to the church in Laodicea, "Behold, I stand at the door, and knock: if any man hear my voice, and open the door, I will come into him, and will sup with him, and he with me" (Rev. 3:20). The invitation to sit at a common meal was one which expressed intimacy of fellowship in the world of antiquity.

On the other hand, the whole question before the reader in chapter 5 is the question of the purity of the church. In verse 4, the judgment that is to be exercised is to be exercised "when you are gathered together." There can be little question that Paul had not here trailed off into the subject of concourse at the various meals that a person might take. Therefore, the conclusion must be that the Corinthians were told not to partake of the Lord's Supper with such individuals.

If this reasoning is accurate, we now have before us the procedure Paul desired the Corinthians to follow, a procedure which is still applicable to churches today. Once again, having followed the explicit instructions of Jesus as given in Matthew 18:15–18, in the event that those should fail, the church, when it is gathered together at the Lord's table, is to take official action at that point to exclude an erring and unrepentant brother from the Lord's table. For such a brother to be excluded from the opportunity to hear the word of God would be unthinkable. On the other hand, one of the major aspects of the Lord's Supper is its fellowship nature; to exclude one from the Lord's table would be a very public and official way of indicating to him that he was not in fellowship, communion, or harmony with the saints of God. With little doubt, this is the action that Paul prescribed for the Corinthians, action which should also be characteristic of our churches today. By the same token, it is also altogether appropriate that the meeting of the church at the Lord's table be the time when those who have been excluded, upon repentance, are invited once again to the Lord's table.

5:12 Finally, the church was to be involved in evaluating its own servants. Paul once again returned to the use of rhetorical questions, one of his favorite methods of teaching. The first question he asked, "For what have I to do to judge them also that are without?" might be better translated, "What business do I have judging those who are outside the church?" Obviously, Paul felt that the judgment about which he had been speaking was an internal judgment that had been committed to the church. The second question was intended to encourage the Corinthians to do exactly that, "do you not judge them that are within?" Implied is the responsibility that the Corinthians had to examine carefully those within the life of the church to be sure that the church maintained its purity.

5:13 While the church is responsible for judging those who are within until the time of the judgment seat of Christ, God judges those who are on the outside. It is not the church's responsibility to be concerned about the behavior of those on the outside. The church is to note that behavior as a sure index to the godlessness of society and the need of individuals for a saving, regenerating experience with Christ. Furthermore, the church is to bear its witness to the world, but in terms of judgment, God handles the judgment of those who are without. However, the church is responsible for putting away from itself the wicked individual. This final exhortation ("Therefore put away from yourselves that wicked person") is actually an Old Testament admonition. It occurs repeatedly in Deuteronomy 13:5; 17:7; 19:19; 22:21,24; and 24:7. The frequency of these words has been noticed by the apostle Paul. He picked them up and reapplied them, not to the nation of Israel, per se, but to the church, and insisted that the wicked individual be excluded from the membership of the church.

Judging Angels

1. Enduring Wrong (6:1–8)
2. Evading Wretchedness (6:9–14)
3. Enthroning Righteousness (6:15–20)

Other problems which existed in Corinth must also be addressed. Two problems are the subject of discussion in chapter 6: (1) disputes within the membership of the church which apparently were being taken into the civil courts and (2) the possibility of licentious behavior on the part of some church members.

1. Enduring Wrong (6:1–8)

The first question to be addressed was that of enduring wrong. The subject was approached by making reference to future judgments (vv. 1–3), church judgments (vv. 4–6), and personal judgments (vv. 7–8).

6:1 A strong Greek word (*tolmaō*) indicates certain astonishment on the part of the apostle that the Corinthian Christians would apparently presume to go to the civil courts in matters of dispute. The word "matter" (*pragma*) has evolved into our English word "pragmatic." Here it simply means a matter for litigation. Paul's astonishment at Corinthian behavior was derived in part from his Jewish background. The rabbis were always concerned that the Jews avoid settling matters in the courts of the Gentiles. In the new dispensation, this carried over in Paul's thinking to taking the matters of dispute among God's people before the unjust. Reference to the unjust does not presuppose a critical anaylsis of judicial systems of that day. Paul's experience, in fact, had been such that he probably believed that the civil and criminal courts of the day would be as much disposed to justice as would ecclesiastical courts. Rather, the word "unjust" refers to the fact that the magistrates were not believers and consequently would make their judgments solely on the basis of Roman law. Two important elements would be missing from such judgments . First, the absence of the Spirit of God in the life of the arbiter would make it impossible for him to have the benefit of God's judgment; and, second, his consideration would extend no further than Roman law, thus failing to consider the law of God at many vital points. The protest lodged states clearly that the choice should rather be for believers to present their differences before the saints. Failure to select the right forum would also cause the witness of the believing community to be tarnished, if not destroyed, in the eyes of pagan magistrates. Such jurists would certainly observe the Christians acted no differently from pagans.

6:2 That the saints would qualify as a legitimate body to arbitrate such disputes may be proved by two affirmations. First, Paul asked, "Are you aware that the saints shall judge the world?" If the world is to be judged by saints, does it not follow that the saints provide the best possible forum for judgment even in the smallest matters? Once again, "smallest matters" (*elachistos*) is the superlative degree of "small" (*mikros*) and provides Paul's estimate of the relative unimportance of the matters which apparently were cause for dispute among the Corinthians. He did not consider them of major consequence. As will be shown later, he suspected that they were mostly matters of covetousness.

6:3 A second reason for favoring the forum of the saints is that the saints are also to judge angels. The logic follows that if saints are going to judge spiritual beings, such as angels, how much more then are they qualified to judge the things pertaining to this life? The phrase "pertaining to this life" (*biōtikos*) is derived from the Greek word *bios*, the general word for life which gives us our English word "biology," as contrasted with *zōē*, a word usually referring to a particular quality of life. Therefore, the affirmation is that the saints are certainly qualified to judge in the general matters of life if they are, in fact, to sit in judgment upon angels.

Though the precise sense in which the saints are to judge the world and to judge angels is not explained, the pending judgment of angels is clear (2 Pet. 2:4). Perhaps the saints in some sense participate in the judgment upon these fallen angels. However, the logic of Paul's argument would be diminished if fallen angels are the angels in view. The astonishing news revealed here seems more likely to be that the saints will have the rule over these remarkable spiritual beings whose natures in time have become thoroughly good and who are the messengers of God delegated at times to watch over the saints in this very life.

The sense of this kind of judgment would be that which is revealed when Jesus said, "Verily I say unto you, That ye which have followed me, in the regeneration when the Son of man shall sit in the throne of his glory, ye also shall sit upon twelve thrones, judging the twelve tribes of Israel" (Matt. 19:28). This concept is not so much the idea of judicial reckoning as it is a matter of rule and government. At first, this may seem to be contrary to the spirit of the passage which suggests that those matters now being taken before civil magistrates should be brought before the church. A second consideration, however, will verify the point, showing that Paul was arguing that these matters do not need adjudication in the sense of a court of law, but need instead godly judgment on the part of the congregation.

6:4 The conclusion, then, is logical. If there are judgments and distinctions to be made in matters of significance pertaining to this life, then the church should set as judges those who are the least esteemed in the church. The word translated "least esteemed" (*exoutheneō*) is a word which literally means "to make light of," "to despise," or "to be contemptible." Those who fall into the category of the least significant in the church, then, are said to be adequate judges of these matters.

One is astonished to discover no mention in the passage of bishops, pastors, elders, or deacons. This does not mean that such were not present in the church at Corinth. Rather, the logical conclusion is that both of these groups functioned primarily in spiritual capacities so that judgment rested with the church. The immense importance of a congregational mode of operation in the early church is irrefutable. The development of an ecclesiastical government in which certain men gained ascendancy first over the local congregation and then over a group of congregations is clearly a late phenomenon which lacks precedent in the early church. Nowhere is this more clearly reflected than here.

6:5 Earlier in the epistle, Paul suggested that the things he had said to the Corinthians were not designed to put them to shame (4:14) but merely to remind them of their responsibilities. Apparently this time the case was different. He informed the Corinthians that he was in fact, speaking these things to their shame. The reason for this shame emerges from the rhetorical questions he asked. "Is it true that there is not a single wise man among you?" Or, to press the question still further, "Is it so that there is not a single one of the brethren who is able to judge between brethren who are divided over the issues of this life?" The tacit admission of the assembly that no one in the church was wise enough to ferret out a solution to the problems and that none in their number was able to judge among the brethren was a shameful admission.

6:6 This shameful condition resulted in a state of affairs in which brother was taking brother to the law, and that before unbelievers. Implied is the idea that such behavior placed the entire church under a cloud before the very people who were supposed to be the objects of its evangelistic and missionary endeavor.

6:7 In the next two verses, Paul proceeded in his instructions as though he had accepted the fact that there was not a single man among the Corinthians wise enough to judge among the brethren. It is doubtful that Paul actually accepted this as the case, but it seems that he temporarily accepted it for the sake of argument. Suppose that there was not an able counselor among them. It still follows that the Corinthians are caught in a serious "fault" (*hēttēma*, a relatively rare usage in Greek which apparently originally meant a "loss"). For example, the word is used in Romans 11:12 where its basic significance may be clearly observed: "Now if the fall of them [the Gentiles] by the riches of the world, and the diminishing [*hēttēma*] of them the riches of the Gentiles; how much more their fullness?"

Paul was speaking of the loss the Jews have experienced to the benefit of the Gentiles. Basically *hēttēma* is used in the same way here. Paul suggested that there was a "loss" among the Corinthians when they were forced to take one another to the law. That inevitable loss was in fellowship among their own number and in the effectiveness of the church's witness to the world. Consequently, Paul raises the important question, "Why do you not rather take the wrong [*adikeō*, indicating an "injustice"]?" The question of the occurrence of injustice was not even before the apostle. He assumed that such things did occur. The question was, rather, "Why not simply accept them?" In fact, he even goes beyond this and raises the question, "Why not allow yourself to be defrauded" (*apostereō*, derived from *stereō*, which literally means "to rob," and the preposition *apo*, which means "from")? The question was "Why not allow the saints to rob you?" This may seem, at first blush, to be a rather harsh verdict, but it must be remembered that Paul was convinced that Jesus was Lord of the church. He was also convinced that God was a God of justice and a beneficent Heavenly Father who protected the interest of His children. The underlying conclusion was that the Lord might be counted on to intervene in these matters. Furthermore, even if one does suffer real loss, action that maintained the sanctity and unity of the congregation would certainly have its reward.

6:8 Unfortunately, the Corinthians had done just the opposite of what they should have done. Instead of suffering wrong and deprivation, they had actually behaved unjustly themselves and had even been guilty of robbing their brethren. It is implied that they had done this in part through taking these matters before the Roman courts of the day.

Paul's prohibition against a believer's taking another believer before the law is germane to our own society and needs to be propounded to our modern congregations. Not only does this passage prohibit members of the assemblies from filing suit against other members, but also the entire section constitutes a warning to Christian attorneys who might agree to provide counsel in such cases.

2. Evading Wretchedness (6:9–14)

The church needed to stay out of the civil courts, but it also needed to evade the wretchedness that characterizes the ways of the world. In the section that follows, Paul discussed the pattern of the condemned (vv. 9–10), the purging of the church (v. 11), and the progress of the Christian (vv. 12–14).

6:9 Still another question begins the section, "Do you not know that the unrighteous shall not inherit the kingdom of God?" Surely if there were ever a legitimate rhetorical question, it is that one. One would think that all believers would understand that the unrighteous shall not inherit the kingdom of God. However, Paul had in mind being even more specific and went to great length to discuss specific kinds of unrighteousness (vv. 9–10). Some, such as fornication and idolatry, have been mentioned previously. This time, however, there are four additional words added: (1) "Adulterers" (*moichoi*) describes those who participate in extramarital relationships and so fracture the marriage covenant into which they entered. (2) "Effeminate" (*malakoi*) has the basic meaning of "soft or delicate to the touch." Although it is not particularly used in classical Greek to suggest homosexuality, there seems to be reason for concluding with Conzelmann that the two terms in this verse designating homosexuality or sodomy are designed to distinguish between passive perversion (*malakoi*) and active, aggressive homosexuality designated by the next word to be examined.[25] In any case, *malakoi* certainly suggests a life centered on the sensual, a mode of existence hardly acceptable for a believer. (3) "Abusers of themselves with mankind" (*arsenokoitai*) is actually an unbelievably euphemistic translation. Literally, the word combines *arsen*, meaning "a member of the male sex," and *koitē*, from which comes our English word "coitus," meaning sexual intercourse. Consequently, the word clearly refers to homosexuality or sodomy.

6:10 Five additional classes of people who will be excluded from the kingdom of God are next mentioned. Once again, four of these five have been mentioned in previous passages—notably the covetous, the drunkards, the revilers, and the extortioners. The only addition here are the thieves (*kleptai*), a word which we have preserved in "kleptomania," referring to one who has the irresistible urge to take what is not his.

6:11 The conclusion to be drawn from the above observation is not that the kingdom of God will embrace no one from any of those categories. As a matter of fact, there will be those in the kingdom who at one time have belonged to all of those categories. It is understood that their exclusion from the kingdom of heaven is based upon their failure to repent and seek the forgiveness of God. This is made evident by Paul's statement that at one time some of the Corinthians had belonged to these groups. Despite this former life, however, a life-changing encounter had occurred, resulting in three strategic developments in the lives of all Corinthian believers.

First, the Corinthians were washed. The tendency on the part of commentators to see here an allusion to baptism fails to discern the spirit of the whole passage. The physical waters of baptism cannot eradicate a single sin nor the taint of guilt. However, it is recorded that the 144,000 are "they which came out of great tribulation, and have washed their robes, and made them white in the blood of the Lamb" (Rev. 7:14). Again, Ephesians 5:26 speaks of the "washing of water by the word." Titus 3:5 mentions the "washing of regeneration, and renewing of the Holy Ghost." The washing mentioned here is the purging of the stain of sin from the life of the unbeliever at the moment of conversion. It is associated with the cleansing effects of the blood of Christ and has nothing to do with water baptism.

Second, the Corinthians were sanctified, indicating a new nature of holiness and separation. Had they only been washed, then

---

[25]Conzelmann, *First Corinthians*, p. 106.

they might have recontaminated themselves with the practices of the world, but in addition to the washing they were also separated unto the things of God.

Finally, they were also declared to have been justified in the name of the Lord Jesus Christ. There is no way that any sinner, particularly one who belonged to the list mentioned above, could ever have an acceptable legal standing before God. However, by calling upon the name of the Lord Jesus Christ and standing in Him, the Corinthians, like all believers, were declared to be righteous in the name of the Lord Jesus Christ. Not their own merits, but the merits of Christ's sinless life availed for that justification. All this was accomplished by means of the Spirit of God.

6:12 Certain progress, then, should characterize the Christian life. Paul had spoken much of Christian liberties, but apparently the Corinthian Christian had seized upon that liberty in Christ and fashioned a motto which was not balanced with responsible holiness. Apparently as its repetition in the epistle suggests, the Corinthians were saying, "All things are lawful unto me." Manifestly, even the Corinthians knew that this "all" was not really inclusive of every form of behavior. However, the attitude was much more prevalent than Paul felt tolerable. Consequently, the apostle began to build some limitations into that Christian liberty.

First of all, all things might be lawful, but that did not mean that all things were "expedient" (*sumpherō*, which most literally rendered would be "to bear together"). The idea is that all things are not productive. The Christian, by virtue of his commitment, has accepted the responsibility of so constructing his life as to accomplish the greatest possible good.

A second restriction Paul pointed out is that while all things may be lawful, under no circumstances will he "be brought under the power of any" (*exousiazō*). Literally the term indicates the exercise of authority. The believer must not be subject to anything, other than the Lord Himself, that would become his master.

6:13 There may also have been at Corinth another favorite expression being used to justify certain kinds of behavior. A vestige of it is perhaps found in the statement, "meats for the belly, and the belly for meats." Paul did not refute the statement. In fact, he in effect allowed that it was true. However, he also called attention to the fact that if food was for the stomach, and the stomach was made for food, the day was coming when both would be destroyed. But if this was the outlook for the alimentary canal, it was certainly not the destiny of the body as a whole. The body, destined as it was for glorification, must be carefully used by the Christian. Specifically, the body is not for any kind of sexual license but was for the use of the Lord, and, correspondingly, the Lord was for the body.

6:14 This is especially true in light of what happened to Jesus Himself. God raised Him from the dead, giving Him a glorified body. By that same power, He is also going to raise believers from the dead. Therefore, the body of the believer assumes an importance much greater than would be the case with the bodies of any other form of biological life. As such, the believer must use his body only to glorify the Lord.

3. Enthroning Righteousness (6:15–20)

It is not enough to endure wrong and to evade wretchedness. The Christian is also committed to enthroning righteousness. Therefore, the next section discusses the body of the believers as a member of Christ (vv. 15–17), as a sacred trust (v. 18), and as the temple of God (vv. 19–20).

6:15 The baptism of the spirit is given a clear definition, "For by one spirit are we all baptized into one body" (12:13). Clearly the body in view is the body of Christ. At the moment of conversion, the believer is permanently placed into the body of Jesus Christ. The same metaphor will hold throughout chapter 12 where the discussion of diversity and the use of spiritual gifts will proceed. The whole argument, however, is anticipated in the avowal that the believer's body is a member of the body of Christ. The argument is anticipated because it lends itself nicely to Paul's efforts to show the reprehensibleness of a Christian's engaging in any kind of fornication. Harlotry was rampant in the ancient world, exhibiting itself as a form of religious ritual as well as in the common brothels of the cities. Recognizing this state of affairs, Paul asked the Corinthians another question, "Shall I then take those that belong to the body of Christ and make them members of a harlot?" The anticipated answer is given in the most specific form, *mē genoito*, which means "let it not be."

6:16 The rationale behind the present prohibition again alludes to an Old Testament passage. Another question presents the passage, "Do you not know that he who is joined to an harlot is one body? for two, saith he, shall be one flesh." There is no doubt that Genesis 2:24 does, in fact, refer to the physical union in marriage. It is the logical culmination of the process which begins with a formal declaration of a new first loyalty, "For this cause shall a man leave his father and mother"; the establishing of a spiritual union, "and they shall cleave to one another"; and finally, the physical demonstration of the fact of that spiritual union in that "they two shall be one flesh." Since the act of sexual union is that to which the writer of Genesis obviously refers, then to be joined to a harlot is, in at least some sense of the word, for two to become one flesh. It would be difficult to imagine anything more unthinkable than to join a part of the body of Christ with a harlot in a one-flesh relationship.

6:17 As a matter of fact, this is precisely what the believer will not want to do because he understands that being joined together to the Lord is the same as becoming one with Him in spirit. In this connection, the word *kollaō*, translated "joined," is particularly helpful. It means "to glue," "weld," "attach," or "adhere."

6:18 The believer's body is, therefore, a sacred trust. That being the case, the believer is enjoined not merely to avoid fornication but to take a much more activistic approach and flee from it. *Pheugete*, a present imperative form of the verb meaning "to flee or run rapidly away," may be translated, "continually flee away from fornication." The picture is that of a man who so vividly knows the dangers and the tragedies bound up in a certain circumstance that he not only avoids it but also perpetually, consciously runs from it. One final reason is added for the urgency of that mandate. The giving of this reason has been the cause of considerable difference among commentators. The apostle indicated that every sin is "from without the body," but the man who commits fornication "sins against his own body." The problem in the text is to explain how it is that other forms of iniquity mentioned in previous sections, such as drunkenness and gluttony, are not considered sins against one's own body.

In answer to that question, Leon Morris suggests, "Other sins against the body, e.g., drunkenness or gluttony, involve the use of that which comes from without the body. The sexual appetite rises from within. They serve other purposes, e.g., conviviality. This has no other purpose than the gratification of the lust. They are sinful in the excess; this is sinful in itself."[26] Following a similar line of thinking, Charles Hodge writes,

> This does not teach that fornication is greater than any other sin, but it does teach that it is altogether peculiar in its effects upon the body, not so much in its physical as in its moral and spiritual effects. The idea runs through the Bible that there is something mysterious in the commerce of the sexes and in the effects which flow from it. Every other sin, however degrading and ruinous to the health, even drunkenness, is external to the body, that is, external to its life, but fornication, involving as it does a community of life, is a sin against the body itself, because incompatible, as the apostle had just taught, with the design of its creation and with its immortal destiny.[27]

These two commentators seem to have captured the essence of why *porneia* is viewed as being so hideous in nature. In fact, while fornication is always serious, regardless of whether it involves a believer or an unbeliever, it assumes particularly serious overtones for the believer. To allow those sexual impulses springing from within his own heart to contaminate himself as a member of Christ's body is particularly unfortunate. This does not suggest that other kinds of sin are not serious, but in a society

---

[26]Morris, *First Corinthians*, pp. 102–103.
[27]Hodge, *Corinthians I and II*, pp. 105–106.

preoccupied with sexuality, a society such as that of Paul's day and of our own, the particular seriousness of sexual immorality must be faced by the church.

6:19 Earlier the Corinthians had been informed that they constituted the temple of the Holy Spirit. The expression, as it was noted at that time, seemed to be particularly applicable to the assembled church at Corinth (3:16–17). Now the same expression is used in a form and context which made it very clear that the physical body of the believer was now in view. Paul questioned, "Do you not know that your body is the temple of the Holy Spirit which is in you?" Not only did he affirm that our very bodies constitute the Holy of Holies (*naos*), contrasted once again with the larger temple complex (*hieron*), but also he declared that the body became the temple by virtue of the fact that God, in the person of the Holy Spirit, indwelt the body.

This is one of the most remarkable features of the new covenant. In the old dispensation, the Spirit of God was active and came upon some, but in the new dispensation every individual believer is personally indwelt by the Holy Spirit, rendering him the temple of God. This, of course, adds another dimension to the whole aspect of bodily chastity; namely, the believer no longer belongs to himself.

6:20 The reason is clear. He has been bought with a price. The word "bought" (*agorazō*) is derived from the Greek word for the "market place" (*agora*). The believer has been purchased out of the market for a "price" (*timē*, a word often used to describe those things which are particularly precious). Just as often, however, this word simply refers to the price attached to something. In this case, the suggestion is surely there that the price involved in purchasing the believer was a costly one. The inevitable conclusion, then, is that of an imperative, "glorify God in your body." The word "glorify" (*doxazō*) means "to radiate the presence and ownership of God in one's own body." This is done by abstention not only from sexual sins but also from all of those sins enumerated in the passage. Even this list is not exhaustive.

Nothing is amiss theologically by including it, but the better evidence seems to point to the fact that the passage ends with the statement, "glorify God in your body."

Marry Or Burn!

1. Covenant for the Married (7:1–9)
2. Counsel for the Redeemed (7:10–16)
3. Consistency for the Called (7:17–24)
4. Consolation for the Concerned (7:25–40)

Chapter 7 marks the beginning of a discussion of specific questions addressed to Paul by the Corinthians. The initial questions revolve around domestic problems which constituted major aspects of Christian adjustment in the first-century world. Christian perspectives regarding the home would not have been so decidedly different in a community of Jewish believers, but by now the Corinthian church was predominantly Gentile, and the ethical mores and marital practices of the Roman State were anything but congruent with the high morality of Christian standards. Already conditions existing at the time of conversion alone accounted for many of the almost insurmountable difficulties. Some of these, in fact, are only partially known to us, thus creating interpretive difficulties in portions of chapter 7. One thing that does emerge with crystal clarity is the strategic importance of the home to early New Testament Christians. Though the chapter does not yield itself as readily to outline as most of the other chapters in Corinthians, we shall follow the basic pattern presented above.

1. Covenant for the Married (7:1–9)

In the first nine verses of the chapter, the propriety of marriage is presented (vv. 1–2), followed by a discussion of the privileges of marriage (vv. 3–5) and of the providence of marriage (vv. 6–9).

7:1 The almost shocking avowal which greets the reader is the initial statement that it is good *(kalon)* that a man should not touch a woman. The word "touch" *(haptomai)* does not indicate the total absence of touch but in this regard is used of intimate contact or even coitus. Apparently the Corinthians had sustained considerable influence from ascetic sources arguing that while marriage was not a deplorable condition, those who were serious about their spiritual condition would abstain from marriage. The Corinthians had addressed that question to Paul. His response, however, was far removed from the answer that would have pleased whatever ascetics were among them. The word translated "good" *(kalon)* is a relatively bland word which seems to indicate that it is certainly acceptable for a man to choose a celibate state. This represents a departure from the position advocated in Judaism, but it certainly does not even begin to suggest that the celibate state is in any sense superior or more desirable than the married state. Later in the discussion Paul explained why matrimony might cause additional problems, but there is still no argument here for the superiority of celibacy.

7:2 In fact, because of fornication, Paul suggested that each man have his own wife and each woman her own husband. It is essential that we bear in mind that the term "fornication" *(porneia)* is a word which covers almost every conceivable kind of sexual misbehavior. The prevalence of this in Roman society constituted considerable temptation for those who might otherwise have sought a celibate lifestyle. Furthermore, as will be shown later, celibacy is predicated upon the possession of the spiritual gift (7:7), in the absence of which some form of *porneia* becomes a real possibility. Consequently, for the majority of Christians, marriage is viewed as the most acceptable alternative to the possibility of fornication.

One objection to the way in which Paul stated his case has been raised. Some allege that he was not arguing for the nobility of marriage but for the expediency of marriage in the light of temptation. Some have even gone so far as to suggest that the apostle himself maintained a low view of marriage. However, if the Ephesian epistle be taken as genuinely Pauline (and there can be little doubt about this), then the latter part of chapter 5 provides an exalted view of the home, which would certainly be representative of Paul's domestic theology. The reason such does not appear in the text before us is that this particular question had not been raised by the Corinthians. They only requested information concerning whether or not there was something supraspiritual about the celibate state. Paul's reply was that while the celibate state is good, so is the married state.

7:3 Having underscored the propriety of marriage, the discussion turned naturally to the privileges of marriage. The husband was instructed "to render unto his wife due benevolence," and the wife was told to do the same for her husband. Literally, the expression in the Greek New Testament meant that each partner was required to give what he or she owed. Unquestionably, the statement referred to the sexual union, as can be discerned in the verse which immediately follows. It is possible to argue that the view expressed here is a rather inadequate theology of sex or that Paul failed to appreciate some of the apparent reasons for sexual union in favor of evaluating its necessity in terms of a debt. The answer to that allegation is the same as the answer to the earlier charge. One must remember the nature of the questions that have been addressed to the apostle and realize that he was dealing with a specific circumstance. Apparently, those of a more ascetic tendency in the church at Corinth were arguing that marriages ought either to be dissolved (especially, as we shall see, in the case of believers married to unbelievers) or else, if not dissolved, continued in a state of total sexual abstinence in order to maintain holiness. Paul's point, therefore, was that in marriage itself there is something owed to the other partner. This is in perfect keeping with the explicit language of Proverbs 5:15–19.

7:4 Furthermore, the wife did not have "power" of her own body, but, rather, her husband had that "power" (*exousiazō*, a word that literally means "authority" rather than "power" in the sense of muscular dynamic). Two observations must be made at this point. First, the common man of Paul's day would doubtless have left the case right there. It is interesting, however, that Paul went on to argue that the husband also did not have authority over his body, but rather the wife had that authority. In other words, Paul recognized the full equality of the sexes. There is no way that any other position can be argued as a Christian position. The Bible clearly recognizes the full equality of all believers, regardless of their status in society, their sex, or their age. This does not mean that role assignments have been abrogated. Children are recognized as fully equal with their adult counterparts. As a matter of fact, Jesus used some of His most harsh expressions to describe the punishment one could anticipate if he were the cause of scandal in the "little ones." Nevertheless, children are still informed that they are to be in obedience to their own parents as unto the Lord (Eph. 6:1). It is clear that while they are equal in essence of being, they are subordinate in role assignment. Paul also called for subordination of wives to their husbands in Ephesians 5. Other forms of demand for subordination exist, such as that of the congregation for its pastors (Heb. 13:7,17).

Nevertheless, there is full recognition of the equality of essence between the sexes. Paul showed this by making his statement with great care, demonstrating the full authority of both husband and wife over the body of the partner. One other insight needs to be noticed. Apparently the ground upon which Paul constructed this argument was the expressed command of Genesis 2:24, "and they shall be one flesh." If the husband and the wife in marriage have become one flesh, then they no longer possess sole authority over their own individual bodies but exist as a unit together in marital relationships.

7:5 Now an even stronger term is used to describe those who would advocate sexual abstinence as a way of achieving holiness, "Do not defraud one another." The word "defraud" is used in an earlier passage (6:7) where Paul was obviously speaking of defrauding in exchange of goods and services. Here, however, the word is used in a new sense suggesting that to decide upon a course of sexual abstinence was actually nothing short of defrauding. In the marriage agreement, it was understood by all that sexual union would be inevitable. In fact, this was altogether desirable. Consequently, to turn in a new direction at this point would be misrepresentation of purpose and commitment.

An exception was provided. The exception had with it two limitations. A couple might elect to devote themselves to prayer for an extended period of time. The King James Version adds the phrase "and fasting," but the overwhelming evidence of the better manuscripts does not include those two words. Therefore, in periods where the couple may feel the intense necessity of seeking the face of God, they may devote themselves to prayer and thus a temporary abstinence from the sexual union. The two limitations, then, were these: (1) abstinence was to be out of common consent and (2) was to be limited to a given, special time. Then the partners were to come together again in order that Satan not be given the opportunity to tempt them for their "incontinency." Once again, Paul demonstrated his rabbinical training in this regard. Jewish men frequently took certain vows in which, for a period of time, they withheld themselves from cohabitation for the purpose of giving special time to study the Torah or to pray. Interestingly, however, the wife was not consulted in the matter. Here, once again demonstrating the equality of the sexes, Paul insisted that husband and wife should agree in this matter. The word "incontinency" *(akrasia)* is derived from *kratos*, which means "self control," prefixed by the alpha privative to negate its significance and thus meaning "non control." The suggestion Paul was making was that Satan might very well tempt one or both of the parties because of the lack of control that either might have had in prolonged abstinence.

One additional factor must be noted in this verse. The apostle recognized the existence of a malicious spirit, here identified as "the Satan." The presence of the article (only in the Greek text) does not suggest that he is one among many such malignant spirits, but it does give definite emphasis to the type of adversary he is. In fact, the word itself derives from the Hebrew term *satan,* which means "adversary," "opponent," or "enemy." The enemy is a real personal force with which to be reckoned, and no quarter should be voluntarily given him.

7:6 The apostle next moved to the providences of God in marriage. The discussion begins with a statement that has become the subject of much controversy, particularly among evangelical Christians. Paul stated that he was about to speak by permission rather than by commandment. A similar expression occurs several more times in the chapter. In verse 12 he wrote, "But to the rest speak I, not the Lord." Again in verse 25 the statement was made, "I have no commandment of the Lord: yet I give my judgment." And finally, in verse 40 he suggested, "I think also that I have the Spirit of God." For some, such expressions indicate that these portions of this particular chapter do not carry the same type of inspiration that evangelicals have normally ascribed to the Scriptures. It is suggested that Paul meant he had no sure word from God, that the Spirit had not given definite leadership, and accordingly that he merely intended to express his own opinion.

However, the four statements to which we referred, if taken together, build a very different case. First of all, in this particular verse he did not have a commandment, but he spoke by permission. By whose permission, we may ask? There was no apostolic legate who stood ahead of Paul. He had already demonstrated that he went up to Jerusalem on one occasion, but not to be instructed by apostles or others in a higher echelon. Consequently, it would appear that the permission to which he alluded must have been the permission of the Lord. Far from betraying a lack of inspiration, the very expression itself suggests the extent of inspiration. Paul was unwilling to say anything that was merely his opinion. He would only speak under what he knew to be the expressed leadership of the Spirit of God. Again, verse 25 sheds light on the subject. Paul wrote, "I have no commandment of the Lord: yet I give my judgment." Two questions need to be asked here. First, why would he give his judgment if he had no commandment from the Lord? The answer is rather apparent. He gave his judgment because the Spirit of God had clarified this in his own heart. Second, what did he mean by "no commandment

of the Lord"? He simply meant that during Jesus' earthly ministry, to Paul's knowledge, He spoke nothing of this particular circumstance or situation. That is also the meaning of verse 12,
where he wrote, "the rest speak I, not the Lord." He was referring
to concrete expressions on the issues by Jesus Himself.

All of this was made final by the apostle's expressed confidence that he had the Spirit of God in these pronouncements
(v.40). They most certainly were not just his own opinions.

7:7 The essential element in Christian celibacy was now
brought center stage. Paul confessed that he would be happy to
see every man in the state in which he found himself. It is clear
that Paul was not married. Suggestions that he was perhaps a
widower are interesting, but no evidence has been supplied to
give even the slightest indication that such was the case, except
for the fact that members of the Sanhedrin were normally married. The evidence of any marriage for Paul is simply lacking.
However, he had found this state of celibacy to be the ideal one
for himself, and there is a reason. Paul wrote, "every man has
his own gift from God." The word "proper" is really in the text
only in the sense of "one's own" gift. "Gift" *(charisma)* is the interesting word in the text. This word, which has been incorpo-
rated in discussions of the modern charismatic movement, is one
used by Paul, particularly in 1 Corinthians 12—14, in his discussion of spiritual gifts. Literally, the word means "grace gift."
Twenty-one such gifts are specifically mentioned. Whether or
not these are intended to be exhaustive is not known, but it is
clear that celibacy is one such gift. Those who claim that every
believer should have every gift have simply not considered this
passage. Furthermore, in response to the ascetics who wanted to
argue that celibacy was a more holy estate than marital union,
Paul answered that this was not the case. As a matter of fact, it
was not a matter of holiness or lack of holiness at all. The whole
matter was a question of the sovereignly disposed grace-gifts of
God. If a man had the gift, as some clearly did, then he should
remain celibate. If, on the other hand, he did not have the gift,
then he should marry.

7:8 To the unmarried, therefore, and to widows, Paul concluded that it was good for them if they abode as Paul. Once

again, however, *kalon* is employed, showing in this mild term the acceptability but not necessarily the desirability of the state, especially not in a moral sense. Under the proper conditions it was simply a good and acceptable state of being.

7:9 The limitation is partially there because of the possibility of a loss of self control. So Paul wrote, "if they cannot contain" (*enkrateuomai* basically means "self control"), then they are commanded to marry, since "it is better for them to marry than to burn." Two possibilities have been suggested for the meaning of that phrase. The first is that "to burn" referred to the fires of judgment that might rest upon them in the case of sexual sin. However, there is nothing in the text to suggest such an interpretation. Rather, the whole subject of this verse is the question of self control. Consequently, it was far better to see this second interpretation as being correct; i.e., it is better for them to marry than to experience a problem of self control which might have led to unbridled passions.

2. Counsel for the Redeemed (7:10–16)

There was counsel for the redeemed concerning marital relations: the reaffirmed vow (vv. 10–11), reasoned viability (vv. 12–13), and redemptive vision (vv. 14–16).

7:10 There is a direct command from the Lord which the apostle recalled with reference to those who were married. It was a universal decree that must be understood prior to the analysis of specific cases that might have existed in the Corinthian congregation. The command which we have from the Lord, together with its implied reciprocity, is "let not the wife depart from her husband." The attitude of the authors of Scripture was that of a unified rejection of divorce. It is commonly said in evangelical circles that divorce is recommended in the case of adultery. Nothing could be further from the truth. Even if the so-called "exception clause" in Matthew 19:9 ("except it be for fornication") be granted, still it is apparent that Jesus did not intend that one seek divorce in the case of unfaithfulness; but rather he noted that Moses allowed this "because of the hardness of your hearts," adding that "from the beginning it was not so."

Perhaps the general attitude of the Scriptures toward divorce is nowhere more saliently epitomized than in Malachi 2:16, where the last of the Old Testament prophets says, "For the LORD, the God of Israel, saith that he hateth putting away: for one covereth violence with his garment, saith the LORD of hosts: therefore take heed to your spirit, that ye deal not treacherously." The "putting away" of which the prophet spoke was surely divorce. God does not take a neutral attitude about it but rather, is in the position of hating divorce. One can understand such a position rather clearly in light of the domestic metaphors that abound in Scripture. These models are weakened when the home disintegrates. As a matter of fact, the ideal for the believer's response to unfaithfulness is embodied in the prophet Hosea's response to Gomer, his unfaithful wife. Consequently, it is the direct command of the Lord that the wife is not to depart from her husband, nor the husband from his wife. Marriage is a sacred covenant which is not to be annulled.

7:11 One of the much debated features of the Matthew 19 passage in which Jesus discussed divorce is the question of whether remarriage is allowable. This will also be faced again in verse 15. However, this verse offers an interpretive insight to both of these problem passages. If a wife departed, she was commanded by Paul, with the use of the present imperative of *menō*, to remain perpetually unmarried. The only other option available to her was to be reconciled to her husband. The word "reconcile" (*katallassō*) is the same word used for the reconciliation of man to God through the cross of Christ. It is, literally, "the restoration of a relationship." If a husband or wife leaves the other partner in the marriage, he/she is to remain unmarried or else have a restoration of that original relationship. Therefore, it is apparent that Paul understood the word of Jesus to allow for divorce in the case of unfaithfulness, but under no circumstances to commend remarriage, even for the party against whom the sin had been committed.

7:12 Paul continued to say what the Spirit had given him, but was now speaking without a specific commandment from Jesus (see discussion on 7:6). Apparently the Corinthians had raised a very serious question of what to do in the case of a believing partner who was married to an unbeliever. One assumes that the marriage was consummated before one of the partners became a believer. Evidently some Corinthians with ascetic propensities were arguing that to continue the marriage relationship with an unbelieving partner was a sin of such gravity as to rival fornication. Paul's response was that if a brother had a wife who was not a believer but they were "pleased together" *(suneudoke*ō*)*—literally, they are "both pleased about the arrangement of dwelling together"—then under no circumstances was the believing husband to put away his unbelieving wife.

7:13 By the same token, if the opposite situation inhered (and this is the more frequent circumstance) and the husband was pleased to dwell with the wife, then she was certainly not to leave him.

7:14 Verses 14 through 16 constitute a redemptive vision that should characterize the believing member of a mixed marriage. Without question, these verses constitute one of the greatest challenges for the interpreter in 1 Corinthians. Generally speaking, there are at least three different positions which have been advocated to explain how it is that an unbelieving husband or wife is sanctified by the believing husband or wife, and to reveal precisely in what sense this makes the children holy rather than unclean.

(1) Sanctification is a reference to the legitimacy of the marriage, and the reference to the holiness of the children is to the fact that they, too, are considered the legitimate offspring of the union.

(2) The apostle was speaking of the moral and spiritual impact of the life of the believer on the life of the unbelieving partner as well as upon the children.

(3) The Calvinistic persuasion is that the "federal holiness" of home is in view here. The children of the union of a believer and an unbeliever are held to be a part of the covenant relationship with God through the relationship sustained to the believing parent.

There are problems with all the views. The first view seems to indicate that all pagan marriages are illegitimate while all Christian marriages are legitimate; however, a pagan married to a believer finds his marriage acceptable to God. But there is no indication anywhere in the Bible that marriages where both parties are pagans are considered any less legitimate than those of Christians.

The second view, which is the moral and spiritual influence theory, must face the strange use of soteriological language such as the word "sanctified." This proves not to be, as we shall see in a moment, an insurmountable problem.

The third view, which consistent Calvinists advocate, is incredibly problematic. It may, for example, explain how it is that the children are covered under the covenant relationship, but it leaves unexplained how an unbelieving marital partner who persists in his unbelief is to be considered sanctified. If such is the case, then the word "holy" as it applies to children and the word "sanctify" as it applies to the unbelieving partner in a marriage must be used in very different senses, which appears not be the case at all. Furthermore, despite the objection of Hodge to the contrary,[28] the passage almost certainly precludes the possibility of infant baptism. The children are spoken of as being holy by virtue of their birth, not by virtue of baptism. Hodge's attempted dodge of this is to point out that children were baptized because they were holy, not in order to make them holy. But it is patently evident that the question of baptism is simply not under consideration at all in these verses. Hence, they provide no support for the baptism of infants, as Robertson and Plummer demonstrate.[29]

The conclusion which must be drawn is greatly assisted by a close look at the word translated "sanctified" (*hagiazō*, the basic meaning of which is "to set apart or consecrate"). The sense in which this consecration is to be understood depends completely upon the context and the question being discussed. For example, believers are told to "sanctify the Lord God in your hearts" (1 Pet. 3:15). God has no need for sanctification. The obvious intent of the passage is that the Lord be set apart in a very special

[28]Hodge, *Corinthians I and II*, pp. 117-118.
[29]Robertson and Plummer, *First Corinthians*, p. 142.

119

place in the heart of a believer as his object of devotion. Here is a case where the word "sanctify" has no salvific sense attached to it at all. Whereas in biblical Greek the word refers more often to soteriological matters, the fact is that it does not exclusively have this nuance. The best possible understanding of the passage, therefore, is that even the unbelieving partner in a marriage is set apart to receive the very special blessings of God that come through the union with the believing partner. That this cannot possibly mean the automatic salvation of the unbeliever is indicated by verse 16, where Paul suggested the possibility that the unbelieving partner might be led to salvation. In fact, that distinct possibility is one of the most profound blessings that will be involved as the unbelieving partner is set apart to the blessings of God.

By the same token, the children born to such a union are not "unclean" *(akathartos)*. Rather, they are "holy" *(hagios)*. Once again, there is no thought that the children of such unions are automatically saved. The thought is, rather, that the children of that union are beneficiaries of the sanctified life of the believing partner and are visited by God with special blessings commensurate with the blessings of God showered upon the believing partner in the marriage. This is the only interpretive possibility for this verse that is not replete with so many difficulties as to make the passage almost indecipherable.

7:15 A situation may occur, however, in which the unbelieving partner is not content to dwell with the believer. While there are infinite blessings attendant upon the unbeliever in such a union, there are also circumstances which may be almost impossible for the unbeliever to accept. For example, if the unbelieving partner is basically immoral in his lifestyle, he may suffer continuing guilt which he is not prepared to handle due to the superior morality of the believing partner, or the unbeliever may simply suffer frustration because of the unwillingness of the believing partner to engage in that immoral lifestyle. In these and other cases, what may result is the exodus of the unbeliever. In such a case, Paul wrote, "let him depart." There is, of course, no other option since physical coercion is never an open possibility for the believer. The next phrase, however, has also been the cause of controversy. In such cases, Paul said, "a brother or sister is not under bondage" (*dedoulōtai*, derived from *doulō*, meaning "to enslave"). The question is this: did Paul mean that the brother or sister was no longer the servant of his marital vows, or did he mean that, being free from the unbeliever who was departed, he was also free to remarry? The answer to that question may be provided in verse 11—namely, if one departed a marriage, he or she was to remain unmarried or else be reconciled to the mate. The objection to the application of verse 11 to the circumstance of verse 15 is that there is a change in the circumstances. Apparently, verses 10 and 11 relate to those who are both believers, whereas verses 12 to 15 have to do with the unbeliever's departure, which cannot be prevented by the believing partner. While granting that circumstances are different, it still must be said that the ideal presented by both Jesus and Paul is that the brother or sister who is deserted will remain unmarried. Surely there is no other way to read the entire general direction of 1 Corinthians 7. Apparently, then, not being under bondage does not refer to the freedom to remarry, but rather to the fact that "God has called us to peace," meaning that the believing partner in a marriage is not to pursue the matter in the course of the law or in any other fashion which would generate additional friction.

7:16 The greatest hope is the possibility that in staying with one's mate, even though he may be an unbeliever, the opportunity is there for winning that individual to Christ. Although *sōzō* is used, it is understood that the husband or wife cannot save the unbelieving partner. Rather, the witness given may result in the salvation of such a partner. An instructive passage in this regard is given in 1 Peter 3:1-2, in which Peter urged believing wives to lead their husbands to Christ on the basis of their Christlike behavior.

3. Consistency for the Called (7:17-24)

The discussion now proceeds along the lines of consistency for the called. The distribution of the Lord is observed (v. 17); devotion to a calling is stressed (vv. 18-22); the spiritual domicile of a man is predicated (vv. 23-24).

7:17 The discussion of continuing in one's present status is broached first of all by recognizing that God has made a distribution to every man. This distribution has to do with one's general status in life but apparently also includes the gifts of the Spirit. In fact, the word "distributed" *(merizō)* is normally used with reference to the distribution of gifts. Whatever one's situation in life and whatever his gifts, every man is to walk as the Lord has called. This diversity enables the believing community to penetrate almost every phase of life. While there is a oneness of fellowship in the churches, there is an almost infinite variety of backgrounds and endeavors represented. This is a circumstance so essential that Paul could even say he had "so ordained" in all of the churches.

7:18 This devotion to a particular calling is now pressed still further. Several cases are provided, beginning with the question of circumcision. If a man is called of God (here the calling seems to be with reference to salvation) while in a state of circumcision, he is not to seek to become "uncircumcised" *(epispaō)*. Such a reversal of surgical circumcision might seem to be an impossibility, but in antiquity, due to certain events, a procedure had been developed for reversal. Apparently this came about as a result of the intensity of feeling about circumcision which developed during the Maccabean period. Because circumcision became associated with the religion of the Jews, Gentiles often looked upon it condescendingly as a mark of the despised Jewish religion. Occasionally, Jewish youths would make an effort to efface the marks of circumcision in order to make their way in the Roman world and the Hellenistic culture. Another example of this concerned the athletic events of the day, where Jews, not wishing to be embarrassed in the gymnastics in the palaestra, would seek to reverse the effect of their circumcision.[30] *Epispaō*, which means to "draw" or "drag after," gradually evolved into a medical term which meant "to draw" the prepuce forward in such a way as to effect the permanency of this procedure.[31]

---

[30]Robertson and Plummer, *First Corinthians*, p. 146.

[31]Liddell and Scott, *Lexicon*, p. 658.

A new era is obviously reflected in the mind of the apostle Paul who, being a trained Jewish rabbi, under normal circumstances would have insisted upon circumcision. But in light of the redemption in Christ, one was to continue exactly as he was. There was no longer any necessity for those who were uncircumcised to be circumcised or for those circumcised to seek to reverse the procedure.

7:19 The reason for this was that circumcision amounted to nothing, and uncircumcision amounted to nothing. The only reason that circumcision had been important to the Jews was that it was part of the keeping of the covenant commandments of God. Since circumcision is no longer applicable in the era of the Holy Spirit, the only thing that remained important was the keeping of God's commandments.

7:20 This verse is not simply repetitious. It is, rather, a summary statement designed to impress once again upon the reader that every legitimate form of existence requires the witness of believers. Therefore, men are to remain in the same calling in which they were called. The verse also provides a preface to the second case Paul mentioned.

7:21 The second case concerns the position of a servant (*doulos*, the most common of all terms to describe slavery). Nowhere did the New Testament writers condone slavery. In fact, the passage immediately before us is in a sense a strong reprimand against the practice. Nevertheless, Paul did acknowledge the existence of such and, for the most part, the inability of the slave to do anything about his circumstances. Therefore, if a slave was called of the Lord to salvation, he was told, "care not for it." The word "care" (*meletō*, the present imperative of the Greek verb *mellō*) means "to bestow careful thought upon" or "to premeditate or to study with a view to devising some plan." Another acceptable translation might simply be "to worry." The servant was told, "Do not concern yourself unduly with your status as a slave." However, if, in the process of time, the slave had the opportunity to be made free, then he should by all means take advantage of that offer and avail himself of the opportunities that freedom would bring. The expression "use it" (*chrēomai*) is in its imperative form, meaning "take advantage of it" or "avail yourself of it." Two interesting possibilities present themselves. First, there is a hint that in many cases those who become the children of the Lord may expect the special providences of God to work toward their eventual freedom. There is no promise of this, but circumstances such as those of Philemon and Onesimus in the New Testament surely must have been increasingly the case in the early church. Second, oftentimes when freedom was offered, it was not accepted. The status of a relatively poor freed man in the Roman Empire was often far less acceptable than the status of well-treated slaves. However, Paul recognizes that there are certain desirable freedoms available to men who are not slaves. He, therefore, says, "if freedom becomes a possibility, avail yourself of it."

7:22 There is a sense in which even one who is a slave becomes free in Christ. This verse explains why the instructions of the New Testament continually advise slaves to be obedient to their masters, even to those who are less than kind toward them (see 1 Pet. 2:18–21). No more poignant example of this can be found anywhere than in observing the importance of the spiritual life in the black community of America during the days of slavery. A man might be a slave six days a week, but when he was with God's people on the Lord's day and always in his heart, he was the Lord's free man. In fact, the free style of worship developed in black churches, and sustained even to a large degree today, is classic testimony of the truthfulness of this statement.

The other side of the issue is that one who happens to be free ought not to revel in that freedom to the extent that he forgets that he, too, is a slave. By virtue of his commitment to Christ, he has voluntarily committed himself to a life of service in the Master's kingdom.

7:23 In fact, he has been purchased with a price, and, therefore, he cannot afford to be the servant of men. This admonition has nothing to do with believers who are called while in a condition of slavery but rather concerns those who are free. One who is free oftentimes will enslave himself to others through his business and social life. The caution here is that this should not happen.

7:24 The section is concluded with one last admonition that every man is to remain beside God in the profession or status in which he is called.

4. *Consolation for the Concerned (7:25–40)*

Consolation for those concerned about various aspects of domestic life is the concluding feature of the chapter. One may observe the framing of the lifestyle (vv. 25-28); the facing of the future (vv. 29-35); and the favoring of the virgin (vv. 36-40).

7:25 Apparently questions had also been raised about the treatment of virgins. Once again, Paul stated that he had no specific commandment of the Lord, but he indicated that he was willing to give his mind or opinion (see discussion of 7:6). It is to be noted once again, however, that in the concluding verse of the chapter Paul believed he had the mind of the Spirit in these things. Also, he was speaking on this particular subject as one who himself has obtained the mercies of the Lord in the matter of faithfulness.

7:26 He, therefore, supposed that it was "good" *(kalos)*, the same word used previously to indicate an acceptable, though not necessarily desirable state of affairs, because of the present constraint or compulsion for a man "so to be." The problem is to determine what he meant by the expression "so to be." It is possible that Paul intended his readers to understand the advisability of being like he was, i.e., free from the press of marital responsibilities. Or it is possible that he meant that one was to be as the case he was about to describe (vv. 36-38). A third possibility is that he meant to refer to the passage immediately preceding this one and was stressing that man should remain in the state to which he was called. This latter position is the most probable. What is especially critical in the verse is that one mark "the present distress." Precisely to what this referred is not apparent. Verse 29, which mentions the shortness of time, may be an index to the fact that the verse has prophetic implications concerning the eschaton or the last days. However, Paul could also have been indicating his anticipation of impending distress and persecution in the Roman world. Certainly such distress did in fact develop. A third possibility is that he expected such distress as a harbinger of the coming of the Lord.

7:27 That the concluding expression of verse 26 probably does mean to remain in one's present state in light of the present distress would seem to be verified by this verse. If a man is bound to a wife, he ought not to seek to be loosed. On the other hand, if he is without a wife, then the present distress should be sufficient to keep him from seeking a marital relationship. The expression "loosed from a wife" does not appear to presuppose a divorce nor, for that matter, the death of a mate, but simply the fact that one is not involved in a marital relationship.

7:28 On the other hand, Paul's recommendation falls into the category of the "good" *(kalos)*. There is no moral superiority about the state; an acceptable status is merely ascribed to it. Therefore, he added that if one should marry, he has not sinned in so doing. Correspondingly if a virgin chose to marry, she had not sinned. It was true that one marrying would have tribulation in the flesh. This was not a reference to trials and tribulations experienced between the two partners of the marriage but rather a reference to the additional inevitable concerns within marriage, such as, for example, the responsibility a man would feel in providing the best possible for his family and the agony of soul that he would probably experience in times of distress. However, Paul said he would spare them a further discussion of this at the moment.

7:29 Regardless of the above, one must prepare to face the future. The quote "I say" is a different word from that used before. Previously Paul used *legō*, but here the word changes to *phēmi*. While there is no appreciable difference in the meaning of the two words, the abrupt change signals a special emphasis on what follows. The apostle declared that the time *(kairos)* was short. Did he mean that this was so in an eschatological sense? Some help is probably garnered by an analysis of *sustellō*, derived from a combination of *stellō*, meaning "to send," and the preposition *sun*, meaning "together." The comment, then, did not so much mean short in the sense of only a moment's time, but rather that the time was being drawn together. *Kairos* is sometimes used in a general eschatological way. Sometimes it was used by the New Testament writers, and especially by Paul, to describe the coming of Christ. Apparently Paul meant to say that everything was drawing together toward the time of the Lord's return. In so saying, he was not guilty of date setting nor is it an infraction upon his word that another nineteen hundred plus years have gone while we await the Lord's return. The statement may also be related to the impending distress mentioned in verse 26.

In any case, as a result of the drawing together of the times, certain conditions are inevitable. These are delineated in the latter part of verse 29 as well as in verses 30 and 31. Those who had wives were to be as though they were not married at all. Precisely what Paul intended by this statement must be understood particularly in light of verse 31. Clearly he did not mean that one was to ignore the responsibilities that he had embraced in his marital covenant. It was not an argument for a man's abstinence from sexual intimacy, since that had been precluded by statements in verses 3 and 4 of the same chapter. Neither was it an argument that married couples should fail to care for the things that belonged to marriage otherwise. It merely was an admonition for the couple not to become too intertwined with the things of this life and in so doing neglect seeking first the kingdom of God and His righteousness (Matt. 6:33).

7:30 Other aspects of life are also included. People who wept in sorrow were to be certain that they did not sorrow "as others which have no hope" (1 Thess. 4:13). The Christian certainly will and should weep, but he should realize that those things which cause him to weep are temporal and passing. Those who rejoice should also recognize the limitations of earthly rejoicing. Those involved in the marketplace should not place too much importance on the accumulation of possessions.

7:31 In fact, the summary statement which embraces all of the aforementioned cases and many more is now provided. Those who "use this world" are not to abuse it. The expression "use" is a translation of *chrōmenoi*, which means "to avail oneself of" or "to employ." Those who availed themselves of the various aspects of this world are to be sure that they do not limit themselves to such. The word "abuse" *(katachraomai)* is the same word translated "use," with the prepositional prefix *kata* added, mean-

ing "to use down." The idea is that those who are availing themselves of the things of the world must be careful that this does
not become the sole focus or even the major focus of life because
"the fashion of this world is passing away." The word "fashion"
(*schēma*) gives us our English word "scheme." A scheme of things
is an impermanent pattern that is workable for awhile but then
passes away. Since everything related to the earth is passing and
since the time of its passing is short (v. 29), it therefore follows
that one must not invest too much of himself in the things of the
world.

7:32 Paul then returned to the specific subject of the benefits
of the celibate life. He stressed that he had thus written to ad-
monish the Corinthians to be without "carefulness" (*merimna*,
which means "responsible concerns" or perhaps even "worry").
Paul knew that in the coming distress the Corinthians were going to face sufficient worries and problems without having the
additional concern of marriage. Therefore, he wrote these things
against that day. For example, he said that the man who was unmarried had his responsible concerns associated with the things
of the Lord, and how he might please the Lord.

7:33 However, the married man had a more complex situation. He must be concerned responsibly about some of the things
of the world, at least to the degree that he must please his wife.
This was not even considered optional. If he had entered into the
covenant of marriage, there came with that covenant certain responsibilities. Although these were not antithetical to his vows
and commitment to the Lord, the covenant of marriage did add
to the complexity of life's situations and to the distresses that one
must face.

7:34 Paul recognized also the distinction or difference between
a wife and a virgin. This was simply a continuation of the
thought that he had developed concerning a married man in
verse 33. The unmarried woman might devote herself to responsible concerns about the things of the Lord. She was therefore
concerned about holiness both in body and spirit. However, the
woman who was married must be responsibly concerned about
the things of the world, at least to the degree that she must please
her husband. This did not indicate that there was any lack of ho-

liness in body or spirit bound up in the marital relationship. It was simply a recognition that the focus of her concerns must necessarily be much more extensive if she chose to marry.

7:35 Further explanation is now given as to why the apostle went to such length to present the virtues of the celibate life. He did it for the profit of the Corinthians and not for the purpose of casting upon them a "snare" (*brochos*, a term which has to do with the trapping of an animal). Paul did not give this reasoning in order to trap the Corinthians but rather for the profit of those who either had the gift of celibacy or else, having faced the termination of a marriage through either death or the departure of an unbelieving partner, might have understood the values involved in the single life they then had. More specifically, he was speaking to them about the things which would enable them in a graceful and comely way to "attend upon" (*euparedros*, derived from *hedra* or "seat") the Lord without distraction. Literally, the meaning is "to be well seated" or, in other words, "to devote oneself assiduously to a particular thing." In this case, the fervency of devotion is statedly to the Lord and is to be accomplished "without distraction" (*aperispaō*, an adverb derived from *spaō*, which means, in its medical sense, "to cause strain, convulsion, or spasm," prefixed by an alpha privitive so that it means "without strain, spasm, or convulsion"). Hence, in this case, a man would avoid the usual difficulties that might be present in serving the Lord if he also had marital concerns. Again, this is not in any sense a prohibition against marriage, only a reminder of the acceptableness of the single life when God gives the gift of celibacy.

7:36 Verses 36 to 38 comprise another one of those very difficult passages in which the Corinthians were in a position to understand what Paul is saying much more easily than we. Obviously, they knew the questions raised and the specific circumstances involved. Since the letter from the Corinthians to Paul is lost and since we do not have recorded anywhere the specific circumstances, the nature of Paul's reply is not easily followed.

The question obviously concerns a virgin and her relationship to "a man," and whether the man in view is her father or her fiance. This distinction is of major consequence in the meaning of the passage. A third possibility consists of a "spiritual marriage," a practice in which spinsters within the church attached themselves to certain unmarried males and took the vows of marriage but never consummated the marriage. The interest in the marriage was not one which involved sexual intimacy but only the protecting hand of the male. The two together gave themselves to spiritual pursuits. However, we have no clear cases of this until the latter part of the second century, and it is doubtful that such spiritual marriages had come to exist as early as the latter half of the first century.

As to the other two possible interpretations, there are problems either way. First, if the virgin daughter of a father was the subject under discussion, one must understand the word "daughter" to be in the text, since it does not actually appear. In the second place, if the father is in view, the statement "behaveth himself uncomely toward his virgin" involves a strange use of *aschēmoneō*, which normally denotes immoral behavior. If immoral behavior is not envisioned here, it is a rare use of the word.

As to the other view that sees the man in the text as being the fiance, that view leaves several other problems also unanswered. Why the couple would be engaged to be married and would still contemplate not marrying is not explained in the text. Indeed, it is sufficiently odd as to make that interpretation almost impossible. This view also renders verse 38, concerning the *giving* of the virgin in marriage, incomprehensible. We are left with the conclusion that what is in view here is apparently the action of a father toward his virgin daughter.

In the ancient world, fathers exercised almost total determination of the time of marriage and the choice of partner for their children, especially for daughters. Conzelmann refers us to the father, Demosthenes, who, before his death, pledged his wife to Aphobos and his daughter, who would be reaching marriageable age in about ten years time, to Demophon.[32] This clearly pictures the practice in secular circles, a custom even more consistently

---

[32]Conzelmann, *First Corinthians*, p. 135.

followed in religious circles. Of course, this means that *aschēmo-neō* does not refer to licentious behavior on the part of the father toward his daughter but only to the question of whether his withholding her from marriage was an acceptable or unacceptable decision. The answer was provided by Paul in the following way. If the virgin had come to the flower of her age, a statement that simply indicates that physically she was now fully mature, then the father might do what he willed in the matter. The verse implies that the father, while having the final determination in the matter, must be exceedingly careful to discern the needs of the daughter in the particular situation. Paul stated that if there was necessity, then the father might feel free to let her marry with full confidence that he was in no sense committing a sin. This would be the case even if he had previously thought that he would retain the daughter in perpetual virginity. In other words, clearly the daughter was going to have considerable opportunity to express her own needs in the matter and would herself largely determine the decision. If the need to marry was there, the man did not sin in allowing it.

7:37 On the other hand, the man who stood steadfast in his heart, not facing any necessity in the matter, was also doing well if he kept his virgin daughter from marriage. The word translated "steadfast" *(hedraios)* makes use of *hedra*, or "seat," which was used earlier in another connection. The word pictures immovability. So the man who stood immovable in his heart's conviction and who faced no necessity put upon him as a result of his daughter's wishes, and had power over his own will so that he was not influenced by criticisms others might offer against his decision, was doing well to keep his daughter a virgin. This is especially to be understood in light of the entire discussion of chapter 7 and the acceptability of the celibate life in light of the impending stresses faced by the Corinthians.

7:38 The summary conclusion is then offered that if the man chose to give her in marriage, he was doing well. If, on the other hand, he chose not to give her in marriage, he was doing better. This was not because of the superior morality or holiness of one state over another but, again, simply because of the stresses that existed and the nature of the coming together of the times.

7:39 One final question is discussed in the chapter. This is the question of the relationship of a partner to the marriage vows in the case of the death of the spouse. Paul simply concluded that the wife was bound by the law as long as her husband was alive. This is an especially interesting insight due to the light it throws on other passages and the possible exception clause in Matthew 19. It is clear that if the husband was still living, the wife was bound by the law to him. Only in the case of her husband's death was she given liberty to marry. Then she might marry whomever she wished, with the one limitation that this time she was certainly responsible for marrying one "in the Lord" or a fellow believer. Without question, this verse also throws light on verse 15 in which it is mentioned that when an unbeliever departed, a brother or sister was not under bondage in such cases. Apparently, a case cannot be made for the authorization of remarriage in light of this verse.

7:40 Even though a widow was free to remarry, Paul stressed one more time that she would probably be happier if she abode in the unmarried state. This was his judgment, but he was quite confident that he had the Spirit of God in making that judgment.

The Bounds of Personal Liberty

1. The Lifelessness of Idols (8:1–8)
2. The License of Indiscretion (8:9–13)

The freedom which believers enjoy in Christ is a responsible freedom. When it becomes a careless expression of the untempered will, it ceases to be conceived properly and becomes a detriment to the work of the Savior. A specific problem had arisen at Corinth relating to the prevalency of idolatry in the ancient world and particularly in that city. The Corinthians had written to Paul asking whether Christian freedom extended to the eating of meat that had been sacrificed to idols. The question, in all probability, had two aspects. First, the existence of guilds which met together in a pagan temple for social purposes and a common meal almost inevitably involved sacrifice of an animal which was then prepared as the entree for the feast. However, even the meat sold in the market place had often arrived there via the temple and thus was actually meat that had been sacrificed to idols. A small portion of the animal, normally the less than delectable portions, would be consumed on the altar as a sacrifice to the idol, while the rest of the meat would be made available for sale. The propriety of eating such meat was also a consideration for the awakened conscience.

1. The Lifelessness of Idols (8:1-8)

Under this heading we will consider knowing the important (vv. 1-3), noting the infinite (vv. 4-6), and nullifying the idols (vv. 7-8).

8:1 The question first addressed is one the Corinthians had raised about eating meat sacrificed to idols. Instead of addressing the question in those terms, the apostle began by anticipating the attitudes of some of the Corinthian Christians. He conceded to being aware of the common knowledge of the Corinthians. The implication was twofold. First, he knew that the Corinthians' knowledge of the fact that idols were nonentities and really amounted to nothing was going to cause them to argue that they had the liberty to eat things that had been sacrificed to idols. Paul would not argue against that premise, per se, but would attempt to enlarge their vision by arguing, in the second place, that knowledge had its dangers and needed to be augmented by another virtue. Consequently, Paul returns to one of his more frequent words and said that knowledge "puffs up" (*phusiō*).

Love, on the other hand, has a tendency to build up. Knowledge is more often used selfishly; whereas love (*agapē*, meaning "self-sacrificing," "other-person-oriented concern"), will inevitably build up not only the object of that love but also the subject doing the loving.

What was done in beginning the discussion of meat offered to idols on this level was subtly to suggest to the Corinthian readers that the answer to their questions may not have been bound up half so much in matters of knowledge as it was in compassion.

8:2 There is also another limitation concerning knowledge. Once a man thinks that he has a thorough grasp of things, he demonstrates that he really does not know anything at all by comparison to what he ought to know. Although something of a cliché, the case remains that when one's intellectual horizons are greatly expanded, it dawns on him that if they have expanded this far, there must also be an infinite realm of knowledge that is yet to be pursued.

8:3 After treating the subject of knowledge as to its inadequacy, Paul returned to the question of love, which is of greater import. Indeed, his statement here seems almost to anticipate the magnificent chapter 13, upon which he built a major portion of his case for the work of the church. Unfortunately, the precise meaning of this verse is not so easy to establish. "If any man love God, the same is known of him," but does the word "same" (*houtos*) refer to God or to man? In other words, does the verse mean if any man love God, the man is known of God; or does it mean if any man love God, then God makes Himself known to the man? Both would be theologically accurate, but the probabilities favor the former conclusion in this particular verse. If a man loves God, God knows about that and enters into a close, personal relationship of "knowing that man." Therefore, the superiority of the virtue of love becomes apparent at the outset.

8:4 The subject now turns directly to the question of food "sacrificed to idols" (*eidōlothutos*, a word which was apparently created by the Jewish community as a substitute for the concept of *hierothutos*, which meant "temple sacrifice"). The word, according to Conzelmann, was constructed "with a polemical edge" against the Greek concept.[33] Derived from *thuō*, meaning "to sacrifice," and *eidōlon*, which means "idol," it is rendered "things sacrificed to idols." The answer to the question about things sacrificed to idols is that an idol amounts to absolutely nothing in this world. The truth of this was common knowledge among the Corinthian Christians. Furthermore, there was no other God except one, and that was the God whom they served. To eat that which was sacrificed to idols, then, was of little consequence as it concerned the help or the hindrance of that particular idol, or of the individual partaking of the food.

8:5 Actually, Paul recognized that there were many that were called god, whether these were gods whose residence was purportedly in the heavens, such as Apollo, or those whose principal residence was supposed to be the earth, such as Poseidon, the god of the sea. There are, in fact, many such gods whose fol-

---

[33]Conzelmann, *First Corinthians*, p. 139.

lowers claimed for them the exercise of lordship over man.

8:6 The declaration of this verse is one of the strongest monotheistic declarations in the Scripture. It occurs in a context in which Jesus was also considered Lord and God, indicating that there was no problem in Paul's mind about triunity—one God and yet three persons within that godhead. The apostle began by stressing that there is one God who is the Father and by whom all things exist. The preposition *ek* is employed in the verse, literally meaning "out of whom all things have come." It is a clear indication that God the Father stands at the genesis of everything that exists. This includes the experience of salvation because we also stand in Him.

In addition to this, Paul spoke of "one Lord Jesus Christ." Literally, the expression means "one Lord who is Jesus Christ." "Lord" (*kurios*) is a term recognizing superiority and, in this case, deity. Jesus, the personal name of the Lord, means "Jehovah is salvation" and describes the mission of the Messiah. Christ (*Christos*), meaning "the Anointed One" or "the Messiah," is the equivalent of the Hebrew *Messias*. There is one Lord, who is Jesus, the Anointed One, or the Messiah.

Now, a similar expression to the one immediately preceding occurs. Of God the Father it is said that all things are *ex hou*, literally "out from Him." There is one Lord Jesus Christ *di' hou*, i.e., through whom all things exist. Jesus is declared, then, to be the agent of the creation of all things, which owe their ultimate origin to God the Father. Furthermore, we exist in our relationship to the Father "through Him"—i.e., through Jesus. This is the only deity whose existence Paul acknowledged.

8:7 Unfortunately, such knowledge does not exist to that same degree in every man. Some of those who had been converted to Christianity out of pagan superstition and idolatry had been genuinely converted but were still struggling with the realities of the non-existence of idols. To these people the idols were still very real forces with which to be reckoned. The King James Version of the text reads, "for some with conscience of the idol unto this hour eat...." However, the more reliable textual evidence points to a word that in Greek looks very much like the word "conscience," but means something quite different. "Conscience" (*suneidēsis*) is a possible rendering, but the passage actually makes much better sense if the word is *sunetheia*, "familiar" or "customary." Therefore, the passage would read, "some with common custom until this day eat this meat as something sacrificed to an idol." In other words, the sense of the reality of the idol to them was such that when they partook of food that had been offered to idols, they could not help but consider the idol and the system of worship associated with that idol. It was inevitable, then, that their consciences (and here there is no question about the way the text reads), being weak, were defiled. The word "defiled" (*molunō*) means "to contaminate." Consequently, it was a very serious offense to them.

8:8 Paul's ultimate conclusion in the matter was that the eating of meat did not actually commend one to God. By eating it one did not gain or advance to abundance, and by refusing to eat it one did not fall short or become defective. It had nothing to do with one's relationship to God and, hence, in reality should not have been a matter of conscience. But this was not the entire story, as we shall note.

2. The License of Indiscretion (8:9–13)

In this discussion, Paul declared that liberty is not free (v. 9), life is not private (vv. 10–11), and love is not simple (vv. 12–13).

8:9 The propensity of the knowledgeable Corinthians to be puffed up was apparently being demonstrated in their abuse of the liberty or freedom which was theirs. A caution was therefore given that they not use their liberty (*exousia*) in such a way that it becomes a stumbling block for those who are weak. *Exousia*, generally translated "authority," was used here by Paul in the sense of the authority to make one's own decisions in these matters. Without at all questioning the actual existence of that authority, Paul warned that it was not to be used in such a way as to cause the weak to stumble. Liberty, then, is not really free. It may be freely given, but there is always a cost involved in its continued usefulness. One of those costs is the concern for others who may be affected in the course of the exercise of one's liberty.

8:10 The Corinthians were also informed that the believer's life was not altogether a private matter. They were told that if a man saw one of the Corinthians who was possessed of the knowledge that idols were nonentities sitting at meat in an idol's temple, it was inevitable that this would be taken by the man of weaker conscience as an invitation to eat those things sacrificed to idols. The result of this was already predicted in verse 7; namely, his conscience would then be defiled. It is in this verse that the extension of the subject is seen.

The question was not just of eating meat which had been sacrificed to idols and then sold in the market place, but apparently some of the Christians were continuing to go to the guild meetings or social gatherings that occurred in the pagan temples. While visiting in those temples, there was always the prospect of being observed by a brother who was a relatively immature Christian still struggling with the whole question of the reality of idols. Seeing a more mature brother at such a place might have caused that brother to be "emboldened" (*oikodomeō*, an interesting word which literally means "to build a house"). Gradually, the word picked up secondary connotations also, such as "to make advancement," or, in this case, to progress to behavior that might be unwholesome for that individual.

8:11 An even more serious prospect than the word mentioned in verse 7 now appears. As a result of the knowledgeability of a mature Corinthian Christian who felt perfect liberty in going to the idol temple or participating in concourse with friends on a social level, now a weak brother for whom Christ died would perish. It is at this point that the verse becomes interpretively difficult.

The term "perish" (*apollumi*) is very strong. Generally speaking, it is used in an eschatological sense of ultimate destruction, not in the sense of annihilation, as noted earlier, but in the sense of removal from all meaning and from God. To add to its strength in this particular verse, the word was moved by Paul to the very first of the sentence, a syntactical maneuver in Greek which, in many cases, provided emphasis in a sentence. The problem is to explain how it was that a brother might face destruction as a result of the actions of a mature Christian's sitting at meat in an idol's temple.

One possibility is that the man had not yet embraced Christianity and was still in the process of examining the possibilities. God's Spirit was dramatically dealing with his soul. He was attending the assembly of God's people, and he was in the process of discovering the inadequacies of idolatry. At that very crucial moment the neophyte saw a mature Christian sitting at a meal in the idol temple and was thereby caused to continue his own idolatrous ways, the result being eternal destruction for one for whom Christ died. The pathos of that closing statement, in such a case, is exceedingly moving.

The other possibility for interpretation is that the word "perish" did not refer to eternal retribution but rather to the perishing of one who was already called a "brother." In the event that the brother failed to achieve all that he should have as a Christian, the effectiveness of his own Christian testimony was in a sense nullified.

Either interpretation would be possible, but it seems that the first is far more likely due to the usual use of the word. One other observation might also be made here. If the first interpretation is the accurate one, then the verse becomes a powerful argument for the universality of the atonement; i.e., Jesus died for the non-elect as well as for the elect. This does not argue universality of salvation but only that the extent of the atonement of Christ included everyone.

8:12 Against the first interpretation is the remainder of the passage. When a man so sinned against the brethren as to strike or smite his weak conscience, he was actually sinning against Christ. The conclusion here is twofold. First, all sin is ultimately sin against God. Second, what may not be a sin in itself may become a sin if in the exercise of one's liberty he is hurtful to others.

8:13 The conclusion is specific and formidable. If eating meat which had been sacrificed to idols offended a brother, then Paul concluded that he would not eat flesh until the end of the age rather than to risk causing his brother to be scandalized. The word translated "offend" is *skandalizō*. The vivid term presents the circumstance exactly. In the exercise of Christian liberty, we must always exercise that liberty with a view to the effect it may have on others. It is a liberty that has definite bounds, recognizable perimeters which must not be violated. Those bounds are the ones that determine the reception of the gospel in any given society. While Christians may rejoice in their considerable liberties, they must always do so in the context of the understanding of their mission on the earth.

Carrying Wealth to Heaven

1. The Ox in the Corn (9:1–18)
2. The Obsession with the Commission (9:19–27)

In 1 Timothy 6, the same apostle who wrote the Corinthian letter stated that just as we came into the world with nothing, we would leave the same way. There, however, he spoke of material wealth. A variety of wealth can be transferred from earth to heaven. In a sense, it is an investment in the heavenly kingdom. In the most intensely personal segments of 1 Corinthians, the apostle offered insight as to the things that really motivated him, as well as his perspective regarding early missionary enterprises.

1. The Ox in the Corn (9:1–18)

In the first section, which constitues a defense of Paul's apostleship and a delineation of apostolic rights and obligations, we will look first at the prerogative of ministers (vv. 1–6), the payment of ministers (vv. 7–14), and finally the pathos of ministers (vv. 15–18).

9:1 Apparently some at Corinth had been willing to strike at the root of the problem. If Paul's authority were to be abridged, his apostleship would have to be denied. Perhaps some had gone that far. Therefore, he began this section rather abruptly by asking, "Am I not an apostle?" As the first proof of that, he asked still another question, "Have I not seen Jesus Christ our Lord?" This statement not only creates the aura of authority but is, in fact, viewed by the whole Christian community as an essential for belonging to the apostolate. Luke provides the basis upon which a successor for Judas was chosen:

> Wherefore of these men which have companied with us all the time that the Lord Jesus went in and out among us, Beginning from the baptism of John unto that same day that he was taken up from us, must one be ordained to be a witness with us of his resurrection (Acts 1:21–22).

Paul recognized the criteria which were established for the selection of a successor to Judas, and later in the book of Acts, his own testimony made constant reference to the fact that he had seen the Lord in a special Damascus Road encounter. He referred to it again in this verse. This argument progressed one step further, however, by asking a second question of the Corinthians, i.e., were they not, in fact, his work in the Lord?

9:2 The last phrase of verse 1 is now pressed still further. If some would not see Paul as an apostle, yet surely the Corinthians would do so because they represented the seal of his apostleship in the Lord. Two things are worthy of mention. First, in a day when many were illiterate, seals were of special importance. Recognizing a particular seal usually meant acknowledging that authority. Paul spoke of the Corinthians as such a seal for his apostleship. The second thing worth noting is that in a sense Paul has here turned their own argument upon them. Since he was the Christian missionary who led the first Corinthian converts to Christ and organized them into a church, if he was not an apostle, then his claim made him a false apostle, and the church at Corinth was the product of a pseudo-apostle. The Corinthians could scarcely afford to argue in such a manner; so the force of Paul's argument was overwhelming.

9:3 One cannot be sure whether this verse refers to the previous two verses or to the verses that follow. Certainly the avowal is applicable to the verses both before and after the statement. Paul spoke of his answer to those who examined him in this. The word "answer" (*apologia*) is a strong term in Greek. A careful look at the word will show the derivation of our English word "apology." The word has slightly altered its meaning across the centuries. For us, to apologize means to express regret. However, originally the word meant an organized, careful presentation of one's position. To give an apology was to state one's logic in such a way as to communicate and convince concerning the propriety of that position or proposal. Paul spoke of giving such an apology.

9:4 A series of questions follow regarding rights that would be expected by him as an apostle and, apparently, by all ministers in the early church. The first question—"Have we not power to eat and to drink?"—apparently bears no relation to previous chapters in which there is discussion of meat sacrificed to idols. What is in view here is the right to eat and to drink at the expense of the churches. The question is designed to elicit an affirmative answer.

9:5 The next question has to do with the authority of Paul to lead about a sister, i.e., a wife, just as the other apostles did. Certain examples are listed—namely, the brethren of the Lord and Cephas. The mention of these apostles and their missionary activities gives a brief and interesting insight into early missionary effectiveness. Clearly "the brethren of the Lord" refers to at least some of the half brothers of Jesus who are mentioned in the gospel account (Matt. 13:55). At least two of them became prominent in the work of the church. One was James, the half brother of the Lord, who, in effect, was the pastor of the Jerusalem congregation at the time of the Jerusalem Council (Acts 15) as well as the probable author of the epistle bearing that name. Jude, apparently the author of the epistle which bears that name, was very probably another half brother of Jesus. At least these two, and maybe others of the half brothers of Jesus, became convinced believers after the resurrection. The verse suggests that they were widely engaged in apostolic missionary endeavors and that while they might never have been to Corinth, their work was known even to the west of the Bosporus. The same, of course, was true of Cephas or Peter. It is already known from the recorded healing of Peter's mother-in-law that Peter was married. In the cases of both the half brothers of Jesus and of Peter, apparently their wives accompanied them on their missionary journeys. These journeys, one may glean, were extensive, and were carried out with the monetary assistance of the churches.

9:6 Still another question concerned Barnabas and Paul and their missionary activity. Did they have the authority to cease working? The work here indicated was not work relating to the kingdom of God. It was a foregone conclusion that they would labor for the kingdom. However, it is also known from Acts that Paul was a tentmaker and that he labored with his own hands to make a sufficient living, never charging the churches, a fact that will be emphasized as the chapter progresses.

9:7 If the apostles had certain prerogatives, the churches, too, had certain responsibilities to the apostles. This would be true whether the apostles and other ministers accepted this participation in their ministry or not. Following his favorite method in this letter, Paul continued to ask questions. He employed three different metaphors, the cumulative effect of which would have been to find common ground at one point or another with almost every person in Corinth. Did men go to war at their own cost? Do farmers plant a vineyard and not enjoy eating the fruit of it? Or who was there who shepherded a flock and then did not drink of the milk of the flock? The answer to these questions was obvious, and the application of the metaphors was no less obvious. One further comment should be made about the three metaphors chosen. There is a real sense in which the ministry is a warfare. There is certainly a sense in which it is a vineyard, a sense to which Paul alluded in chapter 3 when he spoke of the Corinthians themselves as being God's husbandry. And, of course, the metaphor concerning the work of a shepherd is always apropos to the ministry.

9:8 What appears to be a relatively bland statement in this verse is actually of major consequence. Once again, the verse constitutes an argument for apostolic authority and also is significant for presenting the Scriptures as confluently prepared, having been written by man but uniquely inspired by the Holy Spirit. Paul raised the question, "Do I say these things as a man, or is it not true that the law has already said the same thing?" The point was that the law itself was written by the hand of Moses. What Paul was now writing, he was writing as a man; yet there was a distinction between what was written solely by a man and what was written by man under the influence of the Spirit of God. What man may write as man may be pregnant with insight and yet often erroneous. When God speaks through man, however, what is written has all the reliability and dependability of the law.

9:9 Specifically, he referred to a quotation in which the law of Moses ordered that an ox not be muzzled while he worked in the corn (Deut. 25:4). Paul's rhetorical question following this was, "Does God not care for the oxen?" The answer is that certainly He does, and among the provisions made is the order that the ox not be muzzled. Although some ministers may find this analogy a bit uncomfortable, it is clear that Paul was using the analogy to portray the work of the minister and his congregation.

9:10 This verse has a definite connection with the last phrase of verse 9. God does, of course, take care of the oxen, but was the command of Deuteronomy 25:4 for the oxen? The answer is yes, but not primarily for the oxen. This verse asks a question that reveals the real purpose of the statement. Did he make the statement altogether for our sakes? The answer is that it was no doubt written to this end, so that the establishment of an ancient fairness code would guarantee that whoever plowed would plow in actual hope of eating of the fruit of the ground he tilled, and the one who threshed the wheat would also be a partaker of the same kind of hope.

9:11 The conclusion is inescapable. If the apostle had sown spiritual things among the Corinthians, it would be no astonishment that the expectation of reaping a certain amount of the material benefits of the Corinthians would be present. As Paul used the word "carnal" (*sarkikos*, "fleshly"), it referred to those things that ministered primarily to the flesh. He argued that having faithfully labored in spiritual matters, the Corinthians should expect to share in providing those things that ministered to the fleshly nature of man.

9:12 The verse suggests that there had been others who had already exercised this power or authority with regard to Corinthian generosity and who had partaken of these carnal benefits. But in his own case, Paul stressed that although the authority was present, he had never made use of it. Once again, *xrēomai*, translated "used," is derived from the word meaning "to avail oneself of something." Paul had simply not availed himself of what the Corinthians could provide, but instead he suffered all things so that he would not hinder the gospel. "Suffer" (*stegō*) meant originally "to hold off" or "to endure patiently" or "to contain one's self." The idea here is that Paul endured his own circumstances in order to be certain that he did not cause an impediment or a hindrance to the preaching of the gospel of Christ. For him to have accepted remuneration for the task that was his might have created in the Corinthians' minds a suspicion about his motivation or might even have detracted from the freeness of the gospel. Consequently, the apostle chose to endure whatever was necessary.

9:13 However, to continue the demonstration of the rights of the ministers to live from the gospel, still another instance is cited. Once again, Paul returned to asking questions. How did the people live who ministered about holy things in the temple? It is not certain here whether the reference is to the Jewish temple in Jerusalem or to the various pagan temples. The practices would have been similar, but the fact that temple is singular reflects the probability that Paul was referring to the Jewish temple in Jerusalem. There, of course, it is known that according to the law of Moses, the Levites received no possession in the land other than certain cities that were Levitical cities. They were to live off the gifts and offerings of the people. A careful examination of the sacrificial system as revealed in the book of Leviticus will also show that those who officiated at the altar of sacrifice as a part of those sacrificial services often took home a portion of the animal that was sacrificed.

9:14 In the same way the Lord has ordained that those who are preaching the gospel should also have their living from presentation of the gospel. This does not imply that they become hirelings. They are answerable only to God in their messages, but the response of appreciation from the people should make ample provision for them. The reference is doubtless to Numbers 18:21, where it is stated, "And, behold, I have given the children of Levi all the tenth in Israel for an inheritance, for their service which they serve, even the service of the tabernacle of the congregation."

9:15 Once again the apostle returned to the protest that he personally had made use of none of these things. This time, however, the word was not the same one that he had been employing, but rather *chraomai*, a word which contains *charis*, indicating "a gracious favor or bestowal." The apostle had not accepted any of these gracious bestowals. The reason for this behavior on his part was that he would rather die than to have any man "make my glorying void." The word "void" is *kenoō*, which literally means "to empty." Paul evidently experienced great elation of spirit knowing that he had preached the gospel for no other cause than for the love of Christ. He had little to glory in, but he did glory in the cross of Christ. That one should take that away from him through the gifts of material possessions was a thought he did not even want to contemplate. In fact, death would be preferable.

9:16 The concluding discussion of this section focuses on the necessity of preaching the gospel and the resulting reward expected. The apostle explained that in the preaching of the gospel he really had nothing in which to glory. The contrast is with the verses immediately preceding in which he gloried in the preaching of the gospel without charge. In other words, he could only glory in the fact that he had preached to the Corinthians without being a burden to them in the preaching of the gospel itself. The reason for this was that necessity had been laid upon him. The expression "woe is me" is filled with pathos and suggests that the most painful and tragic results would ensue in this life if he did not in fact preach the gospel.

9:17 This does not mean that there is no reward in the preaching of the gospel. To the contrary, if Paul was obedient to the necessity thrust upon him in the preaching of the gospel, if he did this willingly, he would definitely have "reward" (*misthos*). However, if he should do it against his will (obviously here a hypothetical case), it was nonetheless true that he must do it because there had been committed to him "a dispensation of the gospel." "Committed" (*pisteuō*, which we normally translate "to believe") is in the perfect tense, indicating action which occurred in the past and continued in effect without fading. The use of the verb *pisteuō* at this point provides one of the sharpest perspectives as to its actual meaning. As mentioned, it is usually translated "believe," but obviously much more is intended. The idea primarily bound up in the verb is that of total commitment. The words "of the gospel" are not in the text, as is indicated by their italicized form in the King James Version. The word "dispensation" (*oikonomia*) is present, however, and literally derives from *oikos*, meaning "house," and *nomos*, meaning "the law"—hence, "the law of the house." The word, therefore, may be translated "management." Paul affirmed that a certain management had been committed to him. Appropriately, the word *oikonomia* generally represented the position of a slave. Paul's point seems to have been that even if he pursued this preaching unwillingly, the fact of the matter was that a management had been committed to him. He had no other choice but to do it.

9:18 What, then, can he anticipate as a reward? The possibility is that Paul knew that there was reward even beyond what he was about to state. What he did say, however, was that to preach the gospel without charge to the people, being careful not to "abuse" his power in the gospel, was ample reward for him. Once again, "abuse" (*katachraomai*) is probably too strong for this term, which simply means "to use up." The statement suggests that Paul, in preaching the gospel, made the gospel of Christ without charge, therefore not availing himself of the authority that he had in the gospel to charge them or to depend upon the Corinthians for his support.

2. The Obsession with the Commission (9:19–27)

Already it is apparent that Paul had an obsession with the

commission that had been given to him. It was his constant thought and almost his entire interest. In the section that follows, we will notice the deployment of the mission (vv. 19–22), the direction of the mission (vv. 23–25), and the discipline of the mission (vv. 26–27).

9:19 Discussions of evangelistic and missionary strategy often direct themselves toward the consideration of the proper vocabulary for describing the evangelistic task. Soulwinning, for example, has been a popular term and is not without biblical precedent, since the wise sage of Proverbs said, "He that winneth souls is wise" (Prov. 11:30). However, verses 19–22 of the present passage suggest that a different terminology, which could be well employed today, was in use in the early church, at least in Paul's vocabulary. Paul stated that though he was free from all men (a statement referring in part to his free status as a Roman citizen but even more to his status in Christ), yet he had voluntarily placed himself in a position as a slave to all, and this he had done for one purpose—that he might gain the more. "Gain" (*kerdēsō*) is the subjunctive mood of *kerdainō*. It may also mean "to derive profit or advantage" or interestingly, in some cases, "to save or spare oneself." Apparently the saving of oneself is not in view, but it is clear that the saving of others is contemplated. This will be observed again in verse 22. Therefore, Paul chose to use a term from the marketplace to speak of his evangelistic mission. He had made himself the servant of all in order that he might gain as many as possible for Christ.

9:20 What follows is an enumeration of the extent to which this was true. To the Jews he became a Jew in order that he might gain the Jews. This is the second of five uses of *kerdainō*. To those who were under the law, he was under the law that he might gain them that were under the law. There is no implication here that the apostle subjected himself to the rabbinical interpretation of the Jewish law. Unfortunately, the Jews of the first century had, to a large extent, identified the law not only with the Pentateuch or even the Old Testament but also with rabbinical tradition as embodied in the Jewish Talmud. Paul did not suggest that he had been obedient to Jewish interpretations, but he did suggest that he had been obedient to the law of the Old Testament, even to a degree not required in the gospel itself, for the purpose of gaining those who were under that law.

9:21 The opposite polarity is the witness to those who were without the law. The reference here is undoubtedly to Gentiles who were not said to be lawless in their behavior but who simply did not possess the law. The apostle made his approach to them as one being without the law. However, this necessitated a parenthetical statement explaining what he meant. Paul did not suggest that he lived as though there was no law by which he was compelled, but rather he was under the law in Christ. The contrast here is between *anomos* (the word for "law" being *nomos*, prefixed with the alpha privative and meaning "no law") and *ennomos* ("under the law," meaning that Paul was subject to the law of Christ). All of this, however, was to gain those who did not have the law.

9:22 Still additional categories are enumerated. The apostle did not hesitate to become weak so that he might gain a hearing for the gospel among those who suffered likewise. His concluding statement was that he was made all things to all men that he might by all means save some. This final change of vocabulary from "gain" to "save" is significant in two ways. First, it defines precisely what Paul had meant all along by the word "gain"— namely, that the purpose of his ministry was to see to the saving of the lost. Second, the word "save" always indicates the gravity of the circumstances in which men are found. The circumstances are so serious that nothing short of a dramatic rescue can bring about their survival. Paul had access to the information that would lead men into that salvation. This had become the obsession of his life.

9:23 The Corinthians were also involved in this task. All that had been mentioned Paul had done for the sake of the gospel so that he might be a partaker of that gospel with the Corinthians. The word translated "partaker" is *sunkoinōnos*, a word made up on *koinōnos*, meaning "fellowship," and the Greek preposition *sun* added as a prefix. It simply emphasizes the matter of fellowship with the Corinthians.

9:24 In order to make oneself so versatile and to drive oneself as determinedly as was the case with Paul, great discipline is required. It is, in fact, the discipline of an athlete in training. In the concluding section of the chapter, Paul moved to a rehearsal of athletic metaphors designed to demonstrate the discipline of life that is required in the preaching of the gospel. Those who imagine that the preaching of the gospel is a task which requires very little have not pursued it in the same way as the apostle Paul.

Again, a question provides the initial direction of the discussion. Were the Corinthians unaware that all who participate in a race run while only one receives the prize? The word "prize" (*brabeion*) is of uncertain derivation. The word seems to suggest arbitration or judgment, sometimes designating the judge or the umpire in a game. There are cases where it means "wand," or "baton," given as prizes, and it may even on occasion have to do with an official in a religious confraternity. Apparently, the word gradually came to be used as one of the words to describe the reward given for first place in games, such as the Isthmian Games held every three years at Corinth.

There is no suggestion here that only one of the Corinthians would be saved. The suggestion was rather that one must run the race in the proclamation of the gospel with the same determination as that characteristic of an athlete who was striving to win the prize. The command follows, "So run, that ye may receive that reward."

9:25 If one is to compete successfully in any race, the discipline to which he must subject his body is a major factor in his potential success. Those who are going to strive for mastery are "temperate" in all things. The word translated "strive for mastery" is the vivid and picturesque word *agōnizomai*. The English word "agony" is derived from this term. The translation "strive" is, therefore, an excellent one, since it pictures a mental attitude as well as the intensity of physical disciplines necessary to achieve victory in the race.

"Temperate" (*enkrateuomai*) literally means "self control." The competing athlete must rigorously control his body not only in terms of vigorous activity but also in terms of appetite and rest. The astonishing factor for Paul was that athletes did this to obtain a "corruptible crown."

The word "crown" (*stephanos*) referred not to a bejeweled diadem but to the laurel wreath crown that was awarded to one who was victorious in the games. Such a crown, if composed of vegetation, dried and disintegrated rather rapidly. Even in those cases where gold or silver was used to fashion such a crown, decadency was still inevitable. Yet athletes went through all of the agony of preparation in order to win such a crown. However, Paul stressed that the agony through which he had walked was to secure an incorruptible crown. Obviously, the giving of that incorruptible crown is directly associated with the winning of people to Christ. Such a reward is to be gained through the same kind of agonizing preparation and effort exhibited by Paul and will result in the gaining of men for Christ.

9:26 The concept of discipline is continued as Paul wrote that he ran not as "uncertainly" (*adēlōs* which is derived from *dēlos*, meaning "clearly" or "evidently," and the alpha privative prefix which negates the word), thus meaning "I do not run without clarity." The emphasis here was upon the fact that Paul's race was run with a clear goal and according to the most fastidious observation of the rules of the game. Changing to a pugilistic metaphor, Paul said that he did not fight as one who was constantly pounding the air and was thus unable to hit his target.

9:27 Paul's summary statement is important for several reasons. First, he stressed that he "kept under" his body. Once again, an athletic metaphor is employed, but the English translation lacks the color of the Greek term *hupōpiazō*, which literally means "to hit in the face" or "to hit beneath the eye" so as to blacken the eye. It may in some cases be translated "to pummel." As a part of the discipline of his particular race, Paul pummeled himself and captured his body as his "slave" (*doulagōgeō*). These expressions do not imply some sort of ascetic punishment of Paul's body in order to subject the evil materiality of his body to the basic good of his soul. Such a gnostic idea is not present at all. The whole verse occurs in the context of the vigorous discipline of an athlete. Any who have participated in contact sports will immediately recognize the battering that the body must take in order to be prepared for the rigors of the athletic contest. This is precisely what he meant. As Robertson and Plummer put it, "It is perhaps too much to say that St. Paul regards his body as an antagonist. Rather, it is something which becomes a bad master if it is not made to be a good servant."[34]

The reason for this vigorous preparation of the body is provided in the last phrase of the chapter. This phrase, however, has become problematic to some who would construe it as indicating that Paul feared lest he forfeit his salvation. If Paul could forfeit his salvation, then surely loss of salvation is possible for any of the saved. But the whole problem emerges from a much too graphic translation of *adokimos*, translated in the passage as "castaway."

Most of the games, such as the Isthmian Games, the second largest athletic contest of the ancient world, employed a *kērux*, or one who officially called the runners to their starting posts and gave the signal for the initiation of the race. Paul pictured himself in a dual capacity in this concluding phrase, first seeing himself as the *kērux* who called others to the race, and, secondly, as one of the runners involved. The word "preached" is an aorist verb form of *kērux*, so that Paul was identifying the work of the *kērux* in calling the runners to the starting blocks with his own ministry of calling people to Christ. He was concerned lest, when he had called others to the starting blocks, that he himself should become *adokimos*, "disqualified" or "rejected as of little value." The word has nothing to do with loss of salvation. Paul was absolutely certain of his salvation, but he knew that if he did not stay disciplined spiritually, he would not qualify to participate in the spiritual race, the goal of which was to gain men for Christ. To keep from being disqualified as unworthy to participate in this crucial race for souls, Paul therefore disciplined himself rigorously so that he might pass the inspection and participate in the race to which he had already called others.

---

[34]Robertson and Plummer, *First Corinthians*, p. 197.

Eating with Demons

The ethical section of 1 Corinthians is continued in the discussion of chapter 10. Ethics has already been under discussion at several points in the epistle, but now it becomes the focus of Paul's discussion.

1. The Rock in the Wilderness (10:1–4)

In this section, we are told of the grace of God (vv. 1–4), the grade of man (vv. 5–10), and the gravity of the Scriptures (v. 11).

10:1 The filial greeting "brethren" reminds the reader that although what is about to be said is rather intensive spiritual diagnosis, it is nonetheless administered at the hand of one who loves him. Furthermore, the writer had no desire that his readers should be ignorant. He voiced concern about the possibility that they were ignorant of the lessons of Old Testament stories, though they must have known the facts of those stories very well. There began immediately a recounting of the fact that these were the fathers (referring to Jewish fathers) of the faithful, even if they were not of the particular ethnic group primarily present in the church at Corinth. Paul reminded all his readers that the fathers were under the cloud and that all passed through the sea. The reference is to the story of the Exodus, where it is recorded that

> The LORD went before them by day in a pillar of a cloud, to lead them the way; and by night in a pillar of fire, to give them light; to go by day and night: He took not away the pillar of the cloud by day, nor the pillar of fire by night, from before the people (Ex. 13:21–22).

Exodus 14 also records the removal of the cloud from the front to the rear in order to shield the children of Israel, gathered by the banks of the Red Sea, from the approach of the armies of Pharaoh. The pillar of the cloud represented the shekinah glory of God. The word *shekinah* is a rabbinical term developed to describe the significance of this glory cloud which accompanied the children of Israel and the Ark of the Covenant. Literally, the word means "that which dwells." The shekinah cloud is usually described as preceding the children of Israel in the wilderness. In the case of Exodus 14, however, it moves to stand behind them; and in the process of so doing it must have crossed over their heads. Doubtless this, coupled with the mention of the sea, would indicate that the event to which he referred was that critical moment when the children of Israel stood poised on the brink of the sea with the Egyptians closing in from behind. Paul simply noted that they were all under the cloud and, furthermore, that all of them passed through the sea.

10:2 As a part of this experience, therefore, all the children of Israel were "baptized unto Moses in the cloud and in the sea." "Baptize" is not used here in the sense of the faith-witness baptism of the New Testament, i.e., the immersing of an individual in water following his conversion. However, the term is used in this same sense, signifying the complete envelopment of one substance in another, i.e., immersion. This baptism is not related to the ordinance; rather, it pictures people as being entirely immersed into Moses, being enveloped first by the cloud and then by the sea. In other words, they were completely inundated in the experience through which they walked.

10:3 Furthermore, all the children of Israel also ate of the same spiritual food. The reference apparently begins with the crossing of the Red Sea and the beginning of the wilderness wanderings. How would so great a multitude be fed? Each morning when the children of Israel awakened, they found manna, the heavenly substance with the sweet taste, spread upon the ground. This heavenly food Paul referred to as "spiritual meat."

10:4 By the same token, there was the problem of finding water for such a multitude. Paul next called to mind Moses' experience in striking the rock out of which flowed an abundance of water for all the people. This reminded him that the people drank of the same spiritual drink, for they drank of that spiritual Rock that followed them. Being more specific, they drank of the Rock that was Christ. This is no mere allegory. The actual history of the feeding of people with manna and the miraculous rift in the rock are in no sense questioned in these verses. On the other hand, it is clear that Paul was making use of typological language; i.e., these experiences of eating the heavenly bread and drinking the water from the rock really were spiritual experiences of faith as much as they were actual historical incidents. They prefigured the sustenance that would be gained, first of all, in terms of salvation and, second, in terms of general spiritual growth which would be derived from the spiritual food and drink for all men of faith.

The Rock from which the people really drank was none other than Christ. Interestingly, the word "rock" (*petra*) is precisely the same word employed in Matthew 16:18, "And I say also unto thee, That thou are Peter [*Petros*], and upon this rock [*petra*] I will build my church; and the gates of hell shall not prevail against it." In 1 Corinthians 3, mention was made that Jesus Himself apparently is the foundation stone upon which the church is built. Further confirmation is now discovered in this very passage, since the same word that is used in Matthew 16:18 is used here, and it is plainly said that the Rock is Christ. While it is arguable that a different rock is in the mind of Matthew, it is much more likely that in both places Christ is, in fact, the Rock.

10:5 The spiritual sustenance and presence exhibited in the physical experiences of the crossing of the sea and the provision of water and manna were, it would be assumed, totally sufficient to impress upon the minds of the Israelites the power and faithfulness of God. The facts were otherwise. Consequently, God was not well pleased with many of the children of Israel, and the initial triumphant course was thwarted by the intervention of the same gracious God who had saved them from the Egyptians, the sea, starvation, and thirst. Consequently, the children of Israel were overthrown in the wilderness. "Overthrown" (*katastrōn-numi*) gives us our English word "catastrophe." It is derived from the Greek word *strōnummi*, meaning "to spread," and *kata*, meaning "over"—hence, "to spread over" or "to be strewn about." The children of Israel were then subject to catastrophe in the wilderness.

10:6 Just as Paul argued that the verses in Deuteronomy concerning muzzling the ox while it treads out the corn were written for the sakes of those who would come afterwards (9:9–10), so he argued that the wilderness experiences of Israel were examples intended to prevent future generations from making the same mistakes their ancestors had made.

"Examples" (*tupoi*), from which we get our word "types," refers to the outline of an event. For example, on a typewriter one may search out the letter "a." Striking that letter, the element on the typewriter flies forward and leaves an "a" on the paper. Yet it is not actually an "a" on the paper. The only "a" is on the key or the element. What is left on the paper is a perfect reproduction and picture of that "a." Paul's point is that all of the events of the Old Testament were recorded as types—pictures designed to show the believers of subsequent generations how to live and what to avoid. A whole list of these things follows. The first things to be avoided is "lust" (*epithumētēs*), derived from the verb *thuō*, which originally denoted a violent movement of air, water, or some other substance. The sense of *thuō* was "to boil up" as in the smoke of a sacrifice. Consequently, it eventually came to mean, on occasion, "to sacrifice." With the prefix *epi*, meaning "upon," the sense of the word is "to boil upon."[35] Most frequently it has an evil connotation in the New Testament, though it may mean "desire" in a good sense. Whether it is good or evil desire, the picture is that of a "boiling over" of desire. The fathers in the wilderness experienced this boiling over of uncontrolled desire with their wants, without regard for God's will in the matter. Perhaps this is the best definition of lust: whenever one's desire to possess something or someone becomes such that the object is desired regardless of the will of God.

10:7 Idolaters were also present among the children of Israel. The apostle quoted Exodus 32:6, where it is recorded that the children of Israel, upon deciding that Moses would never return from the smoking mountain of God, ". . . rose up early on the morrow, and offered burnt offerings, and brought peace offerings; and the people sat down to eat and to drink, and rose up to play." The tragic story that follows refers to the worship of the golden calf which had been fashioned by Aaron. The people had observed Apis, the sacred bull of Egypt, throughout their Egyptian confinement. The incarnation of the god Apis in the sacred bull was revered just as were the Pharaohs. Upon the death of the bull it was embalmed and placed in a huge sarcophagus, which was in turn placed in what is today known as the Serapium just outside of Cairo. Aaron's golden calf was apparently a reproduction of Apis, an infection in the blood of the children of Israel that reproduced itself again in the golden calves established by Jeroboam at Dan and Bethel in the days of the Northern Kingdom. The licentious worship associated with idolatry is alluded to in the activities of the people.

10:8 Becoming even more specific, the people were also guilty of fornication or sexual license. As a result of this moral collapse, in one day twenty-three thousand of the children of Israel fell. Paul referred to one of the most infamous incidents recorded in the history of Israel, involving the prophet Balaam whose tragic advice to the Israelites led them ultimately to whoredom with the daughters of Moab (Num. 24—25). A plague from God

---

[35]Freidrich Kittel, ed., *Theological Dictionary of the New Testament*, Vol. 3, p. 167.

swept across the children of Israel as punishment for their disobedience (Num. 25:9).

The teaching of the verse is obvious. However, there is one
painful problem. Whereas the Numbers account records the
death of twenty-four thousand, Paul speaks of only twenty-three
thousand who died in the plague. At first sight this difficulty is
an acute one for interpreters of the New Testament who believe
that the Bible is inerrantly and infallibly inspired. However, the
explanation seized upon by more liberal thinkers is even more
unacceptable than the attempts of evangelicals to harmonize the
texts. According to the more liberal thinkers, Paul, a learned
rabbi who studied at the feet of Gamaliel and who was as thoroughly versed in the Hebrew Scriptures and the Septuagint as
anyone, made a glaring faux pas, a mental slip. That the esteemed apostle would exercise such carelessness and endure the
certain embarrassment therefrom is unthinkable.

Gleason Archer has attempted to explain the incident. He
holds that the reference is not really to the incident in Shittim
with the Moabite women (Num. 25:1); rather, the event to which
Paul referred was still the infamous worship of the golden calf
(Ex. 32). In that particular text it is recorded that the Levites slew
three thousand of the people. However, the account refers to others who were slain by the plague (Ex. 32:35). According to
Archer, Paul has given us the combined number of those slain by
the children of Levi (three thousand) plus twenty thousand who
died by plague, but whose numbers are not given in the Exodus
account.[36]

While this is a conceivable harmonization, it seems to lack
probability. The older explanation that the accounts in both
Numbers and 1 Corinthians 10 are using round numbers appears
much more likely. While the Holy Spirit could have seen fit to reveal the precise number of Israelites who fell in the plague, frequently round numbers are used when precise numbers are
unimportant by comparison to the moral, ethical, or spiritual
teaching embraced in the text. One might then appropriately as-

---

[36]Gleason Archer, *Encyclopedia of Bible Difficulties*, p. 401.

sume that the Israelites who died at Shittim numbered between twenty-three thousand and twenty-four thousand. The Numbers account provides us with a rounded-off number just in excess of the number who died, while Paul, under the leadership of the same Holy Spirit, gave the lower number indicating the number of thousands who died without considering the precise number beyond the figure. This may not be an acceptable explanation to all. Perhaps the precise explanation for this has not yet been discovered. Again, it should be stressed, however, that it is an explanation far superior to the one which sees Paul as a forgetful, bungling rabbi who could not keep his facts straight.

10:9 The next example cautions against tempting Christ as some also tempted God and were destroyed by serpents. One reason Gleason Archer's attempt at harmonization in the previous verse seems unlikely is that apparently each verse mentions a different incident to serve as an example for those who would follow after.

This particular incident almost certainly refers to the rebellion against Moses when the children of Israel "spake against God." The rebellion concerned the repulsiveness they had developed for the manna God provided. The result of this sin was the sending of fiery serpents among the people. These venomous beasts extracted a considerable toll among the children of Israel.

A very interesting facet of the interpretation of this verse is the admonition not to tempt Christ "as some of them also tempted." Who they tempted is not specifically stated, but the verse seems to imply that the object being tempted is Christ. Some textual variants read "Lord" rather than "Christ" in this particular verse, but the evidence seems slightly to favor the reading "Christ." If "Christ" is the word that Paul wrote, there is no question but that this is an affirmation of the preexistence of Christ. This would not be strange in light of the avowal of verse 4, but it is a strong statement of the deity of Christ as well as of His preexistence. The result of this particular tempting of the Lord in the wilderness was destruction by means of the serpents. Earlier it was pointed out that the statement "If a man defile the temple of God, him shall God destroy" (3:17) is one which almost always means spiritual destruction. However, it was also pointed out that there are cases where it clearly means physical death. Such is this verse.

10:10 One final example was marshalled by Paul to support his admonition. "Murmur" (*gonguzō*, which means "to mutter scarcely audible but nonetheless clearly communicable utterances of a demeaning nature") is onomatopoeic (sounding like what it depicts). The reference here could apply to several different incidents in the Old Testament, but most likely it refers to the people's murmuring against Moses and the rebellion which resulted in God's determination to smite the people with pestilence, disinherit them, and make of Moses a greater nation (Num. 14). Moses' intercession before God became the catalyst in a new direction for the people of God. The carcasses of a majority of the people fell in the wilderness, destroyed by the destroyer. Other incidents could also be in the apostle's mind.

10:11 Having discussed in the first four verses the grace of God, and then having graded the people, Paul then assessed the gravity of the Scriptures in these matters. All these things happened to the children of Israel, as examples, to be recorded for the admonition of Paul and other believers. "Admonition" (*nouthesia*) once again means "to place in the mind." Paul argued that all of these events had been written to place in the minds of believers the gravity of faithfulness to God. Particularly were these things written for those "upon whom the ends of the world are come." That last expression employs not *cosmos* ("world") but *aiōn*, meaning "ages." The word *telē*, which means a "conclusion" or "climax," and the word *katantaō*, which literally means "to bear or bring down," complete the expression, which may be reasonably translated, "These things are written for our admonition upon whom the climax of the ages is being brought down." In other words, the whole plan and purpose of God with the human family is in its concluding stages with the advent of Christ. The next stage after that will be the conclusion of all things in His triumphant return. The Corinthians were to recognize that they were a special people living in a critical time. All of the warnings had been recorded for them.

2. The Retreat from Waywardness (10:12–22)

The subjects addressed in verses 11 to 22 include conquering temptation (vv. 12–13), communion with Christ (vv. 14–18), and culpability with demons (vv. 19–22).

10:12 The cataloging of the events during the Exodus, especially in light of the prior demonstration of the power of God, is apparently the cause for the serious warning that every man who thinks he is able to stand needs to take special heed lest he should fall. This particular warning is based on two implicit thoughts. First, there is culpability in every man. The best men who ever lived, our Lord excepted, at one time or another deeply and keenly disappointed themselves. The second basis for the warning is bound up in the simple truth that whenever a man is most confident that he stands, at that moment his vulnerability reaches its zenith.

10:13 On the other hand, there is a wonderful promise which the apostle now made to all who underwent such testings. First, the Corinthians were assured that no temptation had taken them except those which were human in nature. The word translated "temptation" (*peirasmos*) may mean "testing" or, on other occasions, "temptation." Sometimes, of course, both ideas are captured in one incident in life. Whichever the case, the author spoke of the Corinthians as being taken by these temptations. *Lambanō*, here used in the perfect tense, may mean "to take" or "to receive." Either idea is adequate in this verse. One may be conceived as the recipient of temptation or as the object assaulted and taken by temptation. Whichever is the case, the comforting aspect is that no one of these temptations is anything other than *anthrōpinos* or "manish." The emphis on the decided "humanness" of temptation again apparently has a twofold purpose. First, the Corinthians were thus reminded that temptation consistently falls into certain patterns and categories which have long since become known to the entire race. Any given temptation might certainly adorn itself in a new dress, but in nature it would not differ from those that had gone before.

The three basic categories of temptation are noted by the apostle John as being the lust of the flesh, the lust of the eyes, and the pride of life (1 John 2:16). The desires of the flesh have remarkable correspondence to the fact that in Genesis Eve noted that the fruit of the tree of knowledge of good and evil was good to eat. A strong similarity exists in the appeal to the fleshly appetite of Jesus in the wilderness temptation when He was asked of Satan to use His powers for His own selfish ends by turning stones into bread (Matt. 4:2–3). By the same token, the desire of the eyes has been compared with Eve's observation that the tree was pleasant to the eyes (Gen. 3:6) and Satan's request that Jesus electrify spectators during the wilderness temptation by casting Himself from the pinnacle of the temple while still sustaining no harm (Matt. 4:5–6). On the other hand, the pride of life bears definite resemblance to the fact that Eve found the fruit of the tree desirable "to make one wise" (Gen. 3:6) and the fact that our Lord was promised that if He would but bow down and worship Satan, Satan would bestow upon Him the authority over all the nations of the world (Matt. 4:8–9). The rather striking coincidence between John's analysis and two specific cases in point apparently provides three major categories into which temptation normally falls. The list of examples (vv. 6–10) is further evidence of the kinds of temptations that impinge upon men as a part of the common human experience.

There is one other important aspect of this mention of the humanness of temptation. Since what believers experience in terms of temptation is a common human experience, one has the assurance that just as men have in the past succumbed to the tempter on occasion, so on other occasions they have conquered the tempter, thereby providing positive evidence that one does not have to succumb continually to temptation. The nature of avoidance, however, is not in what man alone is able to do, but rather it is bound up in the faithfulness of God. God can be counted on not to allow any man to suffer temptation beyond what he is able to endure. God will, in fact, make with the temptation an escape so that every individual will be able to bear the testing. Once again, two sides of the same issue are emphasized. First, God in His sense of fairness never allows a man to be overwhelmed by temptation as with a tidal wave. On the other hand, along with the temptation He always makes a way to escape.

In summary, these are the sterling promises of this verse: (1) There is a limitation placed upon temptation (only what is common to man); (2) God will never suffer exorbitant temptation to come upon His beloved; (3) With each temptation there will be a clear exit for escape.

10:14 Having mentioned the inevitable presence of an exit from temptation and anticipating a return to the discussion of the eating of meat sacrificed to idols, particularly the meat which would actually be eaten in the idol temple, Paul's stern advice to the Corinthians was to flee from idolatry. His counsel was not merely to sidestep idolatry or avoid it, but to race vigorously from its presence.

10:15 The burden of evaluation of what he was saying was placed squarely upon the shoulders of the Corinthians. Paul complimented them by saying, "I am speaking to you as to wise men." Notable is the absence of *sophia*, the word used earlier in 1 Corinthians to describe the wisdom of the world. Rather, the word is again *phronimos*, with which Paul preferred to describe the enlightened logic of the believer. "Since I am speaking to enlightened men," the apostle argued, they were to judge what "I say" (*phēmi*). Once again, the change from *legō* in the first part of this verse to *phēmi* in the latter part of the phrase is apparently a meaningful switch. He was speaking just as other men would, but what he was saying was worthy of the Corinthians' careful evaluation.

10:16 In this verse the subject moves to a discussion of the fellowship at the Lord's table. Even this discussion, however, is not so much an end within itself as it is a preface to a further warning about the dangers of idolatry. Indeed, Paul argued from the viewpoint of exclusiveness. The essence of the argument was that if one was in fellowship with Christ, then he must avoid fellowship with the demonic.

First, Paul spoke of the "cup of blessing which we bless" and asked if it was not the "communion" (*koinōnia*) of the blood of Christ. Several words in this verse are important. The word "blessing" is not the usual *makarios* such as we find in the Beatitudes, but rather *eulogia* (prefix *eu*, meaning "good," with *logia*, meaning "a word"). A "good word," then, is a blessing. And "the cup of blessing which we bless," Paul wrote, "is this not the fellowship of the blood of Christ?" Fellowship, referring to what one has in common, focuses here on the common experience that all the Corinthians had of cleansing by the blood of Christ. It was upon the basis of this common experience that they blessed together the cup of blessing. Elsewhere, *eulogia* is used in terms of adoration, "Blessed be the God and Father of our Lord Jesus Christ" (1 Pet. 1:3). The idea of blessing is "to say a good word about God." Here we drink the cup of God's "good word" about us in the cross of Christ, and in so doing we say a good word of praise concerning our Lord. Only those who have experienced together the common benefits of the blood of Christ actually are able to participate in this service of blessedness. By the same token, the bread which is broken, Paul argues, is the fellowship of the body of Christ. Apparently the practice of the early church was to break pieces from a common loaf and then eat, thus reminding themselves that they together constituted the body of the Lord Jesus Christ.

Two important reminders which are perennially present in the Supper are hereby placed before us. First, we are reminded that as we drink the cup of blessing in the Lord's Supper, we testify to the common experience of being cleansed by the blood of Christ; and second, as we eat from the common loaf, we are reminded of our common experience of living as the body of Jesus Christ.

10:17 That thought is pressed still further. The importance of the symbolism of each person's breaking a piece from the same loaf is that it stresses the individuality of our salvation, "we being many," and yet the commonality of our experience as being "one body" in Christ. The design of the apostle's argument here evidently was not advanced without memory of the divisions within the church at Corinth as well as of the particular problem he was facing specifically in these verses. Thus the emphasis upon unity in the body of Christ returns once again.

10:18 The apostle then returned to illustrations from the Old Testament to document that about which he spoke. He called attention to Israel and spoke of the "Israel after the flesh." This strange statement seems to suggest that there were two different ways in which the word "Israel" might be employed—a fleshly Israel and a spiritual Israel. This, of course, is precisely the case. Paul took that same theme in Romans 9:6, where he stressed that "they are not all Israel, which are of Israel." In other words, there was a "spiritual Israelite," i.e., one who had been faithful to the laws and promises of God. On the other hand, "Israel after the flesh" had itself largely become a stranger to the promises of God. Under no circumstances should this be taken to imply that "Israel after the flesh" has no further place in the program of God. Romans 9:10-11 repeatedly emphasizes that God is yet going to deal with national Israel. In any case, "Israel after the flesh" serves as an example here in the sense that those who ate of the sacrifices were partakers of the altar. The reference is to what transpired especially in the peace offering discussed in Leviticus 3:1-17.

The peace offering generally expressed peace and fellowship between the offerer of the sacrifice and his God. Hence, it was a communal meal. It is described as a thank offering, sometimes as a votive offering, and again as a freewill offering. When the sacrifice was brought by the worshiper, the fatty portions were burned on the altar of burnt offering. The wave breast and the heave shoulder (the right thigh) were left with the priest as his portion, but the remainder was to be eaten in the court by the offerer and his family. Sometimes a portion of it would be taken home and eaten on the following day. In the case of the slaying of the passover lamb, the family also partook of that sacrifice. The point being made was simply that the priest, and sometimes the offerer of the Jewish sacrifice, were partakers of the sacrifice which was made. The very sacrifice to which they looked as an atonement for sin also became a part of them through the eating of the animal sacrifice. As such, they symbolized the fellowship of forgiveness which was theirs.

10:19 The application can now be made since the props have all been placed in order. In previous verses, Paul had suggested that when one comes to the Lord's table, he approaches as a partaker of the fellowship of the cleansing blood of Christ and of the fellowship of the body of Christ. He had also suggested that the fellowship was symbolized in the partaking of the elements of the Supper, just as in the peace offering of the Old Testament the fellowship of forgiveness was symbolized by the people eating a portion of that offering. In light of this, the apostle now returned to his approach of asking rhetorical questions. "What then do I say [*phēmi*]? Is the idol actually an entity, or is the food sacrificed to idols of any actual importance?" The anticipated and correct answer is "no"; idols do not have life, and the food offered to them is no different in its qualitative substance than any other food of which a man might partake.

10:20 The further anticipated conclusion is that as a consequence of the above answer, I may eat food sacrificed unto idols without reservation. It was at this point, however, that the argument of Paul turned in a different direction—one that was somewhat surprising to the Corinthian readers. Whereas in a previous discussion of this matter (ch. 8) Paul hinted at the wisdom of abstention from meat offered to idols, he now espoused a more demanding position. He began by affirming that the Gentiles were actually sacrificing to devils and not to God. "Gentiles" (*ethnē*) simply means "the nations." It encompassed the whole Greco-Roman world and beyond, since the offering of the sacrifices to the gods constituted a common component in many religious faiths.

The things that the Gentiles sacrificed, they sacrificed to devils (*daimonion*), which should be translated "demons." The precise etymology of "demon" is not clear. Forester suggests that the commentators are probably correct who suggest that the original word meant "disruption" or "rending apart," giving rise to the conception of the demon as that which "consumes the body." The word "demon" is used in a great variety of ways. In the literature of the Greeks, sometimes the gods, especially the lesser deities, are pictured as demons. On other occasions, anything that constitutes an unknown super-human power is relegated to the world of the demonic. Almost inevitably demons are presented as rulers of human destiny and are often connected with misfortune and distress. Many of the Greek religions and philosophies spoke of the possibility of men being possessed by demons.[37] The

---

[37]Kittel, *Theological Dictionary*, Vol. 2, pp. 1–20.

concept of demons in the New Testament is similar in some ways to those conceptualizations present in the Greek religions. The similarity is at the point that the demons are pictured as personal, malignant spirits, the authors of much of the evil in the world. The added New Testament emphasis relates them directly to Satan, the prince of the demons, and would apparently identify these demons as being fallen angels. These malignant, fallen spirits are mentioned as being chained (2 Pet. 2:4) until the day of judgment. Apparently this incarceration does not include all of the angels who "kept not their first estate." Some are still able to practice their maleficent intentions in the human family.

As noted earlier, the Greeks often identified their gods as demons, particularly in the case of the lesser gods. It is not surprising then that Paul used the Greeks' own words with the Judeo-Christian understanding of the word and suggested that when the Gentiles made sacrifice to idols, the sacrifice was actually being made to fallen malignant spiritual beings; and it was Paul's desire that the Corinthians not have anything in common (i.e., no fellowship) with demons.

10:21 Next the impossibility of dual fellowship is asserted. One cannot drink both the cup of the Lord and the cup of demons. One is not able to be a partaker of the Lord's table and at the same time sit at the table of demons. "Partaker" (*metechō*) is complementary to the word *koinōnia* or "fellowship" in that it derives from *echō*, meaning "to have," prefixed by the preposition *meta* ("with"), thus meaning "to have something with another." The idea is that it is impossible to have fellowship with the demons and the Lord at the same time.

10:22 Thus far the argument has been that (1) those who sacrifice to idols are sacrificing to demons, and (2) one cannot have a common experience with both the Lord and demons. The third phase of the argument is once again presented in the form of a rhetorical question. Would the Corinthians then provoke the Lord to jealousy? Did they think for a moment that they were more powerful than God? The suggestion is rather obvious. Since the Corinthians had proclaimed at the Lord's table their fellowship with Christ, for them then to approach the table of demons would provoke the Lord to jealousy. The case was exactly the same as if a man pledged his vows of marriage to a woman and then became promiscuous in his sexual behavior. His lack of faithfulness to his wife would provoke her to jealousy. In the pledge of his vows of fidelity, the man would have indicated a fellowship with her alone, which he then actually prostituted. The Corinthians would be doing the same thing if they prostituted their allegiance to Christ by eating at the table of demons. Of course, in the case of a man and his wife, the man might very well be stronger than his wife, but such is not the case with the Corinthians. To have God jealous over His people is a potentially hazardous circumstance. Paul simply raised the question, "Are you able to live promiscuously and still stand against God?" The answer anticipated was an emphatic no.

3. The Recompense of Winsomeness (10:23–33)

There is a reward and a recompense of winsomeness (vv. 23–33). The basic discussion still concerns meat sacrificed to idols, but it now proceeds along the line of the Christian's responsibility to those among whom he works. Note the edification of the elect (vv. 23–24), the evangelization of the lost (vv. 25–30), and the emulation of the church (vv. 31–33).

10:23 Paul then returned to the familiar expression, apparently popularized by the Corinthians, "all things are lawful to me." It is twice repeated in this same verse. As usual, Paul did not refute the accuracy of the statement, he merely pressed the corollary aspects of it by saying, first, that all things were not expedient. "Expedient" (*sumpherō*) means "to bear together." All things may be lawful, but not everything is best to bring things to a wholesome conclusion. In the second place, all things do not edify or build up. Paul was suggesting that Christian behavior could never be predicated simply upon the grounds of what might be lawful. Further questions must be asked concerning whether or not certain behavior accomplished the ends of a Christian. Furthermore, the question must be asked as to whether this behavior would result in constructive forces working in the lives of believers.

10:24 The King James Version suggests that the subject of this verse is wealth; "Let no man seek his own, but every man another's wealth." But the word "wealth" is in italics, which simply means that it was added by the translators for clarity's sake. The truth is that the issue before us was not clarified but confused by the addition of this word, because the subject at hand has nothing to do with the acquisition of material possessions. Rather than wealth, the discussion is "well-being." This verse is a logical conclusion for verse 23. The believer does not determine his ethical posture in life based on that which is lawful, but on that which is constructive and brings things together in a fruitful way because he is responsible for seeing not only to his own well-being but also to the well-being of others. While there is freedom in Christ, there is also bondage in Christ. The bondage is that commitment to the Savior which guarantees that a man will want to do only those things which contribute to the well-being of the kingdom.

10:25 The above statements are now specifically applied in three possible scenarios which represent circumstances likely to have occurred at Corinth. The first one concerns those things sold in "the shambles" (*makellon*), a reference to the Greek marketplace. By even mentioning the *makellon*, Paul thus acknowledged that much of the meat sold had been trimmed from animals sacrificed to idols. Nevertheless, since there was very little opportunity to ascertain whether or not this was the case, Paul simply told them in this particular situation to go ahead and eat it, asking no question for conscience sake.

10:26 Part of the rationale for proceeding on this basis is that the whole earth is actually the property of the Lord with all of its fullness, and that certainly includes the animal kingdom, the vegetable kingdom, and, in fact, all that exists. The further fact that the meat may have been sacrificed to idols is neither here nor there, since all of it ultimately belongs to God. This is actually an Old Testament quotation from Psalm 24:1 and elsewhere.

10:27 A second scenario is now predicated. In some cases the Corinthians would be invited to go to a feast by those who were unbelievers. The King James Version seems to indicate that some necessity was placed upon the believer to go. The word translated "dispose," however, is *thelō*, which means "to want" or "to desire." The case is very simple. Unbelievers invited believers to go to a feast. The believers desired to go. Paul does not indicate that this behavior constitutes being "unequally yoked together with unbelievers." Rather, this was the kind of social contact that was essential if the Christian was to be effective in his task of evangelization. So if he wished to go, he was to eat whatever was placed before him without asking any questions because of conscience.

10:28 The first two possible circumstances are such that Paul gave his permission to eat even what might have been sacrificed to idols. The third scenario is very different. If a man should have invited the Corinthians to a feast and declared that what he was about to serve was a temple sacrifice (*hierothutos*), then the believer was to abstain from eating for the sake of the one who had disclosed to him the origin of this meat. Not only was the believer to abstain from eating the meat for the sake of the one who revealed to him the origin of the meat, but also he was to abstain for the sake of conscience. Once again, in the King James Version the phrase "for the earth is the Lord's, and the fullness thereof" appears. However, the best textual evidence seems to indicate that this has been an addition based on the earlier appearance of the same words. Indeed, if it had been a part of the text that Paul wrote, it would break the train of thought with verse 29, which is an essential explanation to the concluding phrase of this verse, if that phrase is "and for conscience sake."

10:29 The conscience in view in verse 28 is not the conscience of the believer but the conscience of the person who had invited the believer to the feast and revealed to him that they were to partake of meat sacrificed to idols. Paul's concern was that the conscience of the weaker individual not be defiled. One may legitimately ask what is the difference in the two different reasons given for abstention from such a meal. In verse 28 Paul wrote that the believer was to abstain for "his sake that showed it," and the second reason given and explained in verses 28 and 29 is that he was to abstain for the sake of the other man's conscience. Apparently the distinction has to do with the effect of the believer's behavior in terms first of witness and second of example. The person who had invited him to the feast was to be the object of his compassionate concern with a view to evangelization. Not only that, but he was to be certain that he did not set an example, the following of which could result in the defilement of conscience in the unbeliever or weak brother.

In conclusion, Paul stressed that his own liberty should not be subject to the judgment of another man's conscience. In other words, the apostle was arguing that he had every right to sit at meat with this particular individual. The fact that the other man's conscience may be defiled did not make it wrong for Paul to eat in the sense of personal moral culpability. It did, however, make it unwise for Paul to eat and, therefore, sin in the sense of failure to be properly concerned about the life of another.

10:30 Apparently the concluding statement of the previous verse was added in reaction to criticisms offered against those who, realizing that idols were in fact nonentitites, had eaten meat sacrificed to idols. Paul spoke of the situation as though he himself were a part of it. "If I partake of this meat by grace, then why is there evil spoken of men concerning that for which I have given thanks?" The use of *eucharistō* (I give thanks) and *chariti* (by grace) apparently were designed to show that Paul, and perhaps others like him, accepted the food of which they partook as being the product of the grace of God. It was that which He had provided. Mature believers gave thanks to God for it and, with these two circumstances prevailing, found it impossible to understand why others would speak evil of them. Robertson and Plummer suggest that since it is impossible to give thanks to God for a pleasure one knows to be wrong, it follows that the pleasure is actually an innocent one.[38] The word "evil spoken of" is actually *blasphēmoumai*, transliterated into English as "blaspheme." Literally, it means "to deride" or "to reduce to insignificance." Earlier Paul had argued that the wisest course of action was not to eat of things sacrificed to idols. On the other hand, he

---

[38]Robertson and Plummer, *First Corinthians*, p. 223.

was now arguing that the strong who did eat under certain circumstances should not become the objects of derision.

10:31 The conclusion of the whole matter, which the church is to emulate, is given in the concluding three verses. Whether a man is eating or drinking, or whatever other pursuit of life he may have, he is to be certain that what he does is to the glory of God. "Glory" (*doxa*) may be defined as a public manifestation of an inner reality. The statement, then, is simply that whatever the Christian does he must always be concerned about what kind of shadow his public behavior casts upon his continuing relationship with God and His kingdom. He is to be certain that the actions of his life will bring glory and honor to God.

10:32 The second question he must ask concerns the impact of any action upon Jews, Gentiles, and the church of God. "Offense" is the colorful *aproskopos*, which is a combination of three words—*koptō*, meaning "to hit" or "to smite," *pros*, meaning "in the direction of" or "toward," and the alpha privative which negates the whole thing. The word then means "not striking" in the direction of the Jews or the Gentiles or the church of God.

10:33 The concluding verse of the chapter constitutes Paul's own testimony in this regard. He had sought to please all men in all things by not seeking his own profit but rather the profit of other men, especially to the end that they might be saved. This affirmation was in complete agreement with his previous avowal (9:19-26), in which he stressed that the entire posture of his ministry was determined by those things that would enable him to do the most in the cause of evangelism. The profit of the many, notably their personal salvation, was of primary importance to Paul.

Behaving In Church

1. Women Prophets (11:1–16)
2. Wicked Pretenses (11:17–22)
3. Worthy Practices (11:23–34)

The Christian's behavior, wherever he happens to be, is crucial to the effectiveness of his witness. However, almost unthinkable would be a circumstance in which believers behaved in an unseemly fashion when the church was assembled together. Yet apparently there were instances in Corinth, and perhaps threats of additional ones, in which this actually transpired. The clear misbehavior was associated with the celebration of the Lord's Supper. Other incidents may have revolved around the participation of women in the services of the church. In the first section, therefore, Paul examined the glory of God (vv. 1–4), the glory of man (vv. 5–12), and the glory of woman (vv. 13–16).

1. Women Prophets (11:1–16)

11:1 Numerous commentators have noted the obvious. Verse 1 logically accompanies the concluding argument of chapter 10. A new direction altogether is charted with verse 2. However, even though there is technically an unfortunate chapter division, verse 1 belongs to the entire epistle. The simple command urged the Corinthians to be followers of Paul, even as Paul also is a follower of Christ. The word employed for "follower" (*mimētēs*, which gives us our English word "mimic") is not the word we would expect in certain circumstances. Most literally, Paul suggested that the Corinthians reproduce in their lives the same pattern that they saw in his because his life was patterned after the life of Christ.

Paul was suggesting that he attempted to pattern his own life after the inoffensive behavior of our Lord, sometimes refusing to take advantage of the liberties that properly belonged to him in order to satisfy the demands of the kingdom. The Corinthians were to do the same.

11:2 Even though there were troubles in the Corinthian congregation, the whole picture was certainly not dark. Paul praised the congregation at two particular points. First, they remembered him in all things, and, second, they kept the ordinances as Paul had delivered them.

Regarding the first, there is some division of opinion. Some commentators have suggested that the reference is to monetary support for Paul. Almost certainly this is not the case since Paul repeatedly indicated that his labor among the Corinthians was purposefully accomplished without any necessity for his support from the church. Consequently, the statement "that you remember me in all things" must be closely related to "keeping of ordinances" and is surely Paul's commendation of them for keeping in mind his teaching at every point.

Though the church was divided and in serious strife, the impact of Paul's ministry was still clearly felt. Particularly he spoke of the keeping of the ordinances as he had delivered them to the church. The word "ordinances" *(paradosis)* is derived from *didōmi*, meaning "to give," and *para*, meaning "beside." Therefore, "ordinances" refers to those things that are given to a group, a word usually translated "traditions" in the New Testament. Most of the uses of the word have a negative connotation in the New Testament. The gospel writers used it to refer to the traditions of the elders and the traditions of men in contrast to the express word of God. Nothing could be clearer than that the Lord went out of His way to demonstrate that the traditions of the elders (the rabbinical interpretations of the Old Testament) were notably inferior to the law and the prophets. Büchsel is in error when he says, "For Paul Christian teaching is tradition and he demands that the churches should keep to it since salvation depends on it."[39] Nothing could be further from the truth. Paul's whole argument in the book of Galatians, and much of the book of Romans, was that salvation was a matter of God's grace appropriated by faith and had nothing to do with tradition. It is true, however, that the apostle Paul used the word "tradition," both here and in 2 Thessalonians 2:15 and 3:6, in a positive way, though elsewhere he used it in a more negative sense. The word itself is, of course, neutral. When used in this positive sense, it apparently referred to the whole matter of church order, including deportment in church, church discipline, baptism, the Lord's Supper, and order and approach to worship.

11:3 Having warmly commended the Corinthians for areas of faithfulness, the discussion now turns to the behavior of women in the assembly of believers. The text itself does not confirm abuses at Corinth, but the mention of the adornment of women in chapter 11, coupled with a return to the discussion of the right of women to speak in the church in chapter 14, suggests the possibility of a rowdiness and aggressiveness on the part of some of the female constituents at Corinth. Therefore, Paul proceeded first of all to establish the order in the church, insisting that the head of every man was Christ, the head of the woman was the man, and the head of Christ was God. In light of the growth of the feminist movement in recent years, considerable discussion has arisen over this passage.

In an attempt to avoid the implication normally drawn from this verse, Scanzoni and Hardesty attempt to argue that the word "head" (*kephalē*) does not mean anything other than source.[40] They argue that Christ, as the agent in creation (John

---

[39]Kittel, *Theological Dictionary*, Vol. 2, p. 172.
[40]Letha Scanzoni and Nancy Hardesty, *All We're Meant to Be*, pp. 30–31.

1:3), is the source from which man came. By the same token, according to the Genesis account, woman was taken from the side of man; hence, the source or "head" of woman is man.

The position of Scanzoni and Hardesty runs into great difficulty, however, with the concluding phrase of the verse. If they are correct about the basic meaning of *kephalē*, the concluding phrase, "the head of Christ is God," at least implies that there was a time when Christ did not exist just as there was a time when man and women did not exist. Christ, therefore, finds His source of origin in God the Father. Such an interpretation is at variance with everything else the New Testament teaches and is in clear disharmony with the apostle himself in his discussion of Christology in Philippians 2 and Colossians 1.

"Head" obviously must mean something other than "source," just as the word "head" in the physiology of the Bible cannot possibly mean "source." What can be said, however, is that the concluding phrase of verse 3 clearly eliminates any possibility of masculine superiority. Since Christ is in fact God, the phrase "the head of Christ is God" cannot possibly indicate inferiority of creation or standing. By the same token, the statement "the head of the woman is the man" implies neither inferiority of the woman nor superiority for the man. On the other hand, role assignment is clearly in view. From the beginning, God established a certain order which is to exist in the universe in general and in the affairs of men in particular. The order is inviolable. In this order, God has ordained subservience of men to God, because the head of every man is Christ. Furthermore, in that order, God ordained a subordination in office through the incarnation of God in Christ. This subordination, nevertheless, was not a subordination of essence. There was never a time when Jesus was anything less than fully God. On the other hand, He voluntarily accepted the role of a servant in order that He as a man might perfectly keep the law of God and therefore make acceptable atonement for the sins of the human family. This explains why Jesus could say, "He that hath seen me hath seen the Father" (John 14:9), and still say "My Father is greater than I" (John 14:28). In essence He was the same as the Father, but in office He had subordinated Himself to the will of the Father in order that He might perfectly keep the law.

From this consideration it is possible to understand precisely what Paul meant when he said "the head of the woman is the man." Here again is subordination of role assignment. There is no subordination of essence—both man and woman are made in the image of God and as such are equally able to know and experience God and to function as the servants of God in the world. Nevertheless, God has arranged the circumstances of life so that all men are ultimately responsible to someone. Because the home is the first and most important of God's institutions, those same circumstances of order exist within the home and should be honored by all of society. Therefore, woman has been made subordinate to man in office.

11:4 Beginning with this verse, the remainder of this chapter is replete with difficulties which the interpreter to some degree must face in the dark. The problem of 1,900-plus years of separation from the social circumstances in Corinth and the ancient world are nowhere more keenly felt than in a passage such as this. Little agreement exists among major commentators as to the precise social practices that existed in the first century. In fact, the more one investigates the more he discovers that the problem is complicated by a divergence of social custom, which to some degree flowed along geographical and ethnic lines, thus indicating the absence of unanimity of opinion.

Paul made a distinction in the adornment of men and women who would pray and prophesy in the church. Although some have felt that the matters here discussed relate to society in general or perhaps even to the privacy of one's own home, the tenor of the entire chapters would indicate that the assembly of believers was in view. The first problem to be solved must also be faced in verse 5, i.e., the question of the "head," which is said to be "dishonored."

A man who prayed or prophesied with his head covered dishonored "his head," but did "his head" refer to the portion of his anatomy that sits upon his shoulders, or did it refer to Christ, who is said to be the "head of every man" in verse 3? The problem is solved by the principle of contextual interpretation, since there seems to be a continuum of thought between verses 3 and 4. Therefore, the head to be dishonored, if a man should pray or prophesy with his head uncovered, is the Lord.

The strangeness of this argument is reflected in the modern Jewish practice of wearing the *yarmulke* during the reading of the Torah. Some of the Hasidim never venture forth in public without their heads covered, and almost all Jews use a covering when the Torah is read. The genesis of this practice is somewhat difficult to determine but certainly belongs to an ancient tradition extending as far back as the Mishna; hence, apparently by the first Christian century it was common Jewish practice to read the Torah or to pray only when one's head was covered. The Talmudic literature indicates that there were two reasons for this practice. The first was to show reverence for God and the second to indicate the shame of the sinner who stood before God.

This radical departure from such Jewish practice on the part of the rabbinically-trained apostle who sat at the feet of Gamaliel, the most learned of the first-century rabbis, is an oddity which begs for explanation. Some have imagined that the apostle was already doing battle with the impact of the Judaizers who occupied such an important place of discussion in the book of Galatians. If this was the case, then Paul was urging a dramatic break with Judaic practices in order to emphasize that the Christian faith was not an attempt to put "new wine in old bottles."

On the other hand, seemingly the congregation of believers at Corinth was a predominantly Gentile congregation. Therefore, one must not merely ask concerning Jewish convention but also concerning the social practices among worshipers in the Gentile cultures. Here the picture is even more clouded. Among the Greeks, who had such infinite admiration for the aesthetics of the body, the tendency seems to have been away from the veiling of men or women for appearances in public, whether religious or nonreligious. The further west one traveled, the more this seems to have prevailed as the practice of the people. In the East, however, the practices of the modest veiling of women, and perhaps even the covering of the head of men in prayer, were much more prevalent.

In light of the confusion that exists in our information about the social order of the first century, it is better not to speculate from the viewpoint of custom but rather simply to allow Paul to develop his argument on the theological platform he espoused in the following verses. The argument in this regard is not difficult to follow. The problem is then to determine whether Paul's mandate for the appropriate adornment in worship was to have universal significance and hence be binding on the church until this day or whether the passage is in fact an argument based upon the particular culture of Corinth and the Peloponnesus and in effect, an argument that for one deliberately to dishonor the social customs of his milieu will run the risk of bringing shame to the individual believer, to the assembled body of Christians, and to the Lord Himself.

One thing emerges as certain—in the congregation at Corinth men were not permitted to cover their heads when they prayed or prophesied. This apparently constituted a distinct break with Jewish custom and is a statement which may have been necessitated by the presence of a certain number of Jewish converts in the predominantly Gentile church in Corinth. For one to pray or prophesy with his head covered was "to dishonor" his head. The word "dishonor" *(kataischunō)* literally means "to make ashamed" or in this case, "to bring shame upon." Therefore, men were prohibited from covering their heads during the activities of prayer or prophecy, since this would bring shame upon Christ, who is "the head of every man."

11:5 On the other hand, women who prayed or prophesied with heads uncovered were said to dishonor their heads also. Again the reference is to verse 3, where it is said that "the head of the woman is the man." Many commentators suggest that in Corinth women identified themselves as basically promiscuous by appearing in public with heads unveiled. Some have even suggested that the unveiled head and perhaps the short cropped hair or even a shaved head were the distinctive marks of a Corinthian prostitute. The evidence for this, however, is lacking. To the contrary, as mentioned earlier, the women of Greek culture tended to be "liberated," at least with regard to the social customs of adornment, to a degree almost unknown in the East. That Gentile women appeared in pagan temples with heads uncovered is probable. Furthermore, this does not seem to have been a mark of dishonor in any way. Consequently, it is best once again to understand the custom Paul sought to implement in the church at Corinth as one which is introduced purely for the theological reasons which are established in verses 7 to 9.

The word "uncovered" *(akatakaluptō)*, is derived from *kaluptō,* meaning "to veil," and the preposition *kata,* which basically means "down." The derived meaning of *katakaluptō* would be "to veil down" or in all probability, "to veil the face." The alpha privative prefix negates the word so that the expression means "not to veil oneself." The argument is simply that for a woman to pray or prophesy with her head unveiled is to bring shame upon her "head," who according to verse 3 is the man. Further, Paul argued that if a woman is to pray or prophesy with unveiled head, she might as well have her head "shaven" *(xuraō,* a word which literally means "to shave with a razor"). The assertion here must be understood in the light of verse 15, in which Paul argued that a woman's long hair is given to her as a mark of glory. For her to subject her hair to the razor would be for her to suffer the loss of her glory. This would be a shameful condition and would almost certainly bring sorrow of heart and shame to her husband. Paul argued that there was no difference between the shaved head and prayer or prophecy with the head uncovered. Whatever the social conditions were in Corinth or in Judaism, it is clear that Paul has admonished Corinthian women who prayed or prophesied in the church to do so with heads veiled.

There was one additional matter of interest in this verse. Apparently Paul was arguing that women might, in fact, lead in public prayer or prophesy in the church. The discussion of the nature of prophecy itself will be reserved for chapters 12 to 14. For the moment the question is how to reconcile this particular liberty in the light of two other passages in the New Testament. In 1 Corinthians 14:34–35, women were told that they were to "keep silence in the churches: for it is not permitted unto them to speak; but they are commanded to be under obedience, as also saith the law. And if they will learn any thing, let them ask their husbands at home: for it is a shame for women to speak in the church." A similar passage occurs in 1 Timothy 2:11–12 where women were told to "learn in silence with all subjection." Further, Paul says, "I suffer not a woman to teach, nor to usurp authority over the man, but to be in silence."

The question is an obvious one: How can verses ordering the silence of women in 1 Corinthians 14 and 1 Timothy 2 be reconciled with 1 Corinthians 11:5, which seems to indicate Paul's approval of praying or prophesying by women in the assembled church? Actually, the two passages which seem to be in contradiction with this one are, with careful analysis, the very passages which explain the whole situation and prevent an actual discrepancy from being imagined.

Three observations must be noted (1) 1 Corinthians 11:5 is not the only New Testament reference in which women are clearly allowed and even encouraged to speak in the church. The daughters of Phillip the evangelist were among those who prophesied (Acts 21:8-9). In Titus 2:4 the aged women are counseled to "teach the young women...." Aquila and Priscilla were both involved in the instruction of Apollos (Acts 18:26). From these passages it becomes apparent that women were allowed to speak in the assembly, but the circumstances in which that contribution was to be made are clearly specified. (2) The reference in 1 Corinthians 14:34 forbidding women to speak in the churches uses the strong word for "silence" *(sigaō)*. This verse appears in the context of the discussion of Corinthian glossolalia. The verse fails to make substantial sense unless the reference is, at least primarily, to the matter of speaking in tongues. Women are not forbidden all speech but speech that is disruptive in any way. (3) In 1 Timothy 2:11-12 the word "silent" *(hēsuchia)* is a much less emphatic word than *sigaō*, which is used in 1 Corinthians 14. *Hēsuchia* refers to a general attitude of quietness of demeanor. Women are specifically commanded in 1 Timothy to learn in quietness of attitude and subjection of spirit. They are specifically forbidden to teach or in any other fashion to usurp authority over men. This insistence is not drawn from any supposed inferiority on the part of the woman but rather from two theological arguments: the priority of Adam's creation and Eve's deception by the serpent.

When these matters are given full consideration, it becomes clear that women were free to participate in the activities of the early church in almost any fashion so long as wives were in subjection to their own husbands, were modest in their apparel, and were not attempting to command authoritarian positions over the men in the churches.

One other problem exists in the text. The text merely refers to every "woman" *(gunē,* a word which conceivably referred not only to married women but also to single women, young women of marriageable age, and widows). Even if this passage encompasses all of these, the mandate is understandable since nothing is to be done in the church to create disorder or indicate immodesty among any of the women.

11:6 The whole point of modesty now comes to center stage. If a woman was not veiled, Paul argued that she might as well be "shorn." This condition, like that of being uncovered, was said to be a condition of shame. It has already been noted that among unveiled Greek women there was in all probability no indication of immodesty, but the Eastern custom and the consistent practice of Judaism was to veil a woman in any public appearance. This constituted not only a public declaration of her loyalty to her husband, if married, but also demonstrated a basic modesty. Even if such a custom was not practiced among the Greeks and Romans in Corinth, it would have been understood and doubtless to some degree honored.

The word translated "shorn" in verse 6 is not the same as the word translated "shaven" in verse 5. "Shorn" *(keirō)* may mean simply "to cut short the hair." There is some evidence to indicate that lewd women in Corinth may indeed have identified themselves as such by the wearing of very short hair or perhaps, on occasion, even the complete shaving of the head. Whether this be the case or not, verse 15 once again makes very clear that the long hair of the woman is a distinctive feature which constitutes her glory. Therefore, she is reduced to shame with short cropped hair or shaven head. By the same token, Paul argued that she is reduced to shame if she stands to pray or prophesy in the church of God with her head uncovered. Such action would mark an immodesty, thus calling attention to her physical beauty more than to the content of her prayer or prophecy. In addition to that, it would be the dishonoring of her husband. Although the text does not indicate for sure that the word *keirō* means in this case "to cut very short," it would appear from the general description that what Paul was opposing is not the trimming of a woman's hair, or even the cutting of it, but rather any handling of a woman's hair which would create a hair style similar to what might be observed among men. In other words, the entire chapter seems to be a clear call for decided distinctions between the sexes.

11:7 The background theology out of which the previous discussion has proceeded is now set forth. Men are not to cover their heads when praying or prophesying in the assembly because man was made in the image and glory of God. On the other hand, since the woman is the glory of the man, she is to have her head covered when she prays or prophesies in the church. It is worthy of note that the apostle did not indicate that the woman is in the "image" and glory of man, thus making the two clauses to be not strictly parallel. The reason for this is obvious. The woman was created just as much in the image of God as was the man. In this there is a return to the affirmation of essential equality between male and female.

What then is intended by the statement that man is in the image and glory of God? "Image" is the Greek word *eikōn*, which gives us our English word "icon." Unfortunately, in English an icon is almost always associated with an idol or with some physical attribute. That obviously is not the intention of the Greek word or of the passage below. As Susan T. Foh has noted in her excellent analysis, *Women and the Word of God*, the nature of the image of God can be evaluated only in terms of conformity to Christ.[41]

The two passages in the New Testament which refer specifically to the likeness or the image of God are Ephesians 4:24 and Colossians 3:10. These passages seem to indicate that the image of God in man is bound up in man's moral and rational capacities. The specific qualities mentioned are true righteousness, ho-

---

[41]Susan T. Foh, *Women and the Word of God*, p. 56.

liness, and knowledge. Both male and female originally possessed all three of these qualities. Neither does the verse imply that the woman is in no sense to be construed as the glory of God. Any creature made in the image of God certainly does reflect the glory of God. The emphasis, however, is that since man was the first to be created, there is a sense in which he uniquely reflects the handiwork of God as the first earthly creature made in the image of God. The woman, on the other hand, was made as a "help meet" for the man, and because, in a sense, she owes her origin to him, she is the glory of the man.

11:8 The last observation is confirmed as precisely what Paul had in mind by this explanatory verse which affirms that man is not of the woman but woman of the man. The preposition "of" *(ek)*, generally speaking, indicates "out." The idea here is that man was created directly by the hand of God, but woman, though also made by the hand of God, was literally taken from the side of man. The King James version says that God took a rib. "Rib" *(tsele,* Hebrew) is generally translated "side." God took a portion of the side of the man and from that he made the woman. It is woman's origin from the side of the man that caused Paul to say that the woman is "the glory of the man."

11:9 A further point of Paul's theology was enunciated when he declared that the man was not created for the woman but the woman for the man. Here the question is not so much the origin of the two as the purpose of the two. Man was made to have dominion over the other positions of the created order. Whether or not this idea of dominion is a part of what it means to be made in the image of God has been vigorously debated. Since the exercise of dominion is to some degree a rational capacity, it is reasonable to assume that such would be a part of being made in the image of God.

Both male and female share in dominion, but in the case of the female it is specifically noted in Genesis 2:18 that God said, "It is not good that the man should be alone." So that man might enjoy the fellowship of another of the same genus, God created the woman. The argument here is that since the woman was made for the man, she should demonstrate a recognition of her purpose and a faithfulness to her "head" by honoring her husband through the covering of her head when she prays or prophesies. Once again, this verse implies no reduction of the status of a woman to an inferior position—only a clear role assignment as a part of the purpose of God in creation.

11:10 Few verses have puzzled commentators any more than this one. The word translated "power" is not most often so translated. *Exousia* is better rendered "authority." A woman needs to have "authority" on her head because of the angels. Two insights are discernible from this affirmation. First, the veil with which the woman covered her head was not merely a decorative covering but served a decisive purpose in communicating "authority." In other words, a woman's veiled head indicated her submission to her husband as well as to God and, as such, also constituted a protection for her.

The necessity for this "authority" on her head is said to be "because of the angels." "Angels" *(angelos)* may mean "angel" in the sense of the specially created order of spiritual beings which repeatedly appear as special emissaries of God on the pages of Scripture, or the word may be used in its more general sense as "messenger." In the first sense, Hebrews 1:14 speaks of angels as "ministering spirits sent forth to minister for them who shall be heirs of salvation." The second sense of "messenger" apparently is the one intended in the messages given to the "angels" of the seven churches in Revelation 2 and 3, in which "angel" apparently referred to the pastor or messenger of each local congregation. These two meanings may be extended to three possible interpretations in this particular passage.

(1) The "angels" are those who constitute the pastoral leadership of the Corinthian congregation. If this is the proper view, then it would have to be argued that the veiling of the women who pray or prophesy in public would not only be an indication of the submission of those women to the authority of God and to the authority of their husbands, but also to the spiritual authority of the pastors in the churches. In favor of this view is the rather logical development that may thus be observed in Paul's argument as he gave reason after reason, most of which related to the local congregation at Corinth, for the wearing of the head coverings.

(2) "Angels" is a reference to fallen angels who might take advantage of the relatively immodest exposure of the unveiled woman as she prayed or prophesied, lusting after her or even seducing her as, it is argued, was done when the sons of God (fallen angels) saw the daughters of men and cohabited with them (Gen. 6:1–2). The evidence against this view seems so overwhelming as to make it unworthy of consideration. In the first place, it builds the interpretation of a difficult passage upon a highly questionable interpretation of still another obscure passage. It is not at all apparent that the "sons of God" in Genesis 6 should be construed as fallen angels. The Scriptures do clearly declare that fallen angels exist (2 Pet. 2:4 and Jude 6). Some of these fallen angels, described as being chained and awaiting the day of judgment, may still be at large in the earth. Most evangelical scholars believe that the malignant spirits we call demons are actually fallen angels, most but not all of whom have been reserved in chains of darkness until the day of judgment. However, there is no evidence that fallen angels who are spiritual beings can appropriate to themselves bodies capable of cohabiting with human women. Furthermore, there are other possible interpretations of Genesis 6 which are much less beset with problems. In addition to that, it is highly unlikely that Paul would have made any reference to the attendance of evil angels or fallen angels upon the services of worship at Corinth. Furthermore, it is less than clear exactly how these evil angels could be deterred from whatever their evil enterprises might have been by the presence of veiled women, since as spiritual beings they would not be hampered in their observations by material clothing.

(3) "Angels" refers to good angels, who are featured by Paul as in regular attendance in the services of worship at the church at Corinth and doubtless elsewhere as well. Such a view recognizes the employment of angels exactly as Hebrews 1:14 suggests. Angels are "ministering spirits sent forth to minister for them who shall be heirs of salvation." It appears that much of the object of angelic ministration has to do with the saints of God; so that their presence in services of worship would not be peculiar. Hebrews 13:2 suggests that Christians should "Be not forgetful to entertain strangers: for thereby some have entertained angels un-

awares." Again the suggestion seems to be that angels are attending the saints of God, perhaps participating in their own spiritual worship even as the churches assemble for worship. Favoring such an interpretation would be the fact that unless there is strong evidence, as in Revelation 2 and 3, to suggest some other meaning for "angel," then it is best to understand its usual connotation of a spiritual being created for the work of God. The Hebrews passages, as has already been indicated, give further evidence to sustain the presence of the angels ministering to the saints.

If the latter view is correct, then the sense of the passage would be that in light of exalted heavenly visitors who, though unseen, may well be present at Corinthian worship, women ought to demonstrate their submission to their own husbands and to God out of deference to these exalted spiritual beings.

11:11 Verses 11 and 12 demonstrate that Paul had developed a mild mistrust about certain propensities among the Corinthian believers. Already he had written to the Corinthians certain things which they had misinterpreted and misapplied. He now registered some concern that they might misunderstand and misinterpret what he had just said to the extent of reducing a woman to an inferior object. Consequently, he went to some length to demonstrate that what he had been discussing was role assignment and order. Therefore, he concluded that the man is nothing without the woman, and the woman is nothing without the man in the Lord. These words suggest again the language of Genesis 2:24, "and they shall be one flesh." Even though there is role assignment, there is, nonetheless, essential equality within the performance of those roles. The man does not exist independently of his wife, and the wife does not exist independently of her husband, but in the Lord they have become one flesh.

11:12 Earlier Paul argued that the man did not come from the woman; rather the woman was taken from the side of the man. However, such is the case only with the first couple. Since the original creation, God ordained the observable means of procreation through which the human family has multiplied itself across the generations. Consequently, it was also true of the Corinthians that just as the woman was taken out of the man, so, in the case of all the Corinthians and all other men dwelling on the first-century earth, was each of them taken from the woman. And even this process ultimately resides in the providences of God so that while in original creation woman was taken out of the man, she was thus taken and created by God. In the present reproductive processes, male children emerge from the wombs of their mothers; yet even that process is ultimately of God, for nothing exists outside of His creative genius. The impact of these two verses establishes beyond any shadow that the rules for attire while praying or prophesying are designed to engender respect rather than disrespect for both husband and wife.

11:13 The remaining verses of the discussion of the attire of women who were involved in prayer and prophecy take the turn of a certain appeal to naturally observable states. First, Paul encouraged independent and honest judgment on the part of the Corinthians by saying, "Judge among yourselves." The construction is emphatic since the word "you" *(humeis)* is included. "You" is already a part of the verb *krinō*, but when added as a form of its own, it places stress upon that personal pronoun. Literally the passage may be translated "You yourselves judge the situation. You do not need an apostle. There is no necessity for a spiritual revelation in this matter. It is something that you yourselves can judge." The matter that he asked them to judge was the comeliness of a woman praying to God with head uncovered. According to Liddell and Scott, the word "comely" *(prepō)* originally meant something that was fitting or pleasant to the eyes.[42] The question seems to be: "Is it not possible that even your eyes, unblessed as they are by divine revelation, are offended by the sight of a woman praying to God without her head covered?" Almost certainly the reference here is not to silent prayer but to a woman to whom attention would be drawn because of her audible, public prayer.

11:14 The comeliness of a woman praying in a veiled state should have been apparent to the Corinthians because nature itself seems to teach that if a man has long hair, it is a dishonor to

---

[42]Liddell and Scott, *First Corinthians*, p. 1461.

him. Paul recognized that nature is not responsible for short hair in men and long hair in women. On the other hand, nature itself seemed to have provided that men and women would maintain a clear distinction between the sexes. One of the ways by which this takes place would be relatively short style of men's hair as compared to the longer style of women's hair.

Renaissance art has not aided modern man's perception of men of antiquity, since most of the Renaissance artists painted biblical scenes with men sporting long hair. The very fact that Samson, who had taken a Nazarite vow, did not allow a razor to come upon his head is clear indication of the fact that this was an unusual state of affairs. Generally, men throughout all biblical periods wore hair styles shorter than women. Indeed, except in the rare case of the Nazarite vow, long hair was considered a mark of shame to the man. This time the word "shame" is different from that which appears and is translated "dishonor" in verse 5. There the word was *kataischunō*, "to make ashamed." Here the word is *atimia*, which literally means "without honor." In other words, for a man to have long hair rendered him void of honor. He was recognized as being out of step with convention and, perhaps, even as being of questionable morality.

11:15 By the same token, a woman's long hair is a glory to her, and her hair itself constitutes a covering for her. There is one remarkable vocabulary occurrence in this particular verse. The verse not only states that a woman's long hair is a glory to her (a radiant expression of her acceptance of God's role for her) but also that her hair is given to her, as the King James Version translates, "for a covering" *(anti peribolaiou)*. This construction is unusual in that the Greek preposition *anti* almost invariably is used as a preposition of substitution. Literally, the verse might be translated: "Her hair is given to her in the place of a covering." While this literal translation clearly satisfies the grammar of the sentence, it is almost certain that Paul did not really mean to imply that a woman's hair was sufficient covering when she prayed or prophesied in public. Her hair is a glory to her, but the additional covering is to be used as a way of expressing her subservience to both her husband and the Lord.

11:16 Apparently the apostle Paul either expected some negative reaction to what he had just said, or the word translated "contentious" referred to those in Corinth determined to rebel against the prescription Paul had given. Either way, Paul did speak of some who were "contentious" *(philoneikos)*, a word far more colorful in Greek than in English. Actually, it is derived from *neikos*, which in classical Greek meant "a quarrel," "strife," or "feud" and is here combined with *philos*, meaning "love." Therefore, Paul wrote that "if there are those among you who love strife or who enjoy quarrelsome or feuding behavior," then they need to know that we have no such "custom" *(sunētheia)*. Of interesting derivation, the latter word combines *hēthos*, which originally referred to a haunt or an abode and in the process of time eventually came to stand for a custom, with the Greek preposition *sun*, which simply means "with." So Paul affirmed that there is no place in the churches of God for anyone who simply loves the quarrel. What is forbidden here is not argumentation but the love of a quarrel. Anyone who enjoys confrontation and combativeness is still in need of the working of specific spiritual graces in his own heart.

2. Wicked Pretenses (11:17–22)

The subject now changes to a discussion concerning the behavior of the Corinthians as they approach the Lord's table. We shall view certain wicked pretenses which had evolved in the church at Corinth: detrimental assemblies (vv. 17–18), divided acolytes (v. 19), and disturbing abnormalities (vv. 20–22).

11:17 The thoughtful and kind language of the previous sixteen verses moves rather abruptly to a tone of greater severity. Paul could not praise the Corinthians concerning their assemblies because he was persuaded that when they came together it was not for the better but for the worse. It is not clear whether Paul was referring to all their assemblies or only to those assemblies in which the church partook of the Lord's Supper.

No definitive information exists to tell us precisely how often the early church observed the Lord's Supper. Apparently there was some difference among the churches as to the frequency of its observance. Some churches possibly partook of the Lord's

Supper at every gathering. Others apparently practiced what became known as a "love feast," a common meal among the brethren which culminated in a deeply moving observance of the Lord's Supper, thus reminding the assembly of the central event of redemption, the atoning death of Christ. The Corinthian church obviously had such a "love feast" as is indicated by one of the problems that existed at the time of the observance of the Lord's Supper. The fact that the entire following discussion relates to the Lord's Supper would seem to suggest that this is an assembly of the Corinthian saints for the observance of the Lord's Supper.

11:18 Paul's first objection was that he had heard from certain witnesses that when the Corinthians came together there existed divisions, and although Paul did not want to believe what he had heard, he had been pressed to that position as a result of the reliability of the testimony of believing what he had heard, at least in part. The word translated "divisions" is *schismata*, which has given us our English word "schism" with its connotation of wrenching an irreparable division. This English nuance of the word is stronger than its Greek counterpart. Maurer makes mention of the fact that the word is rare in secular Greek. It is used to describe the formation of cliques and the inciting of divisions and separations from a fraternity or a society devoted to Zeus. The punishment of such divisiveness was severe.[43]

The conditions that existed in Corinth had not yet reached the point of the irrevocable division that results in the parting of ways and the institution of new assemblies. However, an actual division, which was perhaps fourfold, had in fact occurred in the church. Paul wrote of this division especially in light of the celebration of the Lord's Supper, which, as he pointed out in chapter 5, is a fellowship feast in which the church ought to celebrate its oneness as the body of Christ. Because of the *schismata* or divisions in the church, the Lord's Supper had actually become a hypocritical feast depicting how far the church at Corinth had strayed from one of its most basic goals—namely, the unity of

---

[43]Kittel, *Theological Dictionary*, Vol. 7, p. 963.

the body of Christ.

11:19 However, the situation suggested to Paul that something even more serious might actually be involved. Paul concluded that there must also be heresies among them. As Thomas Oden has recently noted,

> The leading candidate for one "most ugly issue in theology today" is doubtless heresy. We avoid it like bubonic plague. If we saw someone coming down the street whom we even vaguely suspected might raise the subject of heresy with us, we would find some way of ducking into a hidden place until he had passed.
>
> Why? Because we are programmed to affable religious permissiveness and the rhetoric of compliance. Our least favored interaction pattern as Christian teachers is the role of harsh judge. We detest judging unless we happen to be risklessly judging something that is universally condemned by modernity. This is one reason we are not swift at theology. Few of late have shown the courage to draw even the most elementary distinctions between the truth of the Christian faith and that which differs from it. We know that every affirmation requires the negation of its opposite, so because we do not want to be caught negating anything, we do not make any affirmations either.[44]

Yet despite all of the repulsiveness modernity does, in fact, feel for the word "heresy," it is a word which needs to be a vital part of the theological vocabulary of the church. In the New Testament the word itself has none of the objectionable overtones presently attached to it. In fact, it is used to describe the orthodox faith of our Lord Jesus Christ. The opponents of it described Christianity as a heresy in Acts 24:5 where the same word, *hairesi*, is translated "sect." Tertullus was addressing Felix, the Roman procurator, telling him that Paul was a "ringleader of the sect [*heresy*] of the Nazarenes." The word is also used to describe the Sadducees (Acts 5:17) and the Pharisees (Acts 15:5). Josephus employed the word as a descriptive term for various Greek philosophical schools as well as for the Essenes, Sadducees, and Pharisees. The most basic meaning of the verb form *haireomai* is "to take," "to win," "to seize," or "to take for oneself."

---

[44]Thomas C. Oden, *Agenda for Theology: Recovering Christian Roots*, p. 95.

All of these meanings suggest the idea of a new or different direction.[45] This analysis of the word indicates that the significance of the term denoted a new direction which, if continued, would undermine the foundations of the faith. The difference between orthodoxy and heresy is that orthodoxy continues straight in the glory that has been revealed; whereas heresy is the beginning of a new direction that departs in some fundamental way from a previous position.

God's people oftentimes are uninstructed, naive, and woefully gullible about problems that arise within churches. But the fact is that those who really belong to the Lord will eventually discover in the teachings of those who disrupt the harmony and fellowship of a church theological positions which can only be denominated heresies. As these become apparent, it will also become apparent that God has not approved such false teachers but has made manifest in the church of God those teachers whom He does approve.

11:20 Paul then proceeded with specific instructions about the Lord's table. When the Corinthians came together for their love feast, Paul said, "This is not to eat the Lord's supper." Paul's avowal here is not that their purpose in coming together had not been stated to be the Lord's Supper. He was rather suggesting that while that was a pretense for their gathering, their behavior was such as to make a mockery of the Lord's Supper and reduce it to a mere ceremony void of real spiritual implication.

11:21 The reason for this conclusion was that when they assembled together, the Corinthians selfishly grabbed for bread and whatever else might have been available for eating, and the object of the love feast became greedy and gluttonous self-satisfaction rather than commitment to the servant posture in the body of Christ. Worse still, while some demonstrated selfishness and the need to satisfy their own hunger, others drank until inebriated.

11:22 Paul did not then suggest that the kind of deportment observable at the Lord's table in Corinth was really acceptable

---

[45]Kittel, *Theological Dictionary*, Vol. 1, pp. 180–185.

anywhere. Nevertheless, if one were determined upon such courses of action, Paul asked rhetorical questions: "Do you not have houses to eat and to drink in?" Obviously most of the Corinthians did have a domicile in the privacy of which they could have pursued both meat and drink. "Why, then," Paul continued, "would you despise the church of God?" "Despise" *(kataphroneō)* literally means "to think down upon" the church of God. The allegation of the apostle was that the Corinthians demonstrated in their activities that they had far too little respect for the church of God and the body of Christ. Particularly did they demonstrate this by putting to shame those in the fellowship who were not so blessed with an abundance of food. Paul asked the searching question, "What shall I say to you? Shall I praise you in this?" This time, however, the discussion is on a serious enough note that he does not leave the rhetorical question with its obvious answer. With considerable sternness, he wrote, "In this specific matter, I do not praise you."

3. Worthy Practices (11:23–34)

The concluding section of chapter 11 discusses worthy practices to be maintained by the church at the observance of the Supper: remembering sacrifice (vv. 23–27), reexamining servants (vv. 28–32), and renouncing selfishness (vv. 33–34). One of the most awkward times in the usual observance of the Lord's Supper is the time during the distribution of the elements. Usually people have little idea of what they ought to do. These verses chart a course for productive observance of the Supper.

11:23 It is generally agreed that the account of the Lord's Supper given here may actually be the first recorded account of the Lord's Supper, thus possibly predating any of the gospel accounts. In any case, Paul asserted that what he had formerly delivered to the Corinthians was what he, in fact, had received from the Lord. This information revealed first of all that the initial celebration of the Supper occurred on the very night the Lord was betrayed. This particular occasion was during the week of unleavened bread as the time of the Passover drew near. Scholars debate whether the paschal meal which Jesus observed took place on Wednesday evening with the crucifixion on Thursday, or on Thursday evening with the crucifixion on Friday. Though some of the evidence is not as clear as the scholars would like, it still seems best to regard this meal as having been eaten on Thursday evening. Paul recorded that in the midst of the meal Jesus took bread.

11:24 The first important aspect of the celebration of the Lord's Supper is provided in this verse when Jesus, having taken the bread, is described as giving thanks and then breaking the bread. The phrase "he had given thanks" (*eucharistēsas*, literally "he gave thanks," evolving into the English word "eucharist") indicates that the first important activity in which the church is to participate at the time of the Lord's Supper is the eucharistic activity or the offering of thanksgiving to God. As often as the church celebrated the Lord's Supper, it expressed corporately and individually its thanksgiving to God for the marvelous salvation He had provided.

The second aspect of the feast, to which allusion has been previously made, is also provided. The verse declares that when Jesus had taken the bread, He broke it and said, "Take, eat: this is my body, which is broken for you: this do in remembrance of me." Consequently, the participation of the congregation in the eating of a common loaf pointed to the unity of the body of Christ and reminded them of their fellowship together based on the experience of their common salvation.

The third crucial feature of the Lord's Supper is also present. The disciples are instructed, both here and again in verse 25, that as often as they eat the bread or drink the cup, they are to do it in remembrance of the Lord. Not only is the feast a eucharistic feast and a fellowship feast, but it is also a memorial feast. The most serious disagreements across the years have occurred at this very point. During the Reformation period, Huldreich Zwingli of Zurich was the first of the major Reformers to arrive at the conclusion that this significance of the Lord's Supper was chiefly symbolic in nature. There is evidence that Luther himself temporarily embraced that position but later returned to a position similar to the one maintained by the established church of the era. There are three general positions that have been taken by various Christian communities throughout the generations.

(1) Transubstantiation suggests that the bread and the fruit of the vine are miraculously changed to the actual body and blood of Christ at the time of the mass. Thus, in a sense Christ is crucified repeatedly. The expressions, "this is my body" and "this is my blood," are taken quite literally to represent a transformation of the substance of the elements. Understandably, if this view is correct, one would actually be assimilating the body and blood, i.e., the life of Christ, and in this way partaking of its merits. Among other serious problems associated with this view is the rather obvious criticism that the real body of Jesus sat in their midst with the blood of His life at that very moment coursing through His veins even as He said, "This is my body which is broken for you." Nothing could be more lucidly illustrated as a symbolic statement than this expression. His body was not yet broken, and His blood was not yet shed.

(2) Reacting against the widely received view of transubstantiation but still wanting to maintain the doctrine of the "real presence" of Christ in the Supper, the Lutheran branch of the Reformation eventually developed the theory of consubstantiation. In essence, the view argues that while the elements do not chemically undergo the changes necessitated by the transubstantiatory view, nevertheless, in some mystical and unexplained fashion, the body and blood of Christ are efficaciously present in the elements of the supper. The same general criticisms that applied to the first view apply to this one, including the simple truth that such doctrines are necessitated only by sacramentarian theology, which argues the impartation of grace through means such as the Supper. Since there is convincing evidence that the elements of the Supper impart no grace at all, the third view emerges as the best.

(3) The Lord's Supper is purely a symbolic feast established as a memorial to the most significant event ever to transpire in the history of the race—the atonement of Jesus. Hence, the Corinthians are to partake of it always in remembrance of Jesus' sacrificial act.

11:25 The same procedure is now followed for the cup containing the pressed fruit of the vine. When Jesus had eaten, He took the cup saying, "This cup is the new testament in my blood." The word "testament" is *diathēkē*. Leon Morris, in his book *The Apostolic Preaching of the Cross*, indicates that the word *diathēkē* in nonbiblical Greek included four facets. (1) The *diathēkē* was testamentary rather than contractual; it was the act of one person bestowing benefits upon another. (2) The benefactor of the testament was to receive the benefit only upon the death of the testator. (3) The occasion for the bequeathal of the property involved might have had certain conditions attached to it which must be met before the deposition can be made. (4) The *diathēkē* was something which was always initiated by just one person who assumed the right to the management and distribution of his own assets, even if this was done after his death.[46] All of these characteristics of *diathēkē* in nonbiblical Greek are applicable to the word "testament" as it is used here. Jesus, by reference to a *kainē* (new) *diathēkē* (covenant), indicated that the old covenant was giving way to the new covenant which was prophesied in Jeremiah 31. The terms of that covenant bequeathed to the recipients all the benefits associated with salvation. These were going to be made available as a result of the death of Christ, the testator, but they were conditioned upon the willingness of the benefactors to receive those benefits. Of course, the entire initiative in the matter was taken by Christ. The blood-red juice of the vine was to be a memorial to the blood of Christ, which was shed in order to bring into effect the benefits of the covenant.

11:26 There are two additional purposes for the Lord's Supper in this verse. First, Paul indicated that as often as the church eats the bread and drinks the cup they are involved in the proclamation of the Lord's death. The expression, "Ye do show" *(katangellō)* means "to proclaim a message." Anyone observing the practice of the Lord's Supper, upon inquiry, would certainly be advised of the atoning significance of Jesus' death. Furthermore, that proclamation is made continually "until He comes." In this sense, the Lord's Supper is not only a feast of proclamation but

---

[46]Leon Morris, *The Apostolic Preaching of the Cross*, pp. 82–83.

also a prophetic or eschatological feast. It serves to remind the assembled fellowship that his ordinance will not endure perpetually. It is something that has been commanded for observance in the church only until the Lord returns.

11:27 Obviously the Corinthians had failed to grasp these nuances in the Lord's Supper. In their greed, haste, gluttony, and thirst, all aided by the divisiveness which existed in the church, they had approached the table of the Lord "unworthily." Thus to approach the Lord's Supper, eating the bread and drinking the cup of the Lord "unworthily," was to incur guilt as concerns the Lord's broken body and shed blood. The sense in which such guilt is incurred is revealed in verse 29. "Unworthily" (*anaxiōs*) an adverb which refers to attitude and deportment at the Lord's table. It is not a question of worth or worthiness, since all would be excluded upon that basis. Our worthiness to approach the Lord's table is dependent upon our experience of the forgiveness of sin and full salvation in Christ. The Corinthians failure was that of their generally cavalier approach to the Lord's table.

11:28 The question may then be asked, "How should one approach the Lord's table?" The answer provides the sixth purpose of the Supper. One is to examine himself, and, as a result of this spiritual diagnosis, he is then to eat the bread and drink the cup of the Lord's Supper. "Examine" (*dokimazō*) means "let a man put himself on trial." This trial is not an exposure of himself to the judgment of others, but rather an intense searching of his own heart with the desired end of locating those features of life which may be unacceptable to God. Having confessed these, one is to approach the Lord's table. All six of the purposes of the Lord's Supper are now before us. To review, we have noticed that it is (1) a eucharistic feast, (2) a fellowship feast, (3) a memorial feast, (4) an evangelistic feast, (5) an eschatological feast, and (6) a diagnostic feast. While one scarcely has time to concentrate on each of those elements in any single observance of the Supper, the conceptualization of these purposes will greatly aid in producing a meaningful observance of the Supper and will certainly prevent one from making his approach to the table "unworthily."

11:29 There is, in fact, the possibility that severe consequences will occur when a careless approach to the Lord's table is made.

Those who approach the table in an unworthy manner are actually eating and drinking judgment to themselves due to their failure properly to discern the Lord's body. The word translated "damnation" in the King James Version suggests that for a person, even though he might be a true believer, to approach the Lord's table in an unworthy manner would result in condemnation and eternal judgment. However, this is not at all what is indicated in the text. "Damnation" *(krima)* means "judgment." The kinds of judgment that might be included in this word are delineated more specifically in verse 30. There is no indication that approaching the Lord's table unworthily will result in the loss of salvation or in eternal retribution. Nevertheless, the failure to "discern" *(diakrinō)* or evaluate adequately the Lord's body is the reason for this judgment. Failing to discern the Lord's body apparently is an indication not only of the lack of an understanding of the nature of the Supper itself but also a failure to maintain the fellowship of the body.

11:30 The specific kinds of judgment from God are obviously of a physical nature. Three are specified. Because of the failure of the Corinthians to discern the Lord's body and because of their unworthy approach to the Lord's table, Paul concluded that many were weak and sick among the Corinthians and "many sleep," a euphemism in the English Bible which is not present in Greek. The word "died" is *koimaomai*, a word which gives us our English word "cemetery." The plain affirmation of the text is that some of the Corinthians had persisted so long in their disobedience that they had died. Still others had their condition described as "weak" *(asthenēs*, a word which most frequently describes the condition in which one is left after a long, debilitating illness). Others are "sickly" *(arrōstos*, a word which derives from *hrōnnumi* or *hrōomai*, which meant "to move with speed or violence," or, in the case of warriors, "to rush on"). Gradually the word came to mean simply "health." In addition, the alpha privative is prefixed, making the word mean "without health" or "unable to move speedily"; hence, the carnality of the Corinthians was proving costly to their physical health and even threatening to their lives.

Well-meaning souls frequently object that surely a loving God would not cause or allow such sicknesses for those He loves, and certainly He would not take the life of one just because of carnality in his lifestyle, but the evidence is to the contrary. Ananias and Sapphira lied to the Holy Spirit and died for their deed. Uzzah reached out to steady the ark, but because he touched that which was forbidden, he died by the ark of God. Achan's taking of the accursed and forbidden items cost him his life. Nadab and Abihu offered strange fire before God and were immediately killed. Apparently Simon the Sorcerer barely escaped a similar fate. The facts indicate that God is quite serious. The alternative to the judgment of God is the spiritual introspection prescribed already in verse 28. The advice is repeated again in this verse in light of the information given in verse 30. If a man wishes to judge himself and hence repent, then he will not be judged by God.

11:32 On the other hand, the failure to indulge in this spiritual introspection will result in the judgment of God. The apostle referred to it as the chastisement of the Lord. "Chastisement" (*paideuomomai*) refers to the correction of wayward children. However, the chastisement of God is actually comforting, not only because it acts as a needed corrective in the life of a believer but also because it gives abundant evidence that the believer genuinely belongs to God and is chastised so that he will not be judged together with the rest of the world. The same kind of argument is employed in Hebrews 12:5–11 where it is made clear that chastisement, far from being a reason for agony of soul, is a reason for gratitude to God.

11:33 The conclusion of the whole matter concerning behavior at the Lord's table is that when the brethren come together to eat, they are to learn to wait upon one another. A spirit of selflessness and looking to the well-being of the other is to prevail.

11:34 If a man found himself hungering, then he should eat at home so that when he went to the church of God he might not face the judgment of God. Apparently other minor problems, perhaps related to the observance of the Supper, also existed in the church at Corinth. The phrase "set in order" literally means "to arrange through"; hence, the apostle would work through these problems when he came to be present with the Corinthians.

The Baptism of the Holy Spirit

1. Diversity of Gifts (12:1–11)
2. Distinction in Functions (12:12–26)
3. Difference of Offices (12:27–31)

Scientific textbooks are frequently dated shortly after their release. Other fields of human inquiry have suffered the same obsolescence, even if in some cases several hundred years were required. But if anyone needs proof of the timelessness of the amazing documents that constitute the Bible, he need only consider the insight to be derived from 1 Corinthians 12, 13, and 14, as these chapters relate to the "charismatic revival" in our own era. Apparently much of what was transpiring in Corinth was not at all dissimilar to what is happening in the twentieth century. Generations of Christians have come and gone, seriously deliberating issues that are critical to faith, but infrequently confronted by the problems addressed in these three chapters. Yet in the present era problems similar to those which developed in Corinth have again come to center stage.

1. Diversity of Gifts (12:1–11)

In the first section of chapter 12, Paul discussed the superiority of Christ (vv. 1–3), the significance of gifts (vv. 4–7), and the sovereignty of the Spirit (vv. 8–11). No passage could be more vital for the church today than the three chapters of 1 Corinthians which address these issues.

12:1 Whether the Corinthians had asked a question concerning spiritual gifts or whether Paul had simply been aware of abuses, misunderstandings, and preoccupation with the subject of gifts at Corinth is not certain. Whichever is the case, the time devoted to the discussion of the gifts indicates the seriousness of the problems Paul recognized at Corinth. Two primary words are used for description of spiritual gifts (*pneumatika*, which simply means the "spirituals," and *charismata*, which literally means the "grace-gifts"). The two words apparently are used interchangeably to describe the endowments supernaturally provided by the Holy Spirit to every believer for the purpose of the edification of the Lord's church. They differ not in meaning but in emphasis.

When the gifts are called *pneumatika*, the reference emphasizes their spiritual origins and employment. They are thus not to be construed as natural endowments per se (although they may certainly involve spiritual enhancement of natural proclivities), but they are gifts or abilities provided by the Holy Spirit for the purpose of strengthening the spiritual lives of those who are the objects of these ministries.

When *charismata* (derived from *charis*, meaning "grace") is used, the emphasis is upon the sovereign distribution of those gifts and the undeserved nature of them. Since "grace" refers to the undeserved beneficial acts of God toward men, whether that be in creation, regeneration, or edification, it is clear that spiritual gifts are never deserved by their recipients but are given out of the kindness and mercy of God. Not only are they not deserved, but they also are not selected cafeteria style from the treasure house of God's mercies. They are sovereignly distributed as the Spirit of God wishes.

These *pneumatika* or *charismata* had come to occupy a place of stupendous importance in the church at Corinth. The mystical, mysterious, and ecstatic nature of the various Greek oracles was still an influence with which to be reckoned in the first century.

That the pagan element, having come into the Lord's church in Corinth, would have a tendency toward the reproduction of some of the ecstatic features of their former faith is sad but understandable.

Paul wrote concerning the *pneumatika* because, he said, "I do not wish you to be ignorant." No more crucial words could be said to the church at Corinth or to the modern church than this admonition that we not be without knowledge concerning spiritual gifts. Consequently, there are numerous questions for which we must seek answers in these three chapters. Note some of them here. What is the relationship between spiritual gifts and natural endowments? What categories may be assigned to the various gifts? How many spiritual gifts are there? Do all believers receive spiritual gifts, and, if so, do all believers receive all spiritual gifts? Were some of the spiritual gifts temporary? Do some of the spiritual gifts have more than one expression? Precisely what purpose are spiritual gifts designed to accomplish? And, finally, what prominence should be assigned to the function of spiritual gifts? These are questions which the church at Corinth needed to answer and which Paul answered for them under the leadership of the Holy Spirit.

12:2 The reason Paul admonished the Corinthians in verse 1 is made clear in this verse. He reminded the Corinthian readers that formerly they were Gentiles who were carried away to "dumb" idols. "Dumb" (*aphōnos*) literally means "without a voice"; yet these very idols did exercise power over the populace through maintaining communication with the people via certain oracles, such as the Pythia at Delphi. Consequently, the rather unusual language of the verse suggests that idols, void of voice, nevertheless carried away the people, leading them through the mysterious experiences associated with the mantic oracles. Paul was concerned that in the Corinthian church the worship remain pure and Christ-honoring without reduplication of the characteristic pagan temple worship.

12:3 The ultimate ground of judgment for any religious practice for the Corinthians must be the Lord Himself. Therefore, Paul instructed them that no one speaking by the Spirit of God would ever say that Jesus was "accursed" (*anathema*, derived from *tithēmi*, meaning "to place," and *ana*, meaning basically "up" or "again"). The matrix of the concept is that of rendering to a deity something which was to be for that deity alone; hence, the word came to mean "given up to destruction." For example, in Joshua 7 the children of Israel are told that they committed a trespass in the "accursed thing" because Achan had taken what was "accursed" for himself.

"Accursed" (Heb., *chērem*) refers to the fact that Jericho had been devoted completely to God, and nothing was to be taken by the people. This devotion to God was to be exemplified in the totality of the destruction of that wicked city. One can see rather vividly the derivation of this Hebrew word, since the Arabic word "harem" has a common root with *chērem*. A "harem" referred to those women who were devoted only to a single sheik or tribal chieftain. For anyone else to touch the women of the harem would result in his and, in some cases, her destruction. They were, therefore, called the "harem" or "those devoted."

The Hebrew *chērem* is almost the identical concept involved in the Greek *anathema*. Paul's meaning was that any man speaking by means of the leadership of the Holy Spirit could never say that Jesus was devoted to destruction. The precise meaning of Paul's statement is enigmatic. It is unthinkable that any of the Corinthians had actually made such a statement while speaking in rational discourse. Basically, there are four possibilities: (1) Those who were not used to the ecstatic speech in vogue at Corinth were fearful that those making use of it might by accident curse Jesus or some aspect of His faith. (2) While in such a mantic trance, someone at Corinth, speaking ecstatically, had in fact either called Jesus accursed or else cursed some aspect of the faith of the Lord. (3) Some who claimed to have become Christians were speaking in such a way as to make Jesus merely another member of the pantheon. (4) *Anathema* is used in the general sense, which it had gradually acquired, of blasphemy or derision.

Regardless of which interpretation one wishes to follow, Paul's affirmation is clear. For anyone to be guilty of speaking derisively of Christ or His faith would be ample evidence that he was not speaking by means of the Holy Spirit. Therefore, anything stated in ecstatic utterance that is in any sense contrary to the revealed faith of Jesus Christ is not something that the Holy Spirit has produced. By the same token, no one is able to say "Jesus is the Lord" except as the Holy Spirit inspires that utterance.

Two facets of this declaration are important. "Jesus is the Lord" (*Kurios Iēsous*) constitutes the earliest Christian confession of faith. This confession was frequently upon the lips of the early believers and, in fact, was stated in direct contradistinction to the avowal *Kurios Kaisar* or "Caesar is Lord." Paul's declaration here is not that a man would be prevented from verbalizing the phrase "Jesus is Lord" other than to do so in the power of the Spirit. Rather his statement is to the effect that no man is able to say "Jesus is Lord" meaningfully and truthfully except with the enablement of the Holy Spirit.

12:4 Having established the foundation for the discussion of spiritual gifts, the apostle next began to speak of the diversities of gifts and functions and also of the unity of the Spirit that is essential to their proper function. There are, he declared, "diversities" of gifts. "Diversities" (*diairesis*) is almost the identical word translated "heresies" in 1 Corinthians 11:19. The only difference is that the preposition *dia*, meaning "through," has been added. One recalls that "heresy" basically means "to cut a different direction." *Diaireseis* means "to cut through" and suggests that a division has taken place. Therefore, we are told that there are divisions or diversities of gifts (*charismaton*). The same Spirit gives all of the gifts, but the gifts are diverse in kind and function.

12:5 There are also differences of administrations, but it is the same Lord who has ordained these administrations. The word translated "differences" in the King James Version is the same word translated "diversities" in verses 4 and 6. "Administrations" (*diakonia*) gives us our English word "deacon." A deacon was originally the household slave assigned to wait upon tables. The word gradually came to have the technical sense of a "treasured servant." The word "administrations," therefore, should not be understood in terms of "rule" so much as in the use of those gifts which are involved in waiting upon the ministering to the people of God.

12:6 There are, furthermore, diversities of "operations" (*energēma*, derived from *ergon*, meaning "work"). Our English term "energy" comes from this word. Therefore, Paul seems to suggest that there are various kinds of work that are assigned to the believers. However, it is the same God who energizes in all.

Periodically there have been attempts to take the twenty-one spiritual gifts mentioned specifically in the New Testament and place them in categories, such as administrative gifts, service gifts, etc. This is not objectionable as an attempt to systematize and categorize the information the Scripture provides. However, it is worth noting that only in these three verses does the Bible itself provide anything approaching a categorization of the gifts. Here it would seem that *charisma* is a general term describing all of the activities of the Holy Spirit with regard to the giving of gifts; whereas *diakoni* and *energēma* are descriptive of the division of those gifts into ministering gifts and gifts of labor among the saints of God.

12:7 Another crucial question is answered: For what purpose are the gifts of the Spirit provided? The manifestation of the Spirit is given to every man in order "to profit withal." Two affirmations seem discernible here. First, the gifts of the Spirit constitute a sign of the presence and activity of the Holy Spirit in the church. Hence, they are a "manifestation" of the Spirit. Therefore, the gifts would be one among many ways whereby the world may observe God at work in the life of His people.

The greatest emphasis is placed upon the second reason. The manifestation of the Spirit is given to every man "to profit withal," a translation of a prepositional phrase which literally means "toward the end of bringing all things together." In other words, the gifts are given specifically for edification. They are given to the church so that it may minister to itself in such a way as to keep all things in order.

Indirectly, a third question is also answered in the verse. The gifts of the Spirit are said to be given "to every man." This is a translation of *ekastō*, meaning "to each." The translation "to every man," which might suggest that the gift had been given to both believers and unbelievers, is a little misleading. The translation "to each" properly suggests that *only* the believer, but, by the same token, *every* believer is the recipient of spiritual gifts. In other words, every believer has been given at least one spiritual gift.

12:8 The first listing of these gifts is provided in verses 8 to 11. Additional listings occur in verses 28 to 31 as well as in Ephesians 4:4–16 and Romans 12:3–8. In addition, 1 Corinthians 7:7 speaks of celibacy as a *charisma* or gift, making twenty-one specified gifts. The New Testament does not say whether there are other spiritual gifts besides these.

This verse specifies two such spiritual gifts: the "word of wisdom" and the "word of knowledge." The distinction between the two seems to be that the "word of knowledge" refers to a supernatural comprehension of the facts of a particular situation, whereas "word of wisdom" refers to the supernatural endowment of being able to take what is revealed in the word of knowledge and apply it correctly to the circumstances and situations of life in a pragmatic way. An illustration of how these two function can be found in the supernatural knowledge given to Peter to know that Ananias was lying to him concerning the distribution of the former's property (Acts 5:3). On the other hand, the decision of the brethren to ordain deacons (Acts 6), and to decide the thorny issue of the admission of Gentiles to the church of God (Acts 15), constitute examples of the "word of wisdom"—the ability to arrive at the appropriate practical application of the knowledge God gives.

Both the "word of knowledge" and the "word of wisdom" must be understood to involve special spiritual enlightenment. This is not the mere exercise of human abilities. For example, a man may come to the Scriptures as an unbeliever with an appropriate knowledge of the biblical languages, adequate references, and exegetical commentaries and be able to discern the essential meaning of a text. This he has done by virtue of his training and the general accumulation of interpretive knowledge which is the property of many men. But there are levels of understanding and comprehension that may never be attained this way. John wrote of the only way for attaining special knowledge, an "anointing" (*chrisma*) which the believer has received from the Spirit who abides in him. The result is that "... ye need not that any man teach you: but as the same anointing teacheth you of all things, and is truth, and is no lie, and even as it hath taught you, ye shall abide in him" (1 John 2:27). By the same token, certain applications of God's truth to life's situations go beyond the mere product of the pragmatic mind.

Having stated the supernatural foundations of the "word of wisdom" and the "word of knowledge," it remains to caution that this "word of knowledge" and "word of wisdom" will never, under any circumstance, be in violation of or contradiction with the revealed truth of God as recorded in Scripture. This is the whole point of Paul's statement that, "If any man think himself to be a prophet, or spiritual, let him acknowledge that the things that I write unto you are the commandments of the Lord" (14:37). In other words, whatever happens of an alleged spiritual or prophetic nature must always be in agreement with and subservient to the written word of God.

12:9 Two additional gifts are added: faith and healing. Of course, every believer possesses faith, or he would not be saved (Eph. 2:8–9). However, the faith that is included here as a spiritual gift apparently is an extension of saving faith which enables the possessor almost always to see beyond the circumstances of the moment. Amid the most dire circumstances, faith encourages the brethren by pointing repeatedly to the adequacy of God's power and the perfection of His purpose. It is the compatriot of a vision and confidence in God.

Next the apostle mentioned the "gifts of healings." All healing comes from God. Though it is also recognized that remarkable natural abilities are given to those in the medical profession, the gifts of healing certainly refer to a bequeathal which transcends these natural abilities. Some have suggested that the rather unusual emphasis upon the plural "gifts of healing" emphasizes the fact that the gift is given situationally. It is true that the other option—that there are different kinds of gifts of healing—is highly unlikely and totally unverifiable in the light of Scripture. What might indicate support for the idea that gifts of healings represented gifts given by the Holy Spirit only in certain situations is the fact that even the apostle Paul seems to have possessed the gift, and yet on occasion he either chose not to use it, or did not have it to use.

For example, he healed the father of Publius on the island of Melita (Acts 28:8), but he left Trophimus sick in Miletus (2 Tim. 4:20). In 1 Timothy 5:23 he advised medicinal treatment for Timothy's chronic gastrointestinal problem rather than simply healing him. In Philippians 2:25-27, he felt the helplessness of being unable to do anything about Epaphroditus, who was ill to the point of death but then graciously spared by God. Furthermore, in the case of his own circumstance, his "thorn in the flesh" remained despite three appeals for its removal (2 Cor. 12:7-10). The fact that it was specifically related to the flesh strongly argues for the possibility of some physical malady.

Certainly the gift of healing was principally a gift employed for the authentication of the gospel and of the apostles, who were harbingers of the gospel. This may be observed, for example, in the case of the healing of the paralytic in Mark 2. Jesus forgave the man's sin, but when questioned about His ability to do that, He said, "But that ye may know that the Son of man hath power on earth to forgive sins, (he saith to the sick of the palsy,) I say unto thee, Arise, and take up thy bed, and go thy way into thine house" (Mark 2:10-11). The necessity of such authenticating gifts is clearly reduced by the end of the New Testament era. This is further discernible as one reads the book of Acts.

12:10 The next gift mentioned is the "working of miracles." "Working" (*energēma*) is the same word translated "administrations" in verse 6 of the King James Version. Here in view is the gift of "miracles" (*dunameis*), which are the "temporary supernatural suspension of the laws that govern this world as we commonly observe them."[47] Like the miracles of healing, the temporary suspension and even reversal of a natural law in terms of man's observation was an event normally so spectacular that it, too, had the power of authentication. In Hebrews 2:4 we see the sense in which "miracles" is described as a gift: "God

---

[47]*Criswell Study Bible*, p. 1357.

also bearing them witness, both with signs and wonders, and with divers miracles, and gifts of the Holy Ghost, according to his own will." God, through the gift of miracles, bore witness to the truth of what the apostles were saying.

The second gift mentioned is the gift of prophecy, (*prophēteia*, combining the word *phēmi*, meaning "to speak," and the preposition *pro*, meaning "before"). The problem in determining the exact meaning of "prophecy" is to ascertain whether the word primarily meant to speak about matters before they happened—hence, a "foretelling"—or "to proclaim before the people" the revelation of God—hence, "a forthtelling." The word is used in secular Greek to denote the message of the oracle of Zeus at Dodona in Epirus.[48]

Actually, several factors seem to verify the possibility of a general definition of the word, which in turn carries two sub-expressions. Kramer says of prophecy,

> It denotes appointed men and women and their work, which is to declare something whose content is not derived from themselves but from the God who reveals His will at the particular site. This revelation is through direct inspiration or through signs (*sumbola*) which stand in need of human interpretation. . . .[49]

Kramer has, in effect, provided a reasonable definition for the gift of prophecy even in the midst of his discussion of the use of the word in nonbiblical Greek. Whether we are speaking of prophets in the Old or New Testament, it seems that they were men and women who declared something, the content of which was not derived as a result of thought patterns of their own minds, but rather what God had revealed to them. In some cases, prophecy was of such importance that it merited ultimate inclusion in Holy Scripture (Isaiah, Daniel, Ezekiel, etc.). Much of this prophecy included the foretelling of future events. There were also elements of rebuke, reviews of the gracious acts of God, and calls for repentance, which frequently were unrelated

---

[48]Kittel, *Theological Dictionary*, Vol. 6, p. 791.
[49]Ibid., p. 791.

to the specific question of the future itself.

The New Testament gift of prophecy, then, has two phases associated with it: a gift to know future events and the gift of public proclamation of the word of God. Once again, stress should be laid upon the fact that under no circumstances would any such prophecy even be found contradictory to the revealed word of God found in biblical revelation.

A third gift mentioned is that of "discerning [*dakrisis,* literally "to judge through"] the spirits." The church, especially the group of believers at Corinth, has always had a need for those with the gift of discernment of spirits. John cautioned his readers, "Beloved, believe not every spirit, but try the spirits whether they are of God: because many false prophets are gone out into the world" (1 John 4:1). Any first-century reader would have been only too cognizant of the existence of false prophets.

Prophecy was a phenomenon already associated with the various oracles in their innumerable pagan temples and shrines. In addition to that, even in the Old Testament false prophets, whose messages were conflicting with one another and contradictory to the word of God, claimed to be prophesying in the name of the Lord. In Corinth, it is obvious that many were claiming the inspiration of the Holy Spirit in prophetic utterance, but not all were actually speaking from God. In order to determine what was a reliable prophecy or a legitimate utterance of tongues or just a sincere labor in the vineyard, the gift of discernment of spirits was a much needed one in Corinth, even as it is today.

The last two gifts mentioned in verse 10 relate again to spoken utterance. The first mentioned is "kinds of tongues" and the second "the interpretation of tongues." The two are mentioned together in clear anticipation of 14:27-28, where it is argued that tongues should not be allowed in the assembly except where there is an interpreter. But the question remains: to what does the expression "tongues" refer?

"Tongue" (*glōssa*) demonstrably means the ability to speak various known languages which had not been studied by the one possessing this gift. The purpose of the speaking was twofold: (a) the proclamation of the good news of salvation in Christ to those who otherwise could not have understood and (b) the authentication of the gospel messenger and his message. Two lines of argument establish this as the genuine intent of the apostle and the real meaning of the gift.

First, in 14:21 Paul argued that the law contained the prophecy that God would speak to His people with "other tongues and other lips." This quotation of Isaiah 28:11 most certainly refers to the use of actual existing languages. The second line of argumentation derives from the first instance of the use of the gift of tongues, namely, the Day of Pentecost which is recorded in Acts 2. In that passage when the miracle occurred, the people coming together ". . . were confounded, because that every man heard them speak in his own language" (Acts 2:6). They further expressed their amazement by saying, "and how hear we every man in our own tongue, wherein we were born?" (Acts 2:8). And again, "We do hear them speak in our tongues [*glōssa*, the same word] the wonderful works of God" (Acts 2:11). That the gift of tongues is then a reference to the use of a language, not heretofore studied, for the purpose of communicating the gospel and authenticating the gospel messenger seems irrefutable. The question remaining as to whether or not a second gift of tongues was present at Corinth will be answered in chapter 14.

Interpretation of tongues would be for the benefit of the assembled congregation who could not understand the language being employed for the cause of the gospel. The person to whom interpretation was given apparently did not understand the language being spoken either, but again a supernatural endowment of the Holy Spirit was granted to him. While I would be unwilling to say that God cannot give such a gift of tongues or interpretation of tongues in the present dispensation, it may be demonstrated that the first century need for the authentication of the gospel did indeed pass, and with its passing the occurrence of such a phenomenon is significantly reduced if not altogether absent.

12:11 One can scarcely underestimate the importance of this verse, which stresses that all these spiritual gifts are the product of the same Spirit who has dispersed them to each man according to His "will" (*boulomai*, most often translated "counsel"), a reference to the purposes of God as shared in fellowship by the Father, the Son, and the Holy Spirit. According, then, to the "counsel" of His will, the Spirit chooses which gifts He will bestow upon whom, and He also selects the occasion for the bestowal and determines the use of those gifts. The whole matter is totally bound up in the sovereignty of the Holy Spirit of God.

2. *Distinction in Functions (12:12-26)*

The following sections of the chapter develop not so much the fact or the meanings of the gifts as they concentrate instead on the purpose or the distinction of functions for those gifts. First, observe the baptism of the spirit (vv. 12–13), then the body of the Savior (vv. 14–21), and finally the balance of the saints (vv. 22–26).

12:12 An analogy is often the cradle for truth. Paul utilized such an analogy in speaking of the body of Christ. The human body, he wrote, is just one body, but it is composed of an almost infinite number of members, and not a single one of those is a mere attachment void of functional significance. Paul argued that the same thing is true of the body of Christ. Unfortunately, this is a perception too infrequently comprehended by the church itself. Some members are tacitly viewed as unable to contribute to the well-being of the body, and they are often treated almost as though they were liabilities. But Paul's view was quite different: each is an important member of the body.

12:13 The apostle continued by explaining precisely how a man becomes a part of the body of Christ. The Holy Spirit immersed each one into the body of Christ. Only this critically important verse lucidly explains what is meant by the "baptism of the Holy Spirit." The expression itself is found seven times in the Bible. Most of these occur in the Gospels and generally represent the prophecy of John the Baptist that the one coming after him would baptize "with the Holy Ghost, and with fire" (Matt. 3:11).

Although John prophesied that coming baptism, he did not explain exactly what it meant. Only here in 1 Corinthians did Paul explain exactly what this experience meant. The problem is found in the use of the dative case. In Matthew 3:11 it is recorded that when Jesus comes, He will baptize (*en pneumati*). This is the exact terminology, of course, that is used again in this passage when it is said that we are baptized "by one Spirit" (*en heni pneumati*). The problem is this: should this dative be understood in terms of location—i.e., when Jesus comes, He will baptize the believer in the Holy Spirit, or is it to be understood in terms of instrumentality—i.e., when Jesus comes, He will baptize believers by means of the Holy Spirit.

There are actually three possibilities that emerge from the discussion. (1) This is baptism in the Holy Spirit and is an experience each believer must have sometime subsequent to his salvation experience. (2) This is baptism into the body of Christ administered by the Holy Spirit, a baptism which occurs at the moment of conversion. (3) A combination of the two views is possible in which the baptism John enunciated was fulfilled in a once-for-all experience on the day of Pentecost, when the believing church was immersed in the Holy Spirit. Since that time, the sense of the word in 1 Corinthians 12:13 is normative; i.e., the believer is immersed by the Holy Spirit into the body of Christ at the moment of his conversion.

In order to solve the dilemma, one needs to address three questions: (1) Who is being baptized? (2) Who is the baptizer or the administrator? (3) Into what element is this immersion taking place? A careful reading of this verse in English or Greek gives a clear answer to those questions. First, those being "baptized" were the Corinthian believers. Paul could refer without reservation to all of the Corinthians because, though some might have been baptized by water without salvation actually having occurred, the reference to baptism here is spirit baptism and is applicable only to true believers. Therefore, all true believers have experienced this baptism. The identity of the administrator of baptism is clarified by the answer to the third question—i.e., the identification of the element. Clearly the Corinthians were baptized into the body of Christ. The element in which the immersion takes place is the body of Christ. Not only does the grammar but also the meaning of the passage demands this interpretation, since Paul was in the process of explaining how spiritual gifts were to function within the body of Christ—every individual being a member of that body. This leaves us no other alternative except to see that *en heni pneumati* identifies the administrator of baptism. At the moment of conversion the Holy Spirit immerses every believer into the body of Jesus Christ.

Concerning the three possibilities for interpretation of the passage, view 1 is eliminated altogether. The baptism of the Holy Spirit not only is not an experience subsequent to salvation which every believer needs to have, but also it is never commanded of the believer. Believers are commanded to be "filled" with the Spirit (Eph. 5:18), but they are never told to be "baptized" with the Spirit. Rather they are told to repent and believe, and this verse explains that when that happens they will receive the baptism of the Holy Spirit—i.e., they will be immersed by the Spirit into the body of Christ.

View 3 may be given the benefit of the doubt. Perhaps two different baptisms are envisioned—the one John described as having been accomplished on the Day of Pentecost and then the 1 Corinthians 12:13 baptism of the Spirit as becoming normative thereafter. While that may be plausible, it seems more logical to understand the *en pneumati* in the gospel passages as being used exactly the same way that it is used in 1 Corinthians 12:13, where its usage is not open to question. If that is the case, then view 2 is the correct one. Again, this view would hold that in every instance where "baptism of the Spirit" is mentioned, it should be understood as baptism by means of the Spirit into the body of Jesus Christ.

The importance of each member in the body is then emphasized by the mention of the fact that this baptism includes both Jews and Gentiles, both bondmen and free men. There are simply no distinctions to be made. "Gentiles" is not the usual *ethnē* but is instead *hellēnes*, a more specific designation meaning "Greeks." This may reflect that the church at Corinth had been more successful in reaching the Greek population of the area than the distinctively Roman population. In any case, all—Jews, Greeks, those who were slaves, and those who were free—had been made to drink unto one Spirit. The expression "to drink into one Spirit" emphasizes the assimilation of the Spirit or the indwelling presence of the Holy Spirit.

12:14 The affirmation of this verse is merely the logical conclusion of what has been presented in verse 13. Since the church was a rather strange congregation, bringing together on even footing Jew and Greek, bond and free, Paul therefore reminded them that the body is not just one member but many. This reminder was also given in anticipation of the argument advanced in verse 15.

Obviously in Corinth, preoccupied as they were with the desire to identify and exercise their spiritual gifts, jealousies had arisen with regard to some of the gifts. Possibly the more spectacular gifts were greatly desired by some who did not actually possess them. As we will see in the later discussion, this perhaps led to a fleshly attempt to imitate certain of these spiritual gifts. In light of this, the apostle reminded the Corinthians that the foot is not able to say that it is displeased with its function in the body, since it cannot function as a hand. The sense of the argument is most arresting. The foot of a man is not as observable in public as a hand. Whereas hands are enhanced with rings and other ornamentation, the feet are seldom so decorated. Whereas the hands are seldom covered, the feet are almost inevitably covered. Furthermore, the hand is the instrument of an expressed friendship through the handshake or the caress, while the foot seldom enters into such negotiations. Understandably, then, the foot in this anthropomorphic analogy might experience jealousy or despondency and reply, "I simply do not belong to the body." But the truth is to the contrary. Exhibiting the bejeweled hand in public or helping it arrive at a place where it can shake hands vigorously with a friend is all dependent upon the transportation ability of the foot. Should the recipient of the handshake or the admirer of the bejeweled hand not recognize this truth, it is of no consequence because the body itself knows thoroughly the truth of the affirmation.

12:16 To press the importance of the analogy, Paul simply gave another case—that of the ear experiencing despondency because it happens not to be the eye. The function of both is important, and the impairment of either causes us to view one as "handicapped." But without a doubt, the sparkle, the coloring, and the mobility of the eye make it a much more noticed and appealing member than the trumpet of the ear. But not only does the body know well it would seriously feel dysfunction if deprived of its hearing, it also knows that the absence of the ear would do nothing to enhance the aesthetics of the body.

12:17 The nature of the argument is now turned just slightly. Suppose that out of the jealousy and despondency of the ear for the eye, the whole body were to become an eye. Seeing would not thereby be improved, but there would be enormous forfeiture since the hearing would have vanished. Or if the whole body consisted of hearing, what a loss would be felt in the ability of the nose to catch the whiff of the rose blossom or the honeysuckle.

12:18 The conclusion to the argument is that God "set the members every one of them in the body, as it hath pleased Him." The importance of the thought is to underscore once more the sovereignty of God in the matter of spiritual gifts. When God first fashioned the body of Adam from the dust of the ground, He artistically fashioned it as a part of the most astounding bioengineering process ever, and He determined the function of each organ of the body to contribute to the well-being of the whole. He did not consult with the members of the body He fashioned; He made them to function as it pleased Him. The same is true of the body of Christ, the church. The gifts have been given as God pleased, and they are to function for the good of the whole body.

12:19 This verse may seem to be a mere reiteration of the verse immediately preceding it and thus a redundancy. Quite to the contrary, in verses 19 and 20 Paul was preparing the Corinthians for a different turn in the development of his argument. Therefore, once again he stressed that if the entire body were just one member, it would really not be a body at all. There are, of course, unicellular forms of life. Of these we would never say "there is a body." We would rather say "there is a living cell." To have a body, there must be a multiplicity of organs all functioning together as a unit.

12:20 Paul affirmed that there are, in fact, many members in the body; yet there is to be unity—"there is but one body."

12:21 Having established the twin principles of bodily unity and diversity of function within the body, Paul was now ready to take the argument one step further. Not only should the ear not be jealous of the eye nor the foot despondent because it cannot function as a hand, but also the eye cannot afford spiritual pride and condescension. The eye cannot afford to say to the hand, "I have no need of you," nor can the head say to the feet, "I have no need of you." Suppose the eye beholds a lovely newborn infant. Every desire is there to reach out and cuddle the infant, but the body cannot participate in that activity unless it has the benefit of the hand to grasp. Or again, if the head sees a mountain that it wishes to conquer, whatever its thinking prowess may be, void of its feet, the body cannot make any advance on the mountain, or ever evaluate the grandeurs observable from its lofty heights. So Paul affirmed that every member of the body in its particular function has a definite need of the other members of the body and their functions also.

12:22 In fact, the argument is even more applicable than one might think at first since those members of the body which seem to be the most feeble are absolutely mandatory to its proper function. The comparative degree of the adjective "feeble" (*asthenesteros*) is "weak." There is not great strength, for example, in the human tongue. It is not an organ with the muscular endurance of a bicep, nor does it have any commanding beauty about it. However, it functions not only to provide a portion of the ability of the human body to taste and, hence, to maintain a desire for food and the sustenance of life, but it also has a principal function in the human ability to speak. Consequently, though it is a feeble member, its importance cannot be diminished.

12:23 A second illustration follows. Not only are those members of the body which are weak necessary; but those portions of the body which we tend to view as less honorable bestow abundant honor, and uncomely parts have more abundant comeliness. "Uncomely" (*aschēmonos*) may mean anything from "indecorous," i.e., the feet, to "indecent," i.e., the reproductive and secretive organs. By stressing that we bestow greater honor upon these, Paul apparently referred to the act of clothing. Those organs which fall into the category of being either indecorous or indecent when exposed in public are rendered beautiful and honored by the numerous approaches that the human family makes to adorning such organs. As a result, our "uncomely" (*aschēmonos*) organs have more abundant "comeliness" (*euschēmosunē*), a word which means "gracefulness," "ornamentally embellished," or "pleasing to look at."

12:24 The explanation for such clothing is provided in this verse. Those parts of our anatomy which normally are considered pleasant to the view, such as the face, eyes, hands, etc., have no need of adornment. God has "tempered" (*sunkerannumi*, which means "to blend together") the body in giving more abundant honor to the part which lacked the honor otherwise. God has so prepared our bodies that those portions of it which might otherwise have been despised are the subjects upon which the most abundant honor is actually given. Many commentators feel that this is once again a reference to the matter of clothing and adornment of those organs that are less aesthetically appealing. However, in addition to this thought there may be certain recognition of the intrinsic value of the internal organs which we carefully protect because life itself depends upon their proper functioning.

12:25 God has prepared both the physical body and the body of Christ so that there would be no schism in the body. Once again, *schisma* speaks of a "division." God does not desire any division in the church but rather desires that the entire body should make use of its gifts or functions as an expression of care one for the other.

At this particular point we may glean one of the most important insights concerning spiritual gifts. All through the analogy of the human anatomy to the body of Christ, Paul suggested in effect, that believers are the organs and the appendages of the body of Christ, and spiritual gifts are the functions of those organs as they relate to one another. For example, the stomach and intestines digest food which is then ferried by the bloodstream to the organs of the body. The same bloodstream takes the oxygen filtered by the lungs and distributes it to every panting cell. The organs of the body find their usefulness in the provision that they make for the other parts of the body. Paul was arguing that just as the human body functions in such a way, so the gifts of the Spirit represent the functions of the various organs in the body, and are valuable only as they provide an adequate ministry and service to the other members.

12:26 There is one additional inevitable conclusion to be observed. When one of the members of the body suffers or becomes ill, all the rest of the members suffer with it. When one sustains a substantive injury to one of his appendages, the entire body must often be laid up for rest and recuperation. Furthermore, the entire body feels the impact of the injury in that the body must go to work as a whole to resist infection and to bring healing resources to the assaulted member. Paul's stress on corporate suffering was designed in the first place to remind the Corinthians of the unity which they ought to have felt. In the second place, it was designed as a preparatory statement to the remaining conclusion—namely, when one member is honored, all other members ought to rejoice in that honor. In many respects, this last observation probably constitutes one of the most difficult practices for the church at any time. By alluding to this, in a unique fashion Paul pinpointed the presence of spiritual pride in the exercise of the grace-gifts. He suggested that, instead of becoming jealous and envious with regard to the presence of certain gifts in other believers, one should reach the spiritual maturity to realize that when another's gift is honored and used, it is a matter in which the whole body of Christ is actually honored.

3. *Difference of Offices (12:27–31)*

In this section we will consider the unity of the body (v. 27), the uniqueness of the bequest (vv. 28–30), and the urgency of the best (v. 31).

12:27 The concluding notes of the chapter are initiated with a fresh declaration of the unity-within-diversity theme that has preceded this verse. This time, however, the statement is in the emphatic form. The pronoun *humeis* is used even though it is not necessary to the meaning of the sentence. When this is done in Greek it means that the writer wishes to emphasize that the recipients of his letter are the specific ones he intended. In this way

Paul was stressing that the Corinthians comprised the body of Christ but that each member was important both individually and in terms of the corporate whole.

12:28 For the second time, a listing of gifts appears in the chapter. Some of the gifts which were listed before are reintroduced, while others are mentioned which were not given in the earlier passage. God has established these in the church. Apparently, in addition to the listing there is also intended a prescribed order of importance. First are apostles, second prophets, third teachers. Following after those three crucial offices are the working of miracles and the gifts of healing, helps, governments, diversities of tongues. The first three offices indicated and specifically ordered suggest that these offices belong, at least primarily, to the pastoral leadership of the church. There is no question that the first, the gift of the apostle, ceased with the end of the apostolic era and the death of those thus appointed. As for the prophets, we have already seen that at least one of the functions of the prophet, that of delineating the future through special revelation, also evidently ceased with the coming of the written New Testament. However, the element of prophecy that encompasses public proclamation is still among the spiritual gifts. Certainly the third category of teacher, which may correspond to the pastor and teacher category of Ephesians 4:11, is a gift that continues in the church.

Requirements for apostleship are reasonably specific in the New Testament documents. Four distinct features for apostleship are discernible (see 12:28 and Acts 1:21–24):

For a discussion of "prophet," see notes on verse 10.

"Teachers" (*didaskaloi*) referred to those who were interpreters of the word of God and who had the gift for explaining precisely what the saints of God needed to know about the ways of God. These three offices—apostle, prophet, and teacher—functioned together to provide the spiritual leadership of the early church.

Clearly secondary in importance but nonetheless crucial to the early church was the working of miracles (see v. 10), the gifts of healings (see v. 9), and diversities of tongues (see v. 10). In addition, "helps" and "governments" are added as two important gifts in this discussion. "Helps" (*antilēmpseis*) means "to grasp" or "to take up a matter" over against someone else. The preposition *anti*, which is attached to the verb *lambanomai*, is a substitutionary preposition meaning "in the place of." The vividness and expressiveness of the Greek word is lost in translation. They who had the gift of "helps" were those who had experienced the work of the Holy Spirit in a unique fashion, in the sense of being able to discern those among God's people who were staggering beneath a heavy burden or problem. The possessors of this precious gift are seldom appreciated by the church and even more infrequently accorded the honor they deserve. Yet those who possess this gift go about not only discerning the burdens of others but also often assisting them by becoming a substitute burden bearer for them, having been given discernment as how best to help.

"Governments" is derived from *kubernēseis*, a reference to the helmsman who was responsible for guiding a ship safely through the storms, reefs, and rocks. He was the one who must know the times of the day and the year, the sky, the stars, the currents of air, etc.[50]

A remarkable insight into the meaning of this gift can be discerned from the Septuagint, which uses the word three times, all in the book of Proverbs (1:5, 11:14, and 24:6). Each time the basic meaning of the word is "wise counsel." For example, "A wise man will hear, and will increase learning; and a man of understanding shall attain unto wise counsels" (Prov. 1:5). In each case, *kubernēseis* is translating the Hebrew word *tach'bulah* which also originally indicated steering or directing a ship by means of the pulling of the ropes of the sails. Gradually the word has come to mean "direction," "guidance," or "counsel."

The gift of "governments," therefore, has nothing whatsoever to do with ruling or with any legislative function but should be translated "counsel." While those with the gift of "helps" were helping predominantly with the physical burdens of the people, those with the gifts of "governments" were apparently sharing advice and counsel in critical spiritual and emotional matters.

---

[50]Kittel, *Theological Dictionary*, Vol. 3, p. 1035.

12:29 Consistent with one of his favorite methods of emphasis, Paul once again resumed the asking of rhetorical questions. Are all apostles? Obviously very few ever served in that capacity. Are all prophets? Without doubt there were more prophets than apostles, but even that is a relatively limited group. Are all teachers? Once again the field may have been expanded somewhat, but certainly not everyone has that spiritual gift. Are all workers of miracles? Once again, the field is getting smaller, and the answer has to be "no."

12:30 The questions continue. Do all have the gifts of healing? Do all speak with tongues? Do all interpret? The fact that all of these questions are only answered with a resounding negative but nevertheless that they are all carefully asked is more than ample indication that the Corinthians evidently felt that one had been spiritually slighted and was even underdeveloped spiritually if he did not possess all of the gifts of the Spirit. Furthermore, those who fancied themselves to possess all or most of the gifts apparently were guilty of a condescending attitude toward those who obviously did not. Paul pressed the obvious point that not everybody had all of the gifts. Therefore, a man must take the gifts that he has been given and use them for the cause of the kingdom.

12:31 "Coveting the gifts" (*zēloō*) means "to have strong affection towards" or "to be ardently devoted to." It may, in fact, mean "envious" or "covetous" and is so translated on occasion. Here it is better rendered "ardently desire spiritual gifts." However, there was a particular kind of spiritual gift that the Corinthians were told to desire—namely, the best spiritual gift. There is no way to avoid the clear intention of Paul in this text. He was indicating that some spiritual gifts were intrinsically of greater value than others. Those gifts which involved continuing ministry to the church of God would naturally be of greater significance than those which were only of an authenticating nature. By the same token, those gifts that made a difference in the spiritual life of a believer would reside in a more important category than those which affected his physical life. In this regard, the gifts of tongues, interpretation of tongues, healing, and miracles would all fall into the category of the less important gifts, while gifts such as teaching, prophecy, counseling ("governments"), and others would have strategic continuing importance for the spiritual development of the life of the church.

This does not imply that the other gifts were unimportant or that those who possessed them were to feel slighted in any fashion. However, the latter possibility was a dim one, since the problem seems to have been that those who either possessed or at least thought they possessed the gift of tongues attached such importance to it that they behaved in a condescending manner toward those who did not have it. The command then was that as the Corinthians earnestly desired the spiritual gifts, they should desire the best one.

Some feel that the last phrase of this verse actually belongs with the chapter to follow. Perhaps so. In any case, the import of the verse is clear. Rather than being unduly concerned about ardently seeking spiritual gifts, Paul prescribed a better way. It was not the way of neglecting spiritual gifts but rather a way which enabled one to use them as they were intended.

Love Is Something You Do

1. The Latitude of Love (13:1-7)
2. The Limits of Love (13:8-13)

Perhaps no other chapter in the Bible has been any more profoundly loved, widely quoted, or totally divorced from its context than the "love chapter" of 1 Corinthians. It is a tribute to the lofty literary accomplishment embodied therein as well as to the profundity of its thought that it can, in fact, stand alone or complement almost any other discussion imaginable. The principles elucidated are applicable to relationships in families, churches, or other community groups. However, to understand the nuances of its various phrases, the chapter must be interpreted in the context in which it occurs.

The particular context is a discussion of the use of spiritual gifts in the church at Corinth. Nowhere is it more important for the reader to remember that the chapter and verse divisions contained in all modern translations were not present in the text Paul wrote. That a major interpolation should occur unrelated to the passages before and after is unthinkable.

On the other hand, just as the Corinthians had demonstrated a flagging love for one another in numerous ways, so they have added to that a question of the consistency of their love in regard to the use of spiritual gifts. Although Jesus said that love for one another was the badge of discipleship (John 13:35), nevertheless, they had demonstrated in the following ways the quiescence of that love: (1) the existence of the four divisions in the church (chs. 1—4); (2) the toleration of moral decadence within the church (ch. 5); (3) the willingness to go to the civil courts of law in cases against one another (ch. 6); (4) a concern about their own freedom even when it caused others to stumble (chs. 8—10); (5) their selfishness at the Lord's table (11:20-21); (6) their selfishness and pride concerning spiritual gifts (chs. 12—14). At no point was the lack of love more apparent than it was in the abuse of these spiritual gifts. With this background we are now able to address the subject of the latitude and limits of love in chapter 13.

1. The Latitude of Love (13:1-7)

We will examine the efficacy of love (vv. 1-3) and the ethos of love (vv. 4-7).

13:1 "Though" is a highly questionable translation of the Greek term *ean*. A better translation would be, "If with the tongues of men and angels I should speak." He was not here affirming that he had spoken with such tongues, only suggesting that if this were to be the case he would present merely a parade of sound unless he possessed love. In the verses that follow, many of the spiritual gifts will be mentioned. Prophecy, the understanding of mysteries, the word of knowledge, and faith will all be specified as examples of the possession and use of spiritual gifts.

It is no accident that he began with the question of tongues. There is no indication that the language of angelic tongues is known. Understandably, the rabbis thought that the angels spoke in Hebrew. The biblical narrative itself would seem to suggest that they simply spoke whatever language was expedient in order to communicate with human beings. Whether there is a heavenly language or an angelic tongue per se is not known. Paul simply suggested that if he were able to attain the use of such a lofty language or even if he were able by special spiritual intervention to speak all the languages of the tribes of the earth, he would still be nothing but a cacophony of sound unless he possessed love. Without that love he would merely become as a resounding bronze gong or as a loudly clanging symbol. Both are void of musical scale or significant change of tone and, except when carefully orchestrated with other instruments, are generally painful to the head and ears.

The word translated "charity" in the King James Version is *agapē*. The Greeks used four different words to describe love. *Erōs* is the word which has been borrowed by the English language as "erotic," signifying sexual love, often of a licentious variety. Although the word *erōs* in Greek certainly encompassed sexual love, it was in no sense limited to that form of love. Rather, as Anders Nygren points out in his book, *erōs* is simply appetitive love—love to satisfy a craving or appetite. Its moral tone is neutral, as such, but due to human selfishness and greed often becomes a negative word.[51] *Storgē* was most often used by the Greeks for the love of the family. *Philos* was principally the love of friendship. It can be demonstrated that there are times when particularly *philos* and *agapē* are used virtually interchangeably. Nevertheless, *agapē*, in its essence, was the very opposite of *erōs*. While *erōs* was appetitive, focusing on satisfying personal desires, *apagē* was concerned only with giving to the object of its affection. As John Colet wrote in 1496 or 1497, "Charity is the flower of faith."[52]

Love by definition, then, is that deep concern for the well-being of another which flavors all of one's actions into selfless concern and activity in behalf of others. The absence of such love reduces to nothing whatever virtues there may be in the gift of tongues. As Robertson and Plummer astutely note, there are three conclusions about the use of gifts without love. In verse 1 Paul argued that the absence of love would cause him to produce nothing of value. In verse 2, even with the presence of gifts, without love he himself was of no value. In verse 3, he suggested

---

[51]Anders Nygren, *Agape and Eros*, p. 210.

[52]John Colet, *An Exposition of St. Paul's First Epistle to the Corinthians*, p. 136.

that even though he might exercise numerous gifts, if love is not present he gained nothing of value.[53]

13:2 Paul moved to a consideration of other gifts which were popularly endorsed at Corinth. If one had the gift of prophecy or insight into all mysteries and in addition to that had all knowledge and if he could add to this such all-encompassing faith that he would be able to remove mountains, yet without love he would amount to nothing. This statement is staggering in its content. For one to be a prophet proclaiming the word of God, for one to know the mysteries of the kingdom of God and to have remarkable knowledge of the word and ways of God, further for one to be able to exercise mountain-moving faith, and even then consider himself a total failure is a remarkable affirmation. One begins to understand that a major effort was being made by Paul to convince the Corinthians of the strategic nature of love in the church.

"Mysteries" *(mustēria)* always refers to truths which men could never discover without the special revelation of God. Thus, to know all mysteries would be to assume that one had experienced all there was to experience of the revelation and inspiration of God. Still, Paul concludes, without love "I am nothing."

13:3 Suppose, however, that in addition to the ability to exercise the gift of tongues and all the remarkable gifts and insights of verse 2, a man so greatly valued in society would go even further and bestow all his goods for feeding those in need, and as if this were not enough, suppose he would even give his body to be burned as a sacrifice for others. Would this not be incomparable accomplishment? The answer, of course, is that if one man did all of these things with improper motivation, he would find that it profited him nothing. Furthermore, the only proper motivation is *agapē* love.

There is one problem in the text of this verse. The word translated "to be burned" is *kauthēsōmai*, but many of the best texts read *kauchēsōmai*. The meaning of the two words is entirely dif-

---

[53]Robertson and Plummer, *First Corinthians*, p. 291.

ferent. *Kauthēsōmai* means "to be burned," whereas *kauchēsōmai* is rendered "if I should give up my body for the sake of glory." Robertson and Plummer reject the readings of the better texts in this case, arguing that the verse makes far better sense if understood according to the usual translation.[54] In other words, we are to see that even the ultimate sacrifice that a man could make, if it is made from improper motivation, profits nothing for the man who has made it.

13:4 Even the presence and use of the most remarkable spiritual gifts is inconsequential in the absence of love. But the reader might well ask, "What do you mean by love?" As noted, the concept of *agapē* was a new one, the noun itself having only seven possible appearances in secular Greek. Since all of these possible appearances are in damaged texts, there is the possibility that the word never appears at all and that Richard C. Trench was right when he said, "It should not be forgotten that *agapē* is a word born within the bosom of revealed religion...."[55]

The verb form *agapaō* occurs, but the noun *agapē* seems to be limited to the Septuagint, the Apocrypha, and the New Testament. Given the special nature of this word and its need for definition, the apostle proceeded with a listing of several groupings of two words or phrases each. First, love is "long-suffering" (*makrothumos*, a combination of *makros*, meaning "large or long," and *thumos*, which is the word often employed to depict the anger and rage of man). Therefore, the first characteristic of love is that it is a long time arriving at anger. Note that Paul did not suggest that love is never angry. There are those occasions when a righteous indignation and the activity associated therewith is in order. The point is that this state is seldom reached and only reached in light of the certainty of the will of God because one is so immersed in love that it is difficult for anger to be called forth. Christians need to be given the painful reminder that frequent displays of temper betray the absence, or at least the severe limitation, of love.

---

[54]Ibid.

[55]Richard C. Trench, *Synonyms of the New Testament*, p. 43.

The second word is "kind" (*chrēsteuomai*). Once again this is the only time in which the verb form of this word occurs in the New Testament, and the translation of the King James Version reflects accurately the content of the word. It denotes "a grace that pervades and penetrates the whole nature, mellowing there all that would have been harsh and austere. For instance, wine that has been mellowed by age is called *chrēstos* (Luke 5:39)."[56] It is the flip side of not being swiftly moved toward anger. The disposition of love is a gentle kindness toward all men. Keep in mind that Paul's discussion in chapter 13 concerns love in the light of the particular problems related to the spiritual gifts at Corinth. Some who used these spiritual gifts may have been unkind toward those who did not have them, and anger may well have been generated on the part of those who felt slighted by their absence.

Three negative statements follow. Love "envieth not" (*zēloō*). At this point a careful distinction must be made. The word *zēloō* certainly means "envy or jealousy," but the problem is that the Bible says that our God is a "jealous God" (Ex. 20:5). How can these apparent contradictions be reconciled?

The situation is even more distressing since in 12:31 the Corinthians are advised to "covet" (*zēloō*) spiritual gifts. The answer is found in the question of motivation. If the reason for zealousness or covetousness of spiritual gifts is one's desire to give himself in ministry to the flock of God, then it is a noble covetousness. God is jealous over His people because He earnestly desires to give them the best and hates the destruction brought about by the temper and by sin.

On the other hand, in the church at Corinth jealousy, envy, and covetousness were rampant concerning the desire to possess certain spiritual gifts. Some who possessed these gifts may have demonstrated covetousness in that they rejoiced in their superior favor of having the gift and really preferred that others not join their select group. But love is not envious, and love rejoices when another does well.

---

[56]Spiros Zodhiates, *To Love Is to Live*, p. 71.

Two terms follow which at first seem redundant but are actually vivid additions to the description. First, love "vaunteth not itself" (*perpereuomai*), and love is not "puffed up" (*phusiouomai*). The first word is derived from *perperos*, meaning "a braggart." The idea is that of vocal boasting. *Phusiouomai*, on the other hand, is the inner attitude of exhalted opinion which often leads to the public expression of the *perperos*. The latter word refers to an unrealistic persuasion about one's own importance and a failure to see oneself as a rebellious sinner graciously salvaged by the grace of God, while the former word speaks of the inevitable bubbling over in public speech of exalted opinions of oneself. These two words apparently focus clearly upon one of the major problems in Corinth. Some possessing or claiming to possess the gift of tongues and perhaps other gifts as well were haughty and even boastful about this. As such, they identified themselves as lacking in love.

13:5 "Does not behave itself in an unseemly fashion" is the translation of *aschēmoneō*, a word we have noticed before. The word generally means "to suffer shame because of one's behavior." Perhaps another way to put it would be to say that "love is tactful in its expression." Those concerned about possession of the gifts are reminded that when the gifts become hurtful and generate shameful or tactless behavior then the practitioners of those gifts are demonstrating the absence of adequate love.

Furthermore, love is not "self-seeking." This phrase constitutes one of the most essential attributes of love. It does not seek its own advancement, its own aggrandizement, or its own honor. Love's concern is totally with the object of its affections. Once again, those who employ spiritual gifts for personal benefit have missed not only the entire purpose of gifts but also the development of the kind of love required by the Scriptures.

In addition, love is "not easily provoked" (*paroxunomai*), a word somewhat similar to "long-suffering" (v. 4). The difference is that the emphasis in *paroxunomai* is upon love's refusal to be goaded into mistaken action. Love understands problems and circumstances of life and waits as long as possible to make any kind of motivational judgement or to react adversely to circumstances where there may have been intemperate action on the part of others.

"Thinketh no evil" is one of the most telling of all the terms used to describe love. Literally it is a translation of *logizomai*, a commercial bookkeeping term, and *kakon*, which literally means all kinds of evil and wrong. Thus, the phrase may be translated "does not keep books on evil." Involved here is the frequently voiced and lightly veiled threat, "I will forgive you but I won't forget." Forgiveness that does not involve a maximum effort at forgetfulness, at least to the extent that the matter is forever laid to rest, is not real forgiveness at all. The forgiveness of God in Jesus Christ for the human race is certainly complete, the penalty having been paid by Jesus on the cross. Indeed the forgiveness of God in Christ is the ultimate expression of love.

13:6 In the expression "rejoices not in inquity"(*adikia*, "unrighteousness"), the apostle recognized that the possession of spiritual gifts is no guarantee of spirituality. Spiritual gifts are bestowed by the Holy Spirit upon every believer. Oftentimes those gifts are prostituted, and sometimes they are profaned by ungodly activity associated with them.

The other side of the coin is that one who genuinely loves "rejoices in the truth." The truth emphasized here is both theological and personal. Those who have an *agapē* love for Christ have no difficulty in rejoicing in all the truths revealed in the word of God. An unwillingness to support enthusiastically all the teachings of Scripture inevitably betrays the failure of an individual to love Christ as he should. Furthermore, love rejoices in truth of a personal nature. One is not offended by painful discoveries about himself but rather responds through repentance and confession.

13:7 Four concluding affirmations about love are now made. First, it "bears all things." Once again there is a distinction between this word (*stegō*, which might be better rendered "covers or protects") and "endure," the last word of the verse. For example, in 1 Peter 4:8, love is said to cover a multitude of sins. This affirmation does not imply a cover-up or an avoidance of judgment and justice, it only suggests that the desire of love is always to cover protectively all things so that minimum harm is done to the object of its affection.

"Believeth all things" does not suggest gullibility on the part of the believer. When the Lord said, "Ye shall know them by their fruits" (Matt. 7:16), he indirectly indicated the necessity of careful analysis of circumstances and actions by believers. The point is, as Robertson and Plummer state, "In doubtful cases he will prefer being too generous in his conclusions to suspecting another unjustly."[57] Love, in other words, desires to be able to believe the best about every situation.

Love "hopes all things." There is a quality about love which refuses to accept defeat. Pessimism, doubt, and spiritual reluctance are characteristic of those who have an inadequate love. Where love is present a vision grows. Where love is present one remains optimistic about the intervention of God in the affairs of men. Where love is present there is always hope.

Finally, love "endures all things." "Endures" (*hupomenō*) literally means "to remain under the load." It is often translated "patience" in the King James Version, but here it is better rendered "endurance." Love is not easily quashed. It possesses an incredible resilience that enables it to maintain itself under circumstances that would crush all other commitments. This check list of items is applicable not only to the use of spiritual gifts in the churches but to any situation in which there is a legitimate question of love. It is a check list that needs to be frequently applied by each individual to his own life and relationships.

2. The Limits of Love (13:8–13)

The question must now be addressed as to whether there are, in fact, any limits to love. First, Paul spoke of the abiding nature of love (vv. 8–10), then the enlightening nature of love (vv. 11–12), and finally the prevailing nature of love (v. 13).

13:8 Love never fails or falls. However, the apostle continued by insisting that three of the most coveted spiritual gifts would

---

[57]Robertson and Plummer, *First Corinthians*, p. 295.

eventually cease to exist. In so arguing, Paul was making the principal point that love is superior because it has no temporal limit. While it will continue unto the ages of ages, i.e., throughout eternity, spiritual gifts will have a limited duration and their very time limitation calls attention to their inferiority when compared with love.

Prophecies shall fail; knowledge shall vanish away. The words translated "fail" and "vanish away" are actually the same word. Its lexical form (*katargeō*) means "to render useless or make inoperative." Prophecies are said "to fail," not in the sense that they prove untrue, but rather in the sense that they will simply no longer be necessary. The same is true of the partial knowledge believers possess at the present time. That knowledge shall be far surpassed since "then shall I know even as also I am known" (v. 12). The gift of knowledge will have fallen into uselessness. Tongues, it is said, shall cease. Here the word is quite different from *katargeō*; it is *pauō*, meaning "to cease," "to stop," "to leave off," or "to cause to pause." Also, another change has taken place, as W. A. Criswell indicates: "He uses a different verb, *pauō*, 'cause to cease,' and he changes the voice from passive to middle, *pausontai*, which literally translated means 'tongues shall make themselves to cease' or 'tongues shall automatically cease of themselves.' "[58]

Criswell's mention of the middle voice brings to play a phenomenon in the Greek language which we cannot reduplicate in English. English has active and passive voices but no middle voice. The passive voice emphasizes the subject as acting so as to participate in some way in the results of the action. This is the reason Criswell has translated the passage "tongues shall cease of themselves." The question is left unresolved as to when precisely the end of these spiritual gifts may be expected.

13:9 First Paul dealt with the two he had said would cease. He expressed both their importance and their limitation. Concerning knowledge, we know only in part. Concerning prophecy, we prophesy only in part. The certain intent of the passage was to

---

[58]W. A. Criswell, *The Holy Spirit in Today's World*, p. 177.

remind the Corinthians that while those with the gift of knowledge and those with the gift of prophecy were able to know and to proclaim remarkable insights into the mystery of God, there were limitations upon these gifts. There is an eternity to know and to experience what we at the present see only darkly as in a mirror (v. 13).

13:10 However, there is coming a day when what is perfect will come. When that happens, what is in part shall be done away. Interpretations vary widely about the meaning of *teleios*, a word which has a multitude of possible meanings, such as "fully developed," "complete," "perfect," "without shortcoming," etc. The major possibilities generally advanced by various interpreters are these:

(1) "Perfect" refers to the writing of the New Testament documents, at which point, according to these interpreters, there would be no further necessity for the gift of special knowledge or the gift of prophecy, thus covering both the hortatory and the didactic sections of Scripture, and the need for tongues would also cease since no further authenticating miracles would be needed.

(2) "Perfect" refers to the return of Christ either to take away His church prior to the tribulation or else at the end of the tribulation when He returns to the earth to establish His millennial kingdom. At that particular point in time the church will have no more need for these gifts, and, hence, they will cease.

(3) "Perfect" referred to the eternal heavenly state to which Paul refers in 15:24 when he spoke of delivering up the kingdom of God to the Father after He has put down every enemy.

The problem with the first view is that while the Scripture is perfect in all that it affirms, its perfection lies in its errorlessness—not in its completeness. God has told us in the Scriptures all that we need to know for a successful life and a certain eternity. He has given us much more besides. Nevertheless, it remains that "Eye hath not seen nor ear heard, neither have entered into the heart of man the things which God hath prepared for them that love Him" (2:9). At present we at best see through a mirror darkly. Therefore, it is unlikely that "that which is perfect" refers to the Bible.

The second view, while certainly presenting one who is perfect in the coming of Jesus, is still probably a faulty view in that conditions will not yet be perfect. Even during the millennial age with all the blessings of that era, when Satan is loosed at its conclusion (Rev. 20:7-8), he will have an immediate following from among those who have outwardly submitted to the rule of God during the thousand year reign of Christ but inwardly have never been regenerated. Therefore, "that which is perfect" is probably best construed as a reference to the eternal state of the believer's existence in heaven with God. That is the only time, in fact, which suits the condition, "then that which is in part shall be done away."

The conclusion to be drawn from verse 10, in conjunction with the declarations made in verse 8, is that in the heavenly kingdom there is no longer any need for prophecy or knowledge as special gifts of God. Nevertheless, to at least some extent they continue to exist in the church today. Tongues, on the other hand, constitute another question altogether. The very fact that a different word is used to describe their cessation, and the fact that it is in the middle voice, seem to indicate that these tongues would cease of themselves. This is, of course, precisely what we have recorded for us in the New Testament. Once the gospel has been authenticated through the use of tongues on the Day of Pentecost (once again understood in its Acts reference to be an instance of a language never before formally studied being spoken for the purpose of communicating the gospel) and extended to the Gentiles in the home of Cornelius in Acts 10 and the strange case of the disciples who had known only the baptism of John in Ephesus (Acts 19:1-6), there is no further mention of tongues except in this extended discussion in 1 Corinthians.

Since it is generally conceded that the date of 1 Corinthians makes it one of the earlier New Testament books and since there is no mention of tongues in the later epistles, there is ample evidence to argue that tongues—as a sign gift especially applicable, as we shall see later, to the Jews—had ceased exactly as anticipated in this verse. According to this interpretation, this happened and was expected to happen even before the coming of "that which is perfect." On the other hand, prophecy and the gift of the work of knowledge would continue until the coming of "that which is perfect."

13:11 A further indication that Paul viewed the exercise of these spiritual gifts as primarily a developmental stage of the church is found in this verse. When he was a child, he spoke like a child and had a childlike understanding and comprehension. However, the dawning of manhood and its accompanying maturity enabled Paul to lay aside those things that were characteristic of his childhood. The implication is amply clear. The Corinthians in the excitement of their beginning walk with Christ had reveled in spiritual gifts, particularly those that were more sensational and had greater appeal to their emotional desires. Now they must proceed to maturity, putting away childish things and becoming Christian men.

13:12 Further elucidation of the coming of "that which is perfect" is made in a comparison of our present knowledge with that future knowledge. At the present we see by means of a mirror darkly. Roman glass mirrors were common in the ancient world and especially were those made at Corinth known throughtout the ancient world. My wife's favorite piece in our collection of biblical antiquities is an exquisite alabaster framing of a Roman glass makeup mirror. Some beautiful woman of the first century doubtless used it to behold her image and be sure that all was in place. Yet even the best of these ancient mirrors were not of the same quality as modern mirrors. Consequently, one saw through them "darkly," (*ainigma*, from which is derived the English word "enigma"). The word might better be translated "obscurely" or "with only partial accuracy." In other words, the mirrors into which the people of the first century looked gave only an imperfect image. In fact, any mirror is not the same as beholding, for example, the actual face of a friend.

Consequently, even with the Scriptures, the gifts of prophecy, and the work of knowledge, we are able to see only obscurely the things that God has prepared for us. But there is coming a time "when that which is perfect is come" and we shall see face to face. As a consequence, the partial knowledge that we experience now shall then give way to the opportunity to know even to the extent that he himself is known of God. One must be careful not to press this to the extent of total knowledge. There will never be a time when any created being will know all that God knows, but certainly the knowledge of man will be full and complete "when that which is perfect is come."

13:13 Faith and hope reside alongside love, making a trinity of virtues that every believer ought to have. It is true that each believer will not possess all the spiritual gifts, but it is equally true that every believer should possess faith, hope and love—but of the three, incomparably, the greatest is love.

Edification—The Reason For The Gifts Of The Spirit

1. The Edification of Prophecy (14:1–12)
2. The Essence of Tongues (14:13–25)
3. The Equation of Worship (14:26–40)

The final portion of Paul's discussion of the *charismata* is devoted almost entirely to a comparison between the respective merits of the gifts of prophecy and tongues. Throughout the chapter the superiority of prophecy is everywhere affirmed, and the gift of tongues is reduced to a position of relative unimportance. A fair reading of the spirit and tone of the chapter as well as the letter of the chapter is essential to any who are wooed by the neocharismatic movement in the modern era.

1. The Edification of Prophecy (14:1–12)

As Paul began to speak of the edification of prophecy, he spoke of the desirability of prophecy (vv. 1–3), the design of prophecy (vv. 4–6), and the distinction of prophecy (vv. 7–12).

14:1 The King James Version's "follow after love" is less than graphic by comparison to the Greek *diōkō*, meaning to "pursue vigorously" or "run after." The admonition may even properly belong to the latter part of chapter 13, but it fits equally well in chapter 14, to which it has been assigned. Again, it is in stark contrast to the Corinthians who were ardently pursuing of love, while at the same time being zealous for spiritual gifts. Though the word "zealous" is also vivid, it carries less stress than the command "to pursue love." And insofar as "spiritual gifts" (*pneumatika*) were to be desired, Paul added that they were to desire most of all to prophesy. This expression is the beginning of the apostle's effort to show the clear superiority of prophecy to tongues.

14:2 The King James Version has placed the word "unknown" in italics, meaning that it is not in the text. The whole problem in interpreting this chapter is to determine the precise meaning of tongue, tongues, and unknown tongues. There are basically three positions that have been advocated by various evangelical commentators.

(1) Some feel that every expression of "tongue" or "tongues" in chapter 14 is a reference to ecstatic utterance, a form of speaking which consisted of the assembling of various sounds into a staccato-like concoction of syllables which have no relation to each other and no syntax or semantic structure. Those who hold this view usually recognize that what is being discussed in this chapter is very different from what is discussed in Acts 2 on the Day of Pentecost. Robertson and Plummer, typical of those commentators who take this position, say, "Verse after verse shows that speaking in foreign languages cannot be meant . . . tongues were a sort of spiritual soliloquy addressed partly to self, partly to heaven."[59] Another such expression would be found in Ellicott's commentary, where Shore says, "Against the theory that the gift was one of a capacity to speak various languages, we have three considerations."[60] Shore goes on to mention the use of *dialektos* (which though used in Acts to express languages is not found here), the absence of any trace of the use of the gift of languages in preaching, and finally the fact that the description of the gift

---

[59]Robertson and Plummer, *First Corinthians*, p. 306.

[60]Charles John Ellicott, *Commentary on the Whole Bible*, Vol. IV, p. 340.

in 1 Corinthians is inconsistent with its being a gift of languages.[61]

(2) A second view was proposed by Charles Hodge in the modern era and John Chrysostom in the Patristic period, both of whom held that the gift being addressed in this passage did not refer to any form of ecstatic utterance but explicitly to the use of languages which had never been formally studied.

Concerning this gift of tongues, Chrysostom wrote,

> Wherefore then did the apostles receive it before the rest because they were to go abroad everywhere, and as in the time of the building of the tower, the one tongue was divided into many so then the many tongues frequently met in one man and the same person used to discourse both in the Persian, in the Roman, and in the Indian, and many other tongues, the Spirit sounding with him: and the gift was called the gift of tongues because he would all at once speak divers languages.[62]

(3) The third view, which is advocated by Spiros Zodhiates and this author, is that there are two entirely different "tongues" being discussed in this chapter. Sometimes the discussion focuses on the Acts 2 gift of language, while on other occasions the discussion focuses upon the fleshly imitation of the spiritual gift, which was popular in Corinth at the time. This fleshly imitation approximated similar exercises within the pagan religions of the district more nearly than it did the Acts 2 expression of tongues. Zodhiates argues that wherever the word *glōssa* (singular) is used, the King James translators were justified in adding the word "unknown," since what Paul had in mind was an unidentifiable form of speech that had nothing to do with the Acts 2 "tongues." He points to the use of this in verses 2, 4, 13, 14, 19, and 27. On the other hand, whenever the plural "tongues" is used, such as in verses 5, 6, 18, 21, and 23, one has, in fact, a reference to gift of languages granted upon the Day of Pentecost.[63]

Whether or not the distinction can be maintained on the basis

---

[61]Ibid.

[62]Philip Schaff, ed., *The Nicene and Post-Nicene Fathers*, Vol. 12, p. 209.

[63]Zodhiates, *Tongues? A Study of the Biblical Record from the Greek Text*, p. 74.

of the singularity or plurality of the word may be an open question, but as we shall see in the process of interpretation, Zodhiates is precisely correct in his analysis when he indicates that two different matters are being considered. The legitimate gift of tongues is the one given to the apostles in Acts 2. The Corinthian effort to imitate that gift is under discussion in portions of chapter 14, in which it is contrasted with the authentic Acts 2 gift.

Three things are affirmed concerning this Corinthian imitation. (1) Those who utilized the gift were speaking to God and not to men. This of course is precisely the opposite of the experience recorded in Acts 2, where the gospel of grace was preached to men. (2) The Corinthians did not speak to men, nor did man understand what was being said. This again is in startling contrast to the Acts 2 situation in which the inhabitants of Jerusalem at Pentecost were amazed at hearing them speak in their own languages. (3) In the Spirit, the speaker of Corinthian tongues spoke "mysteries." This last affirmation has been taken as Paul's tacit approval of the practice, based on the general New Testament usage of the word "mystery" (*mustērion*). However, "mystery" may have good, evil, or neutral significances, depending upon the context. Here Paul was not suggesting that the man was speaking the "mysteries of God," a phrase which implies the unveiling of truth that could not be ascertained except through revelation. If that kind of mystery were the subject in verse 2, then it would not be necessary for Paul to insist on an interpreter for the others who listened and apparently even for the speaker himself (v. 14). Consequently, Paul simply stated that whatever one who spoke in Corinthian tongues might have been saying remained a mystery in need of explication. This again is the very antithesis of the pentecostal experience in Acts 2 where clearly those who knew the language being spoken understood its meaning.

14:3 However, the contrast is not simply between the supernatural experience of Acts 2 and the fabricated experience of Corinth but also between the gift of tongues as practiced in Corinth and the gift of prophecy. It might even be fair to say that prophecy is considered far superior even to the phenomenal experience of Acts 2. Prophecy is superior because of its level of accomplishment. Those who prophesy speak to men rather than God. The results may be edification, exhortation, or comfort.

In this verse we are introduced to the important word "edification" (*oikodomē*), which is used repeatedly throughout this chapter and becomes the major canon for establishing the usefulness or relative lack of usefulness of spiritual gifts. The word is made up of *oikos*, meaning "house," and *domeō*, meaning "to build"—hence, the concept of the building of a house is conveyed by the expression. This sense is observable in the fact that in English we frequently refer to a building as an "edifice." "Edification," therefore, means the construction of a serviceable and helpful unit. Biblical preaching when heard and obeyed will inevitably result in the construction of a serviceable unit of life for the listener.

In addition to that, exhortation and comfort are other fruits of prophecy. An unusual word for "comfort" (*paramuthia*) is employed in this particular text in distinction to *paraklēsin*, which is often used to depict comfort and is here translated "exhortation." *Paramuthia* has an unusual etymology. *Muthos*, transliterated into English as "myth," describes a pleasant but possibly untruthful story. Literally, when combined with the preposition *para*, the word means "beside the myth" and originally described the comfort attained as a result of hearing an optimistic story. Gradually, any intent of untruthfulness dropped from the word, and the word *paramuthia* denoted "comfort" alone.

The triple objective of preaching may also be observed in this verse. Effective proclamation ought always to encompass these three elements, though perhaps in varying degrees, depending upon the overall purpose of the sermon. Prophecy should result in the building of a serviceable unit, in the exhortation or calling men to decision, and in comfort through the constant reminder of the intervention of God in behalf of men.

14:4 The stark contrast that existed between the accomplishments of prophecy and that of the Corinthian tongue is now plainly stated. The one who spoke in a tongue only succeeded in edifying himself, while those who prophesied were doing constructive labor in behalf of the whole church. This verse demonstrates clearly the basic selfishness of the Corinthian posture which had already demonstrated itself in the petty divisions within the church membership and in the despicable behavior practiced by some at the Lord's table. It also apparently manifested itself in their preoccupation with a particular gift or at least in their effort to imitate that gift.

14:5 Paul declared his wish that all the Corinthians would speak with tongues, but he added that he would rather they all would prophesy. Two things must be noted in the first phrase. First, the translators of the King James Version left out the inserted "unknown," possibly indicating their recognition that a different kind of tongue was here intended. Paul might have been saying, "I wish you all had the legitimate gift which was given to the apostles in Acts 2." Even if this was what the apostle intended, too much has been made of the translation "I would." It is simply *thelō*, which means "I wish," but by no stretch of the imagination can it be construed as a strong term expressing earnest desire. Already Paul had used the stronger terms for desire in verse 1, when he spoke of following after love (*diōkō*) and desiring (*zēloō*) spiritual gifts. *Thelō* is used here much less emphatically, indicating that Paul would not have minded if they all had spoken with tongues but also expressing his preference that they would prophesy.

The reader is not left to grope for a reason. Paul plainly stated that the one who prophesied was greater than those who spoke with tongues except in those instances where the one speaking in tongues interpreted what he had said so that the church might receive edification. Some difference of opinion exists as to whether or not such an interpretation is even possible in light of verse 14, where Paul wrote that one praying in a tongue prayed with his spirit, but his understanding was unfruitful. On the other hand, if Paul was speaking of the legitimate Acts 2 form of the gift, then very likely the one who spoke would know the meaning of what he said and could himself translate.

14:6 The case is pressed still further by resorting to the usual method of a rhetorical question. Paul suggested that, as he had previously indicated, he might soon be coming to them. He inquired concerning what possible profit there would be unless, instead of speaking in tongues, he spoke to them by way of revelation or knowledge or prophecy or doctrine.

"Doctrine" (*didachē*) generally means "teachings." "Revelation" suggests Paul's apostolic authority and is a tacit acknowledgment that he did possess information given him by God which constituted, as it were, the very voice of God Himself. The activities of passing on revelation or explaining what that revelation means through the word of knowledge or proclaiming it to the people through prophecy or teaching it to them in doctrinal statutes, all constitute activities of edification. These, therefore, are all superior to the use of tongues.

14:7 The argument is basically designed to focus on the limited usefulness of tongues and is now developed by way of illustration. Two forms of musical instruments with which the Corinthians would have had instant familiarity are cited. They are the "pipe" (*aulos*) and the "harp" (*kithara*, from which we get our English word "guitar"). There were several kinds of pipes and harps, but the point is that whether one is using a wind instrument or a stringed instrument, unless there is distinction in sound, a melody will not emerge, and no one will recognize the tune. There is nothing more than a cacophony of sound, which, if audited for any length of time, becomes oppressive and even dangerous. These pipes and harps are called "things without life," an interesting translation of *apsuchos*, which combines the alpha privative with the word *psuchē*, meaning "soul." "Soul" refers to the basic life principle that differentiates animate life from inanimate objects. Paul simply expressed that even those objects which have no animation and no power to think or to will must give a distinction in sound, or else no one will profit by their presence.

14:8 A second illustration with more serious overtones is now employed. If one has to contend only with a din of noise, it may be wearisome, but probably not fatal. The seriousness of the issue at Corinth, however, in the misuse of the gift of tongues is more like the case of a trumpet giving an uncertain sound. "Trumpet" (*salpinx*) refers to the instrument used by the signalmen of a military unit who, by the various kinds of sounds coaxed from his trumpet, would signal the onslaught of the enemy, advance, retreat, or other orders from the command post.

Prior to a day of sophisticated electronic communication, the communication via trumpet was one of the most critical aspects of military science. If the trumpet's sound, therefore, was not clear and certain, the army would fail to prepare itself for the battle. Paul's purpose here was not so much to compare the spiritual warfare of the church with the physical warfare of the world as it was to warn of the dangers of the uncertain sound.

14:9 The comparison was not left to the imagination. The apostle obviously believed in the strategic importance of verbal communication (1:21-23). It was critical that one communicate with clarity. Therefore, he said, "Except one speak by means of the tongue words which are easy to be understood, no one will know what is spoken." "Easy to be understood" (*eusēmon*) brings together the prefix *eu*, meaning "well" or "good," with *sēmeion*, meaning "sign." Therefore, Paul said, "Except you utter good signs, it shall not be known what you are saying, and for all practical purposes you will simply be speaking into the air." The depreciatory tone of the last phrase ought not to be missed by the careful leader.

14:10 Having illustrated his point from the realm of musical instruments, Paul then turned to a more didactic approach. There are any number of "voices" (*phōnos*) in the world, and none of them is without "significance" (*aphōnos*). This play on words involves the use of *phōnos*, which means "voice" or sometimes "language," as it does here. There are many different kinds of languages, Paul suggested, and not a single one of them is non-linguistic. Robertson and Plummer suggested correctly here that the meaning may be "unintelligible."[64] Paul was once again at the business of contrasting the gift given at Pentecost, which was intelligible language, of which there are many in the world, with the Corinthian effort to imitate it, which was *aphōnos*, or "unintelligible" to human understanding.

4:11 In the society of the first century, anyone who did not speak the Greek language and cherish the culture of Hellenism was considered a barbarian. The very word "barbarian" (*bar-*

---

[64]Robertson and Plummer, *First Corinthians*, p. 310.

baros) is onomatopoeic in that it refers to one whose language seems to make no sense and sounds like "barbar." The proof that *phōnos* in verse 10 means "language" becomes very apparent in verse 11, where Paul used the same word "voice" to describe the speech of someone whose language he did not know.

The point here, however, was not to speak condescendingly of those who were not a part of the Hellenistic culture but simply to point out that if one heard another speaking whose language he could not understand, the person was to him a "barbarian," the frequently condescending label used to picture basic inferiority. If that was true among intelligent beings who were actually using communicative speech, albeit the nature of the language was unfamiliar to one listening, how much more severe was the situation at Corinth where, just as it occurred among the pagan oracles, the Corinthians employed ecstatic utterance which could not be understood by anyone. Paul was suggesting that they might very well be viewed by intelligent individuals as barbarians.

14:12 The conclusion of the entire first part of the discussion was now given explicitly. "You Corinthians, therefore, are indeed to be zealous of spiritual gifts, but in that zeal see to it that you seek to excel in edifying the church of God." "Excel" (*perisseuō*) means "to be superfluous" or "to abound." In light of the previous discussion, the Corinthians were cautioned that in their zeal for the possession and demonstration of the spiritual gifts, they were to be certain that they abounded exceedingly in the use of those gifts which resulted in the upbuilding of the church family. Other gifts were to be less emphasized and less frequently employed.

2. The Essence of Tongues (14:13–25)

Further discussion of the Corinthian issue of tongues is the focus of the second section in which Paul discussed the essence of tongues. There is consideration of the liabilities of tongues (vv. 13–17), the limits of tongues (vv. 18–19), and the logistics of tongues (vv. 20–25).

14:13 The charge of this verse is to the effect that if one must speak in a tongue, then he ought to pray that God will give him the ability to "interpret" (*diermēneuō*, derived originally from Hermes, who was the messenger of the gods). In antiquity the gods were conceived as capricious beings differing little from their human counterparts, save in the powers available to aid them in their intrigues. Often they were not on speaking terms with one another and needed arbitration, and there had to be someone to interpret what the gods meant by certain outbursts to their chessmen-like servants below on the earth. That was the task of Hermes, the messenger of the gods, who interpreted among the gods and spoke to humankind also. The prefix *dia* has been added so that its most literal translation is "to interpret through." The Corinthians were thus instructed that the practice of speaking in tongues needed to be enhanced by the gift of interpretation of tongues if it was to be of significant usefulness in the church.

14:14 The reasons for Paul's insistence upon such interpretation was now elucidated. "If I pray in an unknown tongue, my spirit may indeed be involved in the act of prayer, but the understanding is unfruitful." Two things about this verse are important. First, it is clear that what was under consideration was not a known language but rather a rush of unintelligible sounds. Not even the one who uttered these sounds comprehended what was happening, and thus he needed interpretation first of all in order to explain some sense of the matter to himself. Second, Paul did not say that the spirit prayed, but there was no understanding; rather, he said the spirit prayed, but the understanding was "unfruitful." Literally, the word "mind" (*nous*) employed here gives the meaning that "the mind is unfruitful." In the Corinthian experience of tongues, the mind of the believer was completely disengaged and thus not even the whole man was involved in the act of worship. The mind, having been cut adrift, was simply neutralized and, hence, was totally unfruitful or unproductive. This would have to mean that the experience was primarily an emotional one, loosely attached to reality and void of either intellectual or volitional significance.

14:15 In light of the state of mental neutrality that was a part of the Corinthian experience of tongues, Paul advocated a different program. He began by asking his usual question: "What, therefore, is it?" The sense of the question is simply, "In light of what I've just said, what shall I do?" He answered that he knew how to pray by means of the spirit, but he would also pray by means of the mind. When he sang, his singing would also be accompanied by the spirit; but it would not neutralize his mental capacity, since he would also be singing thoughtfully. The verse may indeed suggest that while some of the Corinthians merely spoke in tongues, others were praying and singing with the unintelligible speech, and Paul was saying that it was possible to pray and sing by means of the spirit and also by means of the mind. The apostle thus focused on the fact that while it was possible to do something of some spiritual significance without the use of the mind, it was also possible to involve both the mind and the spirit at one time. The latter case was clearly preferable.

14:16 The first of two examples relating to the effect of tongues upon the audience is now marshaled. What would happen, Paul asked, to the one who occupied the room of the unlearned when he heard the blessing of the Corinthians who were using the Corinthian expression of tongues? The word "blessing" (*eulogeō*) gives us our English word "eulogy." The Greek prefix *eu* means "well" or "good." Attached to the term *logos*, meaning "word," "to bless" is "to say a good word." Any good word said about God would qualify, but it appears that Paul had in mind particularly the offering of prayers of thanksgiving. This is deduced by noticing that the latter part of the verse speaks of a "giving of thanks" (*eucharistia*). The person in question here is anyone who occupies the room of the "unlearned." The word translated "occupy" simply means "to fill full." The word "unlearned" is a translation of *idiōtēs*, which gives us our English word "idiot." However, the connotation present in our word "idiot" is totally missing from the Greek word, which simply means "one's own" and denotes a "private person" in the sense of being contrasted with officials or more mature initiates to an organization. The word is often used of private citizens in contrast to those in public life, such as magistrates.[65] The words used here

---

[65]Morris, *First Corinthians*, p. 195.

indicate that the individuals under consideration were either those who were unbelievers or, more probably, any among the Corinthians who had not had this experience of tongues and, therefore, were laymen with regard to that experience.

The question was simply, "How shall one who is in that posture say "Amen" at the giving of thanks since he does not comprehend what is being said?" "Amen" (*amēn*) derives from the Hebrew and means in both Hebrew and Greek "to affirm something to be true." Here we are granted a look into the activities of an assembly in the early church. Whenever something was spoken, sung, or even offered in prayer to God, it was a common practice for those in the congregation wishing to affirm the truthfulness of the statement to provide record of personal acquiescence by saying "Amen" or, in other words, "let it be so." One of the most interesting uses of this word in the Bible is on the occasion of Jonah's preaching to the Ninevites (Jonah 3:5). The prophet recorded, "So the people of Nineveh believed God . . . ." The word "believed" is *amēn*, meaning that the people of Nineveh acquiesced to what Jonah was preaching.

14:17 The participants in this tongues experience were not questioned as to their sincerity; neither did Paul doubt that they might well have been giving thanks. His point was that no one was being edified, and, therefore, whatever its asset may have been, the Corinthian use of tongues was of limited significance.

14:18 This verse constitutes a significant battleground among interpreters. The statement Paul made was plain enough. He was thankful to God that he spoke in tongues more than all of the Corinthians. Unfortunately, it is not clear whether Paul meant that he personally had the private practice of speaking with unintelligible sounds for his own personal edification, a practice he employed more frequently than any of the Corinthians, or whether he meant that he spoke with more tongues, i.e., languages, than all of the Corinthians put together. If he meant this latter idea, then the verse once again must refer to the use of existing languages which Paul, either by much learning, by miracle, or by both, was able to speak for the purpose of propagating the gospel. John Chrysostom, the golden-tongued orator of Antioch and Constantinople, understood the verse in the latter way.[66] In fact, it was almost unthinkable to imagine the apostle, having so critiqued this Corinthian exercise, turning again and admitting he was the most frequent practitioner of ecstatic utterance. No logic available will indicate anything other than that Paul was speaking of his own use of languages.

14:19 The possible flaw in the above reasoning is found in the content of this verse. "Yet in the church" is an expression which obviously refers to the assembly of believers. Paul affirmed that he would rather speak only five words with his understanding than ten thousand words in a tongue. The solution to the apparent discrepancy to be imagined between verses 18 and 19 is to be found in the fact that Paul was for the moment accepting that the practice which was perpetuated in Corinth was identical to that gift of the Holy Spirit given to the apostles in Acts 2. Elsewhere in the passage it is clear that Paul did not believe that it was the same gift, but for the sake of argument and for stressing a very important point, Paul here allowed that possibility. Therefore, verse 18 does not refer to ecstatic utterance but instead to his linguistic ability. Nevertheless, he was stressing to the Corinthians that whatever ability he may have had, he would rather use just five words with his understanding than ten thousand words in a tongue such as those manifested at Corinth. The statement is arresting when one considers it carefully. Paul had just suggested that whatever the limited benefits of the Corinthian practice of tongues might be, the fact remained that it was more noble and more beneficial to utter only five words that would be understood in the assembly of the saints than to have even a lengthy expression of Corinthian tongues. Modern practitioners of the Corinthian ecstatic utterance need only again to take Paul's statement to heart if they are serious about obedience to New Testament authority.

Five words spoken with understanding are more important than ten thousand in a tongue because others are being "taught" (*katēcheō*, which provides "catechism" or "catechumen," referring

---

[66]Philip Schaff, *A Select Library of the Nicene and Post-Nicene Fathers of the Christian Church*, p. 212.

in the first case to the documents used for basic initial instruction in the significance of the Christian faith and in the second case to the one being thus catechized or taught). The word is derived from *cheō*, meaning "to pour," and the preposition *kata*, meaning "down upon"—thus, "to pour down upon" and eventually "to teach or instruct." The success of anyone functioning as a believer in a hostile world is definitely related to what he understands of the word of God as well as to the power of the Holy Spirit operating within his life. Once he knows what is demanded of him, then the Spirit of God must provide the motivation and strength for faithfulness. Therefore, the catechizing or teaching of the believers assumes paramount importance.

14:20 The tender word "brethren" prepares the hearts of the Corinthians for a searching admonition. "Do not be children in understanding but be babes in malice" is an expression which makes use of two different words for "child." Both are contrasted with the word "men" (*teleioi*) in the latter part of the verse. The first word rendered "children" (*paidia*) refers to a toddler or small child who is beginning to learn some things experientially but who as yet has not real comprehension of the kind of world in which he lives. However, while the Corinthians were urged not to be like the toddler in immaturity and lack of comprehension, they were urged to be even more immature than a toddler in one aspect.

The Greek verb *nēpiazō* derives from *nēpios* and refers to an infant. Literally it renders the phrase, "you are to be innocent as a newborn infant in malice" (*kakia*). The intent of *kakia* in this content is probably "malice" or "maliciousness." Paul was cautioning the Corinthians not to indulge in malicious behavior that would be principally characterized by self-centeredness. In this regard they were to be as little encompassed by maliciousness as a newborn babe would be. In this one way childlikeness was enjoined upon the Corinthians, while childish lack of understanding was depreciated as the Corinthians were asked to be "men" (*teleioi*, "one who is perfectly mature" or "one who fully comprehends and understands") in understanding. "Understanding" (*phrēn*) and *nous*, which has been used previously in the passage, are somewhat interchangeable. J. Oliver Buswell has suggested that *nous* primarily has to do with cognition, i.e., the ability to think and understand, whereas *phrēsin* (derived from the root *phrēn*, meaning "diaphragm or midriff") refers to deep reflection, the pondering of the knowledge that is received by the mind.[67] If Buswell is accurate in his analysis, then the verse constitutes a challenge to the Corinthians not only to understand but also to ponder the things of God in a sense that a toddler would find absolutely impossible. Only the *teleioi* would be able so to ponder the things of God.

Once again the general impact of the verse is to assert the inadequacy of the Corinthian exercise of tongues. Whereas "children" (*paidia*) might be quite content just to make noise which had no particular use, "mature men" (*teleioi*) desire those sounds which are communicative and edifying.

14:21 Paul's next appeal was directly to the Scriptures. He cited Isaiah 28:11 as indication of God's real purpose in the gift of tongues. "With men of other tongues and other lips will I speak unto this people; and yet for all that will they not hear me, saith the Lord." There was also a possible reference here to Deuteronomy 28:49, a similar passage. The Isaiah text arose out of the imminent threat of an Assyrian invasion of Israel. Assyria, as usual, would be "the rod of God's chastisement." This people, whose language was very different from that of the Hebrews, would be a constant threat to the people of God. However, Isaiah was cautioning the people that rather than seeing the Assyrians as a threat, the people of Israel should view them as God's way of calling the people back to repentance.

For the purposes of interpretation of chapter 14, this verse is of paramount importance. There remains no question but that this verse refers to the speaking of intelligible, existing languages—not to ecstatic utterance that has no form or significance. As such, the verse serves as an introduction to the very important contrast that will be made in verses 22 and 23. This is the contrast which, more than any other, establishes the fact that there are really two different kinds of tongues under consider-

---

[67]J. Oliver Buswell, *A Systematic Theology of the Christian Religion*, p. 239.

ation—the gift of tongues as given by the Holy Spirit in Acts 2, and the imitation of the gift as practiced in Corinth.

"Other tongues" (*heteroglōssos*) combines "tongues" with *heteros*, meaning "another of a different kind." Clearly this refers to a different language.

14:22 Just as Isaiah used the foreign tongue of the Assyrian invaders as a sign of the imminent judgment of God, so the gift of tongues constituted a sign for those who did not believe the gospel. The Corinthians were using their ecstatic utterance as a sign for believers in the church, much as modern neocharismatics, to demonstrate that they were, in fact, spiritual. Thus the Corinthian imitation of the Acts 2 gift was featured as a sign for believers. Paul here affirmed that this was not at all the intent of the gift of tongues. The original intent of the miraculous disposition of tongues at Pentecost was as a "sign" (*sēmeion*) for unbelievers.

A cursory reading of the Acts 2 account will undoubtedly reveal this effect of the miracle. When those gathered at Pentecost from every nation imaginable heard Galileans who would normally have been speaking Aramaic proclaim the gospel in an assortment of languages that they obviously had not had opportunity to learn, the conclusion was inescapable: "God has done this." The further point is made that prophecy, while having beneficial effects for unbelievers, also uniquely serves the purpose of the believing community. The contrast pressed concerns the understanding of "tongues," which in its legitimate pentecostal expression was a sign to unbelievers that God was really at work. The church needs no such sign but rather needs the edification of prophecy.

14:23 A hypothetical case is now provided. If the whole church comes together in one place and all are speaking with tongues and those who are unlearned or unbelievers should come, their conclusion upon hearing the widely distributed Corinthian ecstatic utterance would be that these who speak are not rational. The King James Version, "will they not say ye are mad," is a translation of *mainomai*, from which is derived our work "mania," referring to a state of unreality or even hallucination. Paul averred that the unlearned and the unbelievers' natural conclusion about the Corinthian imitation would be that the Corinthians were loosely attached to reality and perhaps were even hallucinating. Once again, the word for "unlearned" is *idiōtēs*, while "unbeliever" is *apistos*, literally "without faith."

The contrast between verses 22 and 23 is startling. In verse 22 we are told that tongues are a sign for unbelievers; yet in verse 23 we are informed that if unbelievers were present when the Corinthians spoke with tongues, their conclusion would be to question the sanity of the Corinthians. These two verses constitute a hopeless contradiction incapable of resolution unless, in fact, there are two different subjects under consideration. This, of course, is precisely what is happening. In verse 22, the apostle was speaking of the actual sign—the gift of tongues—which was given to the apostles in Acts 2. Verse 23, on the other hand, discusses the Corinthian effort to reproduce that miracle—an effort which fell so far short of the authentic spiritual gift that its exercise appeared ludicrous to the very unbelievers who should have been convinced by the sign.

One other interesting consideration in this verse concerns the expression, "if the whole church is gathered together." The words indicate two salient New Testament truths. First, a local congregation of believers, wherever it is gathered, is the body of Christ in fullness of expression, even though geographically it is a local assembly. There is certainly a doctrine of the universal church of all believers taught in the New Testament, but the primary use of the word "church" is in regard to the local assembly. Second, from this passage it may be deduced that there were many meetings of portions of the church in a single locality, but the whole church also assembled together at regularly stated times.

14:24 Again, in contrast to the result anticipated when an unbeliever was faced with the murmur of Corinthian tongues, Paul suggested that in the event all should prophesy, and if in the midst of that prophecy there should come to the assembly one who did not believe or who was unlearned, the results might be calculated to be very different. The unlearned or unbeliever would be convinced by all and judged of all. What makes this particular contrast especially poignant is the fact that verse 22 stresses that tongues are a sign for unbelievers, while prophesying is for the benefit of those who believe and not for unbelievers per se. However, verse 23 suggests that the use of Corinthian prattle will turn away the unbeliever, even though tongues should be a sign to him. The irony of the matter is explicated in this verse. When we prophesy, which is supposed to be for the benefit of believers, it actually has a profound effect on unbelievers and the unlearned in that it is used of God to convince and to judge. "Convince" (*elenchō*) means that the unbeliever is "convinced of all" or "convicted of" his sin and his need of Christ. Furthermore, he is "judged of all" (*anakrinō*). This word does not mean "judge" in the sense of "condemn," but rather it is a forensic term which literally means "cross-examination." The listener is not only convicted and convinced by what he hears, but also he finds himself profoundly cross-examined by the word of God and by the Holy Spirit working to bring conviction in his heart.

14:25 The result of this process is that the secrets or the hidden things of his heart are made manifest. This is not so much a manifestation to others, though that may also happen, as it is an inner manifestation. Men outside of Christ are never sensitive to the extent of their own sinfulness or the love and mercy of the Savior. When the unbeliever is convinced and cross-examined by the word of God and the Holy Spirit, he sees the corruption of his own heart in light of the mercy of God. As a result, he falls on his face and worships God and announces to everyone that God is truly resident within the believing community. One must note carefully the resulting contrast. The anticipated result of the use of tongues in the congregation is the conclusion on the part of the unbelievers that sanity has passed from the practitioner of tongues, but where prophecy prevails in the assembly, there are three anticipated results. First, men are deeply convicted and judged by what they hear. Second, as a result, they fall down and worship God. Third, the report goes out, not that the people are beside themselves, but rather that God truly dwells in them. It is almost impossible to overemphasize this conclusion. Then, as now, there were some who felt that in the use of ecstatic, unintelligible murmuring others would find indication of godliness and the presence of the indwelling Spirit.

Paul insisted that the very opposite was the case. In fact, if we wish true conviction, authentic conversion, and genuine evangelism in which converts testify to the fact that God indwells believers, then the church should specialize in prophesying rather than in tongues.

3. The Equation of Worship (14:26–40)

The concluding section of the discussion of spiritual gifts focuses on an equation for worship. Initially the discussion concerns the benefit of peace (vv. 26–33), followed by the behavior of women (vv. 34–35), and concluding with the blessing of order (vv. 36–40). The focus is on certain rules that were to be the established guidelines for worship at Corinth and in all the churches of the saints. The worship of the church was not, therefore, strictly programmed. Much freedom was allowed, but there were certain principles that would have to be observed. The concluding section of this chapter provides these principles growing naturally out of the discussion of spiritual gifts which occupied the apostle's attention for a considerable portion of the letter.

14:26 The first of seven principles is enunciated in this verse. The church was told that when it came together it may well have been that every member of the assembly had a psalm, a doctrine, a tongue, a revelation, or an interpretation. This listing of possibilities is, of course, only partial. The important consideration is the concluding principle which marks the first of the seven: "Let all things be done with the end result being edification." In effect, Paul was excluding from the assembly the use of any approach or the exercise of any supposed gift which did not, in fact, result in the building up of the assembly. The emphasis here is on the "coming together," which should form the basis upon which the meaning of verse 39 is understood. Paul would not forbid men to speak with tongues, but by the same token he did forbid it in the assemblies unless it resulted in the edifying of the people. One note concerns the use of the word "psalm." The psalms constituted the songbook or hymnal for Israel. The singing of these psalms was a form of musical expression also frequently used in the New Testament church.

14:27 Three principles for worship in a New Testament assembly are provided in this verse. Principle two: "If anyone speaks in a tongue, let it be by two, or at the most by three." This prohibition simply states that in a given assembly of the church there will never be more than three and preferably only two who speak in a tongue. The subject is still "when you come together," and thus the rule is applicable to the assemblies of the saints. Principle three dictates that any speaking in a tongue is to be done "by course" or "one after another." In other words, those speaking in tongues are forbidden to do so simultaneously. According to principle four, there is to be an interpreter whenever speaking in tongues occurs.

14:28 The fourth principle concerning the requiring of an interpreter is expanded in this verse—a testimony to the fact that the apostle wanted to be certain that he was clearly understood in the matter. If there is not an interpreter, the one who thought he might speak in tongues is to keep silent in the church and speak only to himself and to God. The difficulty in this verse is not in understanding the principle but in discerning just exactly how the principle was to be legislated. For example, did a person know ahead of time that he was going to have an experience of tongues, and did he therefore search out an interpreter in advance? Or, on the other hand, was there a call made for an interpreter as soon as the ecstatic utterance began? The third possibility, which would be the completion of the experience before an interpreter was sought, is rendered highly improbable by the fact that the practitioner of tongues apparently was not to speak at all if there were no interpreter. The precise logistics may elude the interpreter, but Paul's point certainly does not. The effect of the principle once again is virtually to eliminate the use of tongues in the midst of the assembled church. The absence of an interpreter means that one who would speak must remain "silent" (*sigatō*), a strong word which calls for absolute silence.

14:29 On the other hand, the prophets were urged to speak, two or three of them, and the others who had the gift of prophecy were to "judge" (*diakrinō*). This word does not imply harshness of judgment or even the offering of a critique—rather, it is the assignment of analyzing the spiritual message being delivered. A good translation would be "to discriminate" or "to discern." Thus we are reminded that one of the gifts given to the church is that of discernment, and Paul was suggesting that such an important gift was to be constantly exercised as one of the most crucial gifts in the assembly. Here the gift of prophecy is used in the sense of one who speaks the word of God before the people. This preaching or interpretation of the word of God must always be subject to the authority of the Spirit of God. Therefore, the gift of discernment assumes a position of importance right alongside that of preaching the word.

14:30 Furthermore, there is always the prospect that a special insight in the word of God may be revealed to one of the prophets sitting by who had not really been scheduled to preach on that particular day. In such a case, the first is to hold his peace. Once again the word is *sigatō*, which means that the first man is simply to cease speaking, take his seat, and allow the one who had been listening to rise and speak. This procedure provides yet another insight into the work of the early church. Presumably the two or three prophets who were to speak had prepared for that task—they had a word from God. Obviously, more than one was frequently involved in the preaching task. However, a wonderful liberty existed within those assemblies so that if the Lord saw fit to provide a unique insight to some who sat by, they, too, could rise and share that perception. In such a case, temporarily setting aside the one who was supposed to speak was not uncommon.

14:31 In fact, Paul concluded that all might prophesy as long as they did so one at a time, because God reveals different things to different people; and as all the people share insights that God has given in His word, the congregation learns and the saints are comforted. The mutual spirit of sharing as well as the work of the Holy Spirit in each member of the congregation is thereby acknowledged.

14:32 The rationale for one prophet ceasing his instruction in order that another, to whom God had spoken, might speak is now suggested in that the spirits of the prophets are subject to the prophets. Once again it is difficult to underestimate the significance of this particular verse. The contrast once again focuses on the difference between prophecy and tongues. In the Corinthian experience of tongues, the spirit of the one who was speaking in tongues was not subject to him. In other words, since the intellect was disengaged the person often was unable to control what he was doing or saying—perhaps a trance-like demeanor was observable—but in the case of prophecy, such was not the case. On the contrary, the spirits of the prophets were "subject" (*hupotassō*) to the prophets. *Hupotassō* is a military term derived from *tithēmi*, meaning "to place," and the preposition *hupo*, meaning "under." It is the voluntary act by which one places himself under the command of the ranking officer. The spirits of the prophets are not out of control, but are in subjection to the prophet himself. Thus, one who has planned to speak may choose to permit another to speak in his place in deference to the moving of the Spirit of God, because the prophet's spirit is controlled by the prophet.

14:33 One can scarcely overestimate the importance of Paul's reminder in this verse. The King James Version has added the explanatory words "the author," but the verse is better rendered without them. The verse simply declares that God is not of confusion but of peace. "Confusion" (*akatastasia*) comes from *kathistēmi*, which means "to be tranquil or stable." The alpha privative prefix reverses the meaning to "disorder," "sedition," or "disruption." The verse then affirms that God is not in disorder, commotion, and tumult. As the entire universe testifies, He is preeminently a God of order, harmony, and purpose. Those aspects of Christian worship which do not reflect that order are immediately suspect.

In addition, God not only is not present in disorder but He also is preeminently a God of "peace" (*eirēnē*), a beautiful word which describes not only the absence of conflict but also a deep tranquility like that of which Paul spoke when he mentioned the "peace of God that passes all understanding" (Phil. 4:7). Consequently, this condition of peace, as opposed to upheaval, for which Paul called in the church at Corinth ought also to be the case in all the churches of the saints.

14:34 The fifth principle for worship is now provided. The women are to "keep silent" (*sigatō*) in the churches. It is not permitted for them to speak. The precise meaning of this verse has been the subject of increasing interest in the present era. Some have interpreted the verse to mean that Paul was prohibiting women from speaking in the church under any circumstances, while others have argued that this was merely a cultural accommodation based on a specific problem that existed in the Corinthian church—hence, its applicability was only to the first-century culture and perhaps even restricted only to the church at Corinth. The difficulty with this latter interpretation is that the women were told to be silent and to remain under obedience "as also saith the law." In the following verse it is stated that "it is a shame for women to speak in the church." Furthermore, Paul's treatment of a similar theme in 1 Timothy 2 makes it clear that there were theological reasons bound up in this limitation, and not merely cultural circumstances.

In 1 Timothy 2:9-15 women are told to "learn in silence" and not to teach or usurp authority over men. The reasons given are theological in nature. The first reason offered is the priority of Adam's creation. The second reason given is Eve's act of transgression in having been deceived. These verses, whatever else they may mean, seem to rule out the possibility of mere conformity to the culture of the first century. There is a real issue here. On the other hand, the first interpretation is also fraught with difficulties. If Paul was saying that women are never to speak in church, then he seems to have been in contradiction with himself when he allowed a woman to pray or prophesy provided her head was covered (11:5). In addition, there are other explicit references to women in teaching roles in the epistles of Paul.

The resolution to this problem is in a consideration of the context. The statement insisting on the silence of women in chapter 14 is in two respects very different from the statement that occurs in 1 Timothy 2. First, the context of chapter 14 is clearly a discussion of spiritual gifts and the misunderstandings and abuses of those gifts in the church at Corinth. Apparently some women in the church at Corinth were the ones who were principally involved in the exercise of speaking in tongues. Paul's fifth principle governing the worship of the church and the use of tongues, then, was a prohibition against women speaking in tongues. In fact, any other interpretation of the statement in verse 34 so wrenches the verse from the context in which it occurs as to make it almost inexplicable. On the other hand, this interpretation fits naturally with the entire discussion and constitutes a fifth principle for governing the use of tongues in the church.

A second major difference between this and 1 Timothy 2 is the language employed. In verse 34, *sigatō* is a strong word meaning "absolute silence"; whereas in 1 Timothy 2 the word for "silence" is *hēsuchia*, a word which primarily has to do with an attitude of quietness—a term which does not imply a prohibition against all speech in the church. In addition, however, there are similarities in the two accounts. It is clear that the expression in 1 Timothy has been given in the context of the importance of domestic life. In the home God has ordained that the husband should be the spiritual leader. The same theme of 1 Timothy 2 is also recognizable in 1 Corinthians 14. Women were to be under obedience "as also says the law." The question may be asked, "Obedience to whom?" The law called for obedience to one's husband. That same theme will be elucidated further in the following verse. In addition to the strong word *sigatō*, meaning "silence," Paul added, "it is not permitted unto them to speak." "Permitted" (*epitrepō*) means literally "it is not turned in their direction to speak." Both of these strong statements constitute only a prohibition for speaking in tongues.

14:35 It is also true that any kind of behavior in the church which would place a woman in decisive leadership over men was forbidden—hence, if women wished to learn anything, they were to ask their husbands at home because "it is a shame for a woman to speak in the church." Perhaps the women in the church at Corinth were not only the principal abusers of this gift of tongues but were also blatant in their questioning of those who stood to prophesy or to teach. Such behavior was not becoming to a woman who was under the authority of her husband. It certainly manifested anything but the "meek and quiet spirit" called for in 1 Peter 3; so women were told that if they wished to question, they were to ask their husbands at home, for it brought shame on the masculine leadership of the church and upon the women themselves for them to speak in arrogant ways in the church of God.

14:36 The rhetorical questions of this verse seem to have been anticipation on Paul's part that there would be objection raised against what he had just written. He knew that what he had said would not be palatable to some of the women and perhaps even to some of the men. Therefore, he began to pose questions about the origin of authority among the Corinthians. "Did the word of God come from you or did it come unto you only?" The impact of the question was to remind the Corinthians that they were not the harbingers of the good news of Christ—rather, Paul had been sent to them with the word of God, and consequently what he said remained the authority of God to them, whether they found it palatable and desirable or not.

14:37 The sixth principle to be observed by the church is enunciated as a result of the preferred answer to the rhetorical question of verse 36. Since the word of God came to the Corinthians by Paul, then any man who considered himself to be a prophet or thought of himself as a spiritual one was to acknowledge that the things Paul had written to the Corinthians were the commandments of God. Two facets of this verse are very important. First, the phrase "those who think of themselves as prophets or spiritual" needs a brief explanation. "Prophets" is clearly understood, but those who thought themselves to be the "spiritual ones" (*pneumatikos*) apparently were the ones who were claiming to have superiority in their spiritual gifts—particularly the gift of tongues as practiced in Corinth. Paul was simply saying that "if a man thus claims to be spiritual and to possess these spiritual gifts, then let him demonstrate that spirituality by acknowledging that the things I have written to you are the very commandments of God."

The second facet of this strategically important principle is the obvious claim on the part of the apostle Paul that what he had written constituted the very commandment of the Lord. This is not an insignificant affirmation. The apostle had in one sentence not only ascribed to his own letter, which we call 1 Corinthians, the very voice and mind of God, but he had also equated 1 Corinthians with the writings of the law and the prophets of the Old Testament. That Paul should declare that what he had written constituted the very commands of God must either be true or the boast of an egocentric fool whose view of himself was hopelessly exaggerated. One needs to look no further than this for an argument for the verbal inspiration of Scripture. Paul was not asserting that his ideas alone were the thoughts of God but rather that the very things he had written were the commandments of the Lord. Furthermore, he suggested that a true test of genuine spirituality and of legitimate prophecy was the willingness of the prophets and those who claimed to be spiritual to accept without debate the things he had written as the very commands of the Lord. Conformity to the words of Paul as being the commandments of the Lord is the sixth principle governing the use of spiritual gifts in the early church.

14:38 On the other hand, the observation that "if any man be ignorant" he was to be let alone in his ignorance was not an unfeeling or deterministic observation. Some of the better manuscripts of this particular passage read "he is not known" rather than "let him be ignorant" (*agnoeō*). If these manuscripts are accurate, the sense of the passage is that "if a man be determined to remain ignorant, then he is not to be recognized by the church of God as a spiritual leader or a prophet." This interpretation not only is most harmonious with the ancient manuscripts but also fits logically into the discussion begun in verse 37. In the event a man was determined not to acknowledge as true what Paul had written, then the church under no circumstances should acknowledge him to be a prophet or a spiritual leader.

14:39 Paul then arrived at the conclusion of the whole matter. The church was to covet the gift of prophecy and was not to forbid speaking with tongues. "Forbid" (*kōluō*) means to "hinder," "restrain," or "prevent." The statement once again emphasizes the relative unimportance of tongues in comparison with prophecy. However, the Corinthians were not to prevent speaking with tongues. Precisely what Paul meant by this must be understood in the light of the total emphasis of chapter 14. The Corinthian effort at tongues had been reduced in every conceivable way to a position of relative unimportance.

In addition to this, six principles governing the use of tongues in the Corinthian congregation have already been given , and a seventh will follow in the last verse. These principles effectively circumscribe the use of tongues altogether in the assembly of believers. Nevertheless, for two reasons Paul said that tongues are not to be forbidden. First, he had already allowed that if one engaged in ecstatic utterance in privacy, while there was no real significance, edification, or meaning to be found in it, it was not thereby evil or wrong. That private experience might be permitted to the person. In the second place, Paul knew that the Acts phenomenon of speaking the wonderful works of God in a language in which the speaker was untutored had really happened. Furthermore, Paul knew that under the right circumstances it might happen again. The necessity for the revival of these sign gifts such as tongues seems to be unlikely, but Paul did allow that possibility.

14:40 The last governing principal for the work of the church, and particularly for governing the use of tongues, is that all things be done decently and according to order. "Decently" (*euschēmonōs*) combines *schēma*, meaning "a temporary pattern," with the prefix *eu*, meaning "good" or "well." In other words, all things done in the church were to be according to a becoming or decent pattern and, furthermore, were to be "in order" (*taxis*). *Taxis* was often used to speak of regulated conduct or of distinctive classes of individuals, such as, for example, priests. The significance of the concept is that there is to be a good pattern and observable order in the churches of the Lord. This seventh principle once again does not prohibit freedom in worship and was not designed to create a high church order with rigidly prescribed rituals. It is only a principle which prohibits spiritual anarchy and uncontrolled outbursts which could nullify the impact of the gospel on those who are lost.

These seven principles, if applied to the services of worship in the assemblies of the saints and especially to the exercise of the gift of tongues, would act as regulators to prevent misconduct in the church—especially that misconduct which may be erroneously ascribed to the Holy Spirit.

Baptism For The Dead

1. Undeniability of the Resurrection (15:1-11)
2. Unassailability of the Resurrection (15:12-19)
3. Unconquerability of the Resurrection (15:20-34)
4. Untaintability of the Resurrection (15:35-49)
5. Unimpeachability of the Resurrection (15:50-58)

One major problem perplexing the Corinthian Christian remained. Chapter 15 deals with the question of the reality of the resurrection. Verse 29, which has been so frequently misinterpreted, has been used as a chapter title to focus on the fact that, if properly interpreted, this verse becomes the sense around which the whole chapter is built.

1. Undeniability of the Resurrection (15:1-11)

An examination of the undeniability of the resurrection will focus on the saving of the eternal soul (vv. 1-2), the sighting of the resurrected Christ (vv. 3-8), and the serving of a gracious God (vv. 9-11).

15:1 "I declare" (*gnōrizō*) literally means "I make known to you." Paul used this word to spell out in very emphatic terms that precise nature of the gospel he had preached. The next phrase makes use of two different forms of "gospel." First, the noun form of "good news" is employed, followed by the verbal form, which is usually translated "to preach" or "to preach the gospel." *Euangelizomai* is in the middle voice, thus emphasizing the subject's participation in the action. In this way Paul stressed his own participation in the gospel he had preached. Furthermore, it was received by the Corinthians, and in that gospel they now " stand" (*hestēkate*, a prefect tense of the verb *histēmi*). The Greek perfect tense tends to speak of an action accomplished in the past, the consequences of which continue infinitely into the future. The expression, therefore, suggests that once the Corinthians received the gospel, they stood in it at that time and continued to stand in it even at the time of Paul's writing. This is another passage that emphasizes the permanency of the salvation bestowed upon us by the Lord.

The order of discussion in the verse is also important. First, the gospel is preached. However, even though it is true and even though it is faithfully proclaimed, the benefits of it must be received by those for whom Christ died. Reception of the benefits, in turn, enables a man to stand in Christ and have assurance of this relationship before God.

15:2 The structure of this particular verse is somewhat difficult, but the general meaning is plain enough. First, it was the gospel that was saving the Corinthians. The verb *sōzō* is in the present tense, indicating continual action. Once again the stress is on the perpetuity and permanence of salvation in Christ. Those who had received the preaching of the gospel were being saved, provided the Corinthians had genuinely grasped the word Paul had preached to them. The King James Version translated *katechō* as "keep in memory," but the term combines *echō*, which means "to have" or "to hold," and the preposition *kata*, which means "down"—hence, "to hold down" or "grasp."

The possibility that the Corinthians had heard the word preached and outwardly acquiesced while inwardly never grasping the real significance of the gospel was clearly proposed by Paul when he suggested that they possibly believed to no purpose or in vain. Robertson and Plummer suggest that "in vain" is not a good translation of *eikē* in this particular case, and they propose that it means "without consideration," "heedlessly," or "rashly."[68] This is the better understanding of the word. The verse in no sense allows for the possibility of the loss of salvation but rather declares the possibility of a hasty commitment to Christ which is less than saving faith, the commitment represented in that seed which fell on rocky ground and sprang up immediately but withered when the heat of the sun scorched it. The reason given for the failure of the seed is that it had no root in itself (Matt. 13:5-6). The same situation is depicted in this verse.

15:3 Paul was not an eyewitness to the events that surrounded the actual crucifixion, burial, and resurrection of Christ. Though he could have been in Jerusalem at the time, it seems rather improbable, since most of Jerusalem apparently was to some degree caught up in the events of that Passover season. Paul stated, however, that he had given or delivered to the Corinthians first of all what he himself had received. Later he would claim an apostolic first-hand experience with the resurrected Lord, but that, as we shall see, was a special appearance of Christ, after the elapsing of a fair amount of time. Consequently Paul wrote, "about these first matters I am speaking to you out of the experience of having myself received the witness about Christ."

The first essential feature of the preaching Paul had heard was that Christ died concerning our sins. The choice of *huper* ("for") alerts the reader to a special use of this preposition, which becomes important in later verses in the chapter. *Huper* in this case means "concerning" or "with reference to" and demonstrates that Christ's death was necessitated due to the sins of the people. No plainer statement could be imagined to the effect that Jesus paid the ransom "with reference to" the sins of the world. His death was a satisfaction of the just demands of the righteousness of God against iniquity. The affirmation that Christ died for our sins is said to be "according to the scriptures." Due to the rela-

---

[68]Robertson and Plummer, *First Corinthians*, p. 332.

tively early date of 1 Corinthians, it is unlikely that Paul had reference here to any New Testament document in circulation at that time, although it is remotely possible that copies of Matthew or Mark might have been available even at this early date. More likely the reference is to the Scriptures of the Old Testament, such as the Suffering Servant passage of Isaiah 53.

15:4 Following His crucifixion, Jesus was buried in the tomb of His wealthy Arimathean disciple, Joseph, but He was raised on the third day, again "according to the scriptures." The fact of the emphasis on the burial of Jesus is important to a full grasp of His resurrection. Observers, in some number, knew of His burial and even saw the body placed in the tomb. There can be no doubt about the facts of His death or burial.

A second observation in this verse is that He was raised again (*egeirō*) on the third day. The verb's perfect tense stresses that He was raised from the dead and continues in that risen state. Its passive voice indicates that He was the recipient of the action of the Heavenly Father when the Father raised Him from the dead. All of this is also said to be "according to the scriptures." The evidence for the resurrection in the Old Testament is not so abundant as for the crucifixion. On the other hand, Isaiah 53:10–12 certainly implies the resurrection of the Suffering Servant, and in the preaching of the early church, Psalm 16:10 was employed in the same way.

15:5 The evidences which support Paul's proclamation of the resurrection of Christ are now gathered. First of all, Paul recalled that the risen Lord was seen by Cephas and then by the twelve. The reference to being seen by the twelve includes the experience in the Upper Room, in which the resurrected Lord appeared to the disciples with Thomas absent and then again with Thomas present (John 20:19–31). Both instances are included under the one heading. He was seen first of all by Simon Peter (Luke 24:34).

15:6 The next reference to the risen Lord was His appearance to more than five hundred brethren. This appearance was "at once" (*ephapax*, combining *hapax*, meaning "once," and the preposition *epi*, meaning "upon," so that the meaning is "upon one occasion"). It is as if the apostle anticipated the argument that some of the early disciples were either hallucinating or were guilty of rapturous desires to have the Lord back again, which resulted in visions and perceptions that were not real. Paul wrote that such was not the case because He was seen alive by more the five hundred brethren at one time. One other salient piece of information is then added. Out of these who saw the Lord alive, the greater part were still alive at the time of Paul's writing of 1 Corinthians. Some had "fallen asleep" (*koimomaomai*, from which is derived our English word "cemetery"). *Koimomaomai* is a euphemism given by Paul to say that some had died, but most were available for any assessment that anyone would like to make of their testimony. It is as though Paul was giving an invitation to the Corinthian doubters to find these people and ask them their experience with the living Christ.

15:7 Still more information is added in that He was seen by James and then one last time by all of the apostles. The latter reference is probably to His appearance to the disciples at the time of ascension. The appearance to James is mentioned in the New Testament only here, and it is not certain which James was intended. James, the son of Zebedee, would be the most likely, but in light of his early martydom it may be that the living witness was a different James. If that is the case, the James in view would more probably be James, the half brother of Jesus and the pastor of the church in Jerusalem—the one who apparently was convinced to become a follower of Jesus by the constraining evidence of the resurrection. James the Less or James the son of Alpheus could also be the figure but that seems less likely. Perhaps in light of the impact of the resurrection upon James, the half brother of Jesus, it is best to see him as intended. The concluding reference to His appearance to all the apostles is a reference to the time of the ascension.

15:8 One last appearance is mentioned by Paul. Last of all, the apostle said, "He was seen by me under unique and remarkable circumstances." Actually ten separate appearances of the risen Christ are recorded. Some of these are not mentioned by Paul. It is almost certain that the apostle knew of all these appearances and, in fact, wrote of at least one and maybe two of which we would otherwise be uninformed. For some reason he did not see fit to refer to all of them.

Apparently he had chosen to refer to the appearances to Cephas (or Peter) and James as witnesses whom the Corinthians themselves would have held in such esteem that they could not be doubted. Furthermore, the appeal twice to the twelve had the advantage of indicating not only a multiple witness to His resurrection but also, again, a witness in which every one of the observers would have been held in high regard. Finally, the mention of five hundred seems to be an effort at establishing a cumulative witness and saying, in effect, that this many people surely could not have been hallucinating.

The ten appearances that are mentioned in the Scriptures are these:

(1) Mary Magdalene and the other Mary (Matt. 28:9; John 20:16–17),

(2) Peter (1 Cor. 15:5; Luke 24:34),

(3) Cleopas and his friend (Luke 24:13–32),

(4) The apostles without Thomas (Luke 24:36–49; John 20:19–24),

(5) The apostles with Thomas (John 20:26–29),

(6) A group of over five hundred people (1 Cor. 15:6),

(7) The seven disciples by the sea (John 21:1–23),

(8) James (1 Cor. 15:7),

(9) The apostles for the Great Commission and Ascension (Matt. 28:16–20; Luke 24:50; Acts 1:6–11),

(10) Paul (1 Cor. 15:8; Acts 9:3–6).

The strange nature of Christ's appearance to Paul is bound up in the fact that this appearance took place as a post-ascension appearance—the only incident of its kind in the history of the church. Its unusual timing is noted by the apostle. The English expression "as one born out of due time" (*ektrōma*) literally means "an abortion." The purpose of the verse is not to suggest a comparison between the timing of an abortion as preceding the regular time for birth. In fact, what transpired was just the opposite. Long after the other appearances of the risen Lord, there was a special appearance to Paul. The sense then of *ektrōma* is this: like the unexpected termination of a hopeful pregnancy with delivery at an unannounced moment, so the resurrected Christ appeared to Paul at a most unexpected moment—a moment that did not conform to what one would have anticipated.

15:9 These thoughts evoked in the apostle a paean of praise to the God who graciously smiled upon him with such an appearance. First, Paul spoke of his inadequacy, expressing the conviction that he was the least of the apostles and really not worthy to be called an apostle. The reasons for his unworthiness went beyond the appalling sinfulness which renders us all unworthy of God's love and extended, in the case of Paul, to the fact that he was an ardent persecutor of the church of God. His position as grand inquisitor for the church of God not only caused Paul much sorrow but also increased his admiration and appreciation for God's grace.

15:10 In this verse, God's grace became the subject of Paul's enthusiasm, for to that grace he owed what he had become. Furthermore, he wanted the Corinthians to be aware that the grace of God was not bestowed upon him without result. In appreciation and gratitude to God for that grace, he labored more abundantly than all of the other apostles. "Labored" (*kopiaō*, from which we derive our English word "copious") reflects strenuous and arduously prolonged labor. That this was no mere boast on the part of Paul becomes apparent in the reading of his epistles and the book of Acts. However, even this labor he ascribed to the grace of God, stressing that it was not he who did it but rather the grace of God that was with him. Not only, then, is the grace of God essential to the saving of the soul, but also it is prerequisite to effective service to Christ.

15:11 Paul's conclusion regarding all of the apostles was that whether they labored or Paul labored, the gospel which had been presented was what they all with one accord preached, and it was also what the Corinthians had believed. The essence of the gospel, then, which had been proclaimed by all the apostles and believed by the true disciples of Christ, was that Christ died for our sins, was buried, and rose again on the third day. Any addition to the essential elements of the gospel is to subtract from the glory of what God has done in Christ.

2. Unassailability of the Resurrection (15:12-19)

In this section Paul alluded to the influence of Greek philosophy (v. 12), employed graphic parables (vv. 13-17), and spoke of great predicaments (vv. 18-19). In this particular section the apostle stipulated seven consequences which would naturally obtain if, in fact, Christ had not risen from the dead.

15:12 In Corinth there obviously were those who were preaching that Christ had not risen from the dead. The pervading ideas of Greek philosophy viewed all materiality as essentially evil and spirituality as essentially good. Consequently, a better state could be anticipated when the imprisoned spirit was liberated from its aging, fleshly burden at death. The Greeks could not imagine the return of the soul to such a prison as the body in some other life. This influence of Greek philosophy may be observed early in its impact on the Sadducees in the day of Jesus. Obviously it was also making itself felt in Corinth. The apostle had just spent time defining precisely the nature of the gospel. He had concluded that both the death and resurrection of Jesus Christ were essential elements in that gospel. Paul's argument, then, took this form: (1) the gospel includes the triumphant resurrection of Jesus; (2) this was the gospel that was preached by the apostles who were themselves eyewitnesses of the resurrected Christ; (3) the number of witnesses to the resurrection provides overwhelming cumulative evidence in its favor; (4) Paul himself had seen the resurrected Christ, although under unusual circumstances; (5) since this preaching was a part of the gospel and was so vividly verified, how could it be that some of the Corinthians were questioning the fact of the resurrection?

It is possible that the resurrection primarily in question was not that of Jesus but that of believers in the age to come. Paul, however, was about to argue that either there is or there is not a resurrection. If Jesus is, in fact, risen, then that lays to rest the possibility that there is no resurrection.

15:13 Such reasoning of the apostle is now specifically applied to Christ and His followers with the seven negative consequences which are inevitable if, in fact, there is no resurrection. The first of these is that if there is no resurrection of the dead, then Christ is not risen. "Resurrection" is a picturesque word derived from *anastasis*, which in turn is made up of the preposition *ana*, meaning "again," and *histēmi*, meaning "to stand" or "to make to stand"—hence, the meaning "to stand again." When one dies he is, of course, no longer able to experience any kind of locomotion or even to remain erect. The continuation of life in Greek thinking did not necessitate such, but the Old Testament obviously anticipated such a reality as the resurrection, and it is also everywhere affirmed in the New Testament. The expression "resurrection of the dead" is literally "resurrection from the dead." Death here refers to the cessation of physiological function, but, Paul declared, out of the state there is a resurrection. If no such reality is possible, then the first conclusion must be Christ Himself is not risen.

15:14 Two additional consequences are provided in this verse. Growing naturally out of the conclusion of verse 13 that if there is no resurrection Christ is not risen, then it must be conceded that if Christ be not risen then the preaching of the apostles and of Paul was vain. Furthermore, since "faith cometh by hearing, and hearing by the word of God" (Rom. 10:17), the faith of the Corinthians was also in "vain" (*kenos*, meaning "empty" or "altogether void of content"). The result of preaching the resurrection of Christ, if there is in fact no resurrection, is that the preaching of the apostles was in vain in the sense that it was sham and hypocrisy. There was form to the preaching and a certain kind of logic inherent in it, but in the absence of truth it was without content and empty of significance. Correspondingly, the faith that the Corinthians had placed in the gospel was also empty. While the apostles preached a lie, the Corinthians believed the falsehood. The latter might have been less guilty than the former, but both were together in the fruitlessness of the preaching and believing tasks.

15:15 A fourth difficulty involves not only the fruitlessness of preaching but the falsity of the witness provided. Interestingly, Paul stressed that the falsehood involved here was of much greater consequence than that of one man's simply deceiving another about temporal or material matters. For one to misrepresent the things of God, regardless of his motive, is the most degrading of all possible falsehoods. The potential for harm involves the fact that the consequences of such a falsehood may not only affect this life but also whatever existence may follow upon physical death. In addition, the nature of the falsehood relates to the most sacred of all relationships—i.e., the relationship between creature and Creator. The possibility that Paul and others would be found to be false witnesses of God is certain if there is no resurrection because they had clearly testified that God had raised Christ from the dead. The expression "we are found" suggests the possibility of investigation. If, upon investigation, it is certain that the dead do not rise, the duplicity of the apostles would surely be discovered since, in fact, they had testified that God raised up Jesus, whom in fact He has not raised.

15:16 At first this verse may seem to be merely a restatement of verse 13, which it is, but Paul's purpose marks the use of a forensic device in which one repeats his major premise in order to be certain that the listener follows the logic. Consequently, the reader is simply reminded once more that if it is a foregone conclusion that the dead do not rise, then the impossibility of resurrection must be applicable to Christ also.

15:17 The fifth inevitable conclusion is unfolded. If Christ had not been raised and the Corinthians' faith was in vain, then they were also still in their sins. This pregnant analysis seems to indicate that salvation through a resurrected Christ not only provided forgiveness for sin but in some significant way also extricated him from sin. The way in which believers are pictured as being extricated from their sins is not that of sinless perfection—a doctrine clearly repudiated by the New Testament—but rather a removal from the overwhelming influence of sin. While believers are still sinners, the power of enslaving sin is somehow broken through the death and resurrection of Christ. However, if there is no resurrection, then the Corinthians, like all other men, were left to flounder in their sins.

15:18 Thus far the consequences which would inevitably follow if there is no resurrection are appalling, but in this verse the apostle Paul also began to reveal the certain confrontation every soul faces with the last enemy—death. The sixth consequence would be that those who have fallen asleep in Christ are, in fact, "perished." Again the terminology is exceptionally vivid. "Sleep in Christ" implies safety, serenity, and confident faith. It also was a reminder to the Corinthians that the faith of those who had believed was definitely a faith in the Christ who would not only forgive them but also raise them up in the last day. If the dead did not rise, then those people who so placed their faith in Christ had perished, and the Corinthians would know them no more.

15:19 The sixth observation related to the life to come, but the seventh and final one, calls attention to the present life: if we have hope in this life only, then of all people Christians are the most miserable because they have gullibly embraced the ultimate falsehood. "Miserable" (*eleeinoteros*) literally means "to have mercy on" or "to be pitied." In this case the latter catches the meaning better than the King James Version translation "miserable," which implies unhappiness.

In the event that the resurrection were not, in fact, true, Christians would, for the most part, still be appreciably less miserable than their pagan neighbors. The concepts bound up in Christian ethics are designed to make life fruitful and happy to a degree far greater than what is normally attained by members of society in general. So the sense of the verse is not that Christians would have a miserable physical existence if the resurrection were not real but, rather, that they are to be pitied above all other people in their gullibility and imminent disappointment. Having devoted their lives to the service of One whom they hope to see and adore in ages to come, they would, in fact, experience no resurrection at all.

3. Unconquerability of the Resurrection (15:20–34)

In this section we see Christ, the first fruits (vv. 20–25), the crisis in death (vv. 26–28), and the challenge in conflict (vv. 29–34).

15:20 Although Paul had, for the sake of argument, allowed the possibility that there was no resurrection in order to enumerate the consequences of such a state, he now wished to reaffirm the resurrection so that there can be no question of the truth. Therefore, he boldly stated that Christ had, in fact, risen from the dead. However, this affirmation had already been made in the early part of the chapter.

What is new in this verse is the connection of the resurrection of Christ to that of the individual believer. Paul concluded that through his resurrection Christ had become the "first fruits" (*aparchē*, combining *archē*, meaning "the beginning," and the preposition *apo*, meaning "from"), thus giving the sense of "from the beginning" or "first." *Aparchē* is a word distinctly associated with the Jewish sacrificial system. The Jews were to bring the first of their flocks or of the harvest of the field as a sacrifice to God out of gratitude for His provision. The word, though it does not actually employ the word "fruits" in its makeup, came to be understood as "first fruits" in the sense of being first or from the beginning. Christ, then, was the "first fruits" of those who slept. He Himself had the experience of the sleep of death as a result of his crucifixion, but in His triumphant resurrection He not only was raised from the dead but also provided promise of the future triumph of all others who would follow him.

15:21 The theological underpinnings of this conclusion date back to the fall. Since through man came death, likewise through man would be resurrection from the dead. There are two important notes to be made. First, the verse is a clear declaration of the full humanity of Jesus Christ. Orthodox doctrine more often has to defend the full deity of Christ and so can become imbalanced on occasion in the pursuit of that defense. However, evangelical doctrine insists on both His humanity and His deity. This verse makes it clear that it was the man Jesus who was raised from the dead. Indeed, such has to be the case since it is impossible for God to die. This is not intended to posit a division of persons for Jesus. Jesus is one person. However, that one person had two distinct natures—human and divine—and by virtue of definition God cannot die. Thus the verse constitutes a strong affirmation of His full humanity.

In the second place, the first phrase of the verse also is instructive in understanding the problem of the origin of sin. It is not possible to attribute sin to God. Sin occurs through the agency of man and his rebellion against God.

15:22 One of the most important concepts in theology is enunciated in the declaration that "in Adam all die." An equally important confidence is expressed in the statement that "in Christ all shall be made alive." The interpreter must determine precisely what is meant by these universal statements. The statement "in Adam all die" could mean any one of three things. The first view makes salvation universal in insisting that the same individuals are included in the two uses of the word "all" (*pantes*). According to this view, everyone follows Adam in death, but Christ secures salvation through His resurrection for the whole race that fell in Adam.

A second view maintains that the discussion here is not a discussion of the righteous dead alone. According to this view the affirmation is that all will, in fact, be raised whether that is the righteous to life everlasting or the unrighteous to eternal punishment. The verse affirms that just as in Adam all died, so as a result of Christ's resurrection there will be the resurrection of all men, even though in some cases that is a resurrection to damnation.

The third view is that the expressions "in Adam" and "in Christ" are the key indexes to the proper interpretation of the verse. According to this perspective the entire human race was in Adam, as Hodge would say, "in both representative and vital union."[69] Since the whole race has thus descended from Adam, all have inherited the sentence of death which was passed upon him. However, only those who are "in Christ," i.e., those who have by faith committed their souls to Christ, are the recipients of the resurrection from the dead.

The impossibility of the first view is shown in such passages as Romans 1 where Paul makes it abundantly evident that those outside of Christ are damned, and that justly so. Consequently,

---

[69]Hodge, *Corinthians I and II*, p. 324.

the apostle cannot have meant here that all who die in Adam are eventually revived in Christ. The second possibility, while perhaps impossible, is highly unlikely. The word "make alive" (*zōopoieō*) is never found in the New Testament as a description of the wicked subsequent to present life. Almost certainly this word refers only to those who are righteous. Furthermore, this entire chapter is devoted only to the discussion of the resurrection of the righteous. Paul knew of a resurrection of the unjust (Acts 24:15), but he did not speak of that in this particular passage.

Consequently, the third perspective, which sees the second "all" as not simply reduplicating the "all" who die in Adam but as referring to "all" of those who are "in Christ," must be the right one. Hence, the verse affirms that all men whose life has sprung originally from Adam will experience death, while all whose second origin or new birth may be traced to a relationship with Christ will be made alive in Him.

There are two additional observations that should be made. First, it is stated that "in Adam all die" (*apothnēskō*, which A. T. Robertson in his *A Grammar of the Greek New Testament* calls a frequentative or iterative present). Literally it should be translated "just as in Adam all continue to die." In addition, the verb is also in the active voice, indicating that man is responsible for his own death. In Adam, man keeps on dying. On the other hand, the second verb, *zōopoieō*, is in the passive voice, indicating that the subject is being acted upon. Consequently, while man brings about his own death, it is Christ, the second Adam, who is responsible for the resurrection of the dead on the last day.

There is one last question which must be addressed. It relates to the sense in which all men die in Adam. Obviously a portion of the result of Adam's sin has been passed on to the entire race. As long as there was access to the tree of life in the Garden of Eden, man did not face the prospect of physical death. The entrance of sin and the barring of access to the Garden clearly signalled the imminence of death for Adam and for his posterity. This explains the strange change of perspective in Genesis 2 and 3. The last verse of Genesis 2 records that the man and woman were naked and unashamed. After their rebellion, they were ashamed of their nakedness and attempted to fashion clothing designed to cover their reproductive organs.

Suggestions that our first parents had entered sexual union and were ashamed of this do not accord with the explicit evidence throughout Scripture that God, as the author of those sexual abilities, looks with great favor upon sexual union within the appointed bounds—namely, marriage. Other proposals, such as the idea that prior to sin our first parents had a halo effect which vanished and thus revealed their nakedness, simply do not do justice to the explicit statements in the Genesis account. Most often no explanation is given for the effort of Adam and Eve to cover the reproductive organs.

The explanation is to be found in this verse. Either by intuition or more probably by revelation, that first historical couple realized that they had passed sentence upon all posterity through their rebellion. The very organs that would be used to perpetuate the race, which should have been most prized, became the objects of shame because by them Adam and Eve would also perpetuate forever the memory of their sinful disobedience to God. The shame involved in constantly reproducing both the sin and its consequences in their posterity caused Adam and Eve to attempt to hide the reproductive organs from open view.

In what sense, then, were we included in the sin of Adam? What has been passed to all the progeny of Adam is not the guilt for Adam's individual sin. Much less are we punished for Adam's iniquity. However, in the fall man's depravity became a reality. No longer was Adam all that God had created him to be. Thus, all born to him were born with a weakness which Adam originally had not possessed. All his posterity was to be born with a proclivity toward evil which guaranteed that in time every individual would willfully follow the example of Adam and sin against God—thus, in Adam all are continuing to die. Happily, all who are in Christ will also be redeemed from that death and experience even the resurrection of the body.

15:23 The anticipated question of the Corinthians as to when this would take place is the next subject addressed. Every man is to be made alive in his own order. In this verse and following, we are provided with a chronology of eschatological events which provide specific information as to the sequence to be anticipated. Christ is declared again to be the first fruits. That resurrection took place three days after His crucifixion under the reign of Pontius Pilate somewhere between the years A.D. 27 and 33. Those who are Christ's, on the other hand, are told that they must conform to the "order" (*tagma*) that God has ordained. *Tagma* implies not only order but also succession, and, hence, it is seen that those who belong to Christ are resurrected at His coming. "Coming" (*parousia*) literally means "being beside."

Christ has been received into the heavens for the time being. Paul spoke of this time between the ascension of Christ and His coming as a period lasting "until the fullness of the Gentiles be come in" (Rom. 11:25). In other words, Paul saw an undetermined length of time which was to be devoted to the evangelization of the Gentile nations. Clearly in Romans 9—11 he anticipated still another period of time in which the nation of Israel would be the object of God's particular activity. Nevertheless, the time of the fullness of the Gentiles would culminate in the coming (*parousia*) of Christ for His own. This period also is pictured as preceding the kingdom age, which will be discussed in the verses to follow.

What happens to those who die in Christ prior to the *parousia*? Paul answered this question in 2 Corinthians 5, where he wrote of a state of "nakedness," by which he meant a disembodied state. The apostle believed that upon physical death a man's spirit went immediately to be with the Lord, alive and vitally experiencing all the glories of God's presence, yet in a disembodied state. At the coming of Christ his body also would be raised and glorified.

15:24 The next five verses focus on the kingdom era, which is generally labeled the millennium in prophetic studies. Following the resurrection of those who belong to Christ at His *parousia*, Paul wrote, "Then cometh the end." However, the addition of the word "cometh" in the King James Version text is especially misleading. The Greek text only says "then the conclusion" (*telos*). What is in view here is not the "end" in the sense of the end of a train, but rather "end" in the sense of concluding sequence.

Again *tagma,* which occurred in verse 23, prevails as the sense in which *telos* should be understood.

The last in the sequence of events here prophesied by Paul is the delivering up of the kingdom of God to the Father. Several important aspects of this declaration must be noted. The expression "the kingdom" has at least three distinct uses in the New Testament. First, there are those occasions when "kingdom" seems to be a reference to the reign of God in the hearts of men. However, it is a mistake to see this nuance as the primary use of the word, as some amillennialists have insisted. The second use of the word "kingdom" is in reference to the heavenly or eternal kingdom. Finally, "kingdom" is used to describe the earthly kingdom, and it is used in this sense here.

Paul had in view the same kingdom age which was prophesied by the Old Testament prophets (Is. 2:1-5; 11:1-9; Jer. 31:31-34; Joel 3:17-21; Amos 9:11-15; Mic. 4:1-5). Furthermore, this aspect of an earthly kingdom is also pictured in Luke 1:31-33 and Revelation 20:1-3. It is described not only as a period of one thousand years' duration but also as a period when peace will pervade the earth in its entirety, when the original productivity of the earth will be restored, and when the domesticity of all animal life will again reflect its pristine state.

During this period Jesus, according to Luke, will reign upon the throne of David, and at the end of the period He shall deliver up this earthly kingdom to God who is also the Father. This will not be done, however, until He puts down all "rule . . . authority and power." These three words may be references to earthly kingdoms, authorities, and powers, but it is more probable that the reference is to spiritual authorities and powers. For example, in Ephesians 6 the apostle Paul spoke of a warfare that the Christian must face with something far more devastating than flesh and blood. These enemies are described as "principalities" and "powers," which are the same words translated in this verse as "rule" and "authority." Actually there is a sense in which the kingdom age will subdue under the authority of Christ not only fleshly powers but also all spiritual powers. Not until all of these have been "put down" or conquered will Christ deliver the earthly kingdom to the Father.

Those who would suggest that there is to be no earthly kingdom age face insoluble difficulties in this particular verse. Nothing could be clearer than that a manifestation of the kingdom of God as here presented is not inclusive of the eternal kingdom. Hence, the kingdom that is before us here, which is also clearly depicted as a kingdom era existing after the resurrection of the saints of the church age, is one that shall be delivered to the Father and thus merged into the eternal kingdom.

15:25 This kingdom age is mandated, Paul wrote, by the necessity of subduing all the enemies of Christ under His feet. When Jesus came initially, He came as the Suffering Servant, but His return will be as the Supreme Sovereign. Thus, those whose hearts were not subdued by the mercy of the cross will find themselves subdued by the mastery of the Christ as He reigns upon His throne.

15:26 The last enemy to be destroyed is death. However, *katargeō* is not the word most often translated "destroy" or "perish." Its usual meaning is "to render useless or unproductive." The idea, then, is that death, as the last enemy of man, shall be cancelled.

15:27 This verse actually begins with an apparent allusion to Psalm 8:6, which prophesies the advent of Messiah and the ultimate hour when all things are placed beneath His feet. This allusion is indicated by the statement "when he saith." "Place under" (*hupotassō*) is a military term. Two interesting matters are clear in this verse. First, the quotation is from a psalm obviously written by a man but clearly understood by Paul to be the very voice of God. The antecedent for the pronoun "he" in the phrase "he saith all things are put under him" is clearly the God who is mentioned in the first phrase of the verse and who put all things under the feet of Jesus. Hence, God uttered Psalm 8:6, a clear indication of verbal inspiration.

It is also interesting to notice that Paul affirmed one exception to all that was placed under Jesus, and that is the Father who is the one who has put all things under the Son. This affirmation does not entail a subordinationist Christology in which Jesus is viewed as something less than God. It only means that the full work of Christ with regard to the salvation of the human family is accomplished in perfect obedience to the will of the Father and, further, that of the kingdoms of this earth, even the millennial kingdom, are ultimately subject to the heavenly kingdom.

15:28 Few verses have been more problematic to evangelical Christians than this verse which, at first glance, seems awfully difficult to square with the trinitarian emphasis. However difficult the verse may be, especially in its English translation, one must remember that the first rule of biblical interpretation is to be cognizant of both the immediate and larger context. In light of Philippians 2 and Colossians 1 and 2 particularly, there can be no question but that the apostle Paul was convinced that Jesus was God in every sense that the Father is God. Whatever he meant in this verse must be understood in the light of those lucid passages.

This verse does declare that when all things, including death, have been "subdued" (*hupotagē*), then the Son of Man Himself shall be subject to the one who had put all things under Him in order that God may be all in all. The problem, of course, is to determine exactly in what sense the Son will be subject to the Father. As we have already seen, it cannot mean that the Son is inferior to the Father in any way. He is not partial deity but is co-equal and co-eternal with the Father and the Holy Spirit.

The last phrase of the verse has suggested to some that the trinity has been a purely functional one rather than an essential one and that at the end of the kingdom era Jesus the Son merges with God the Father in such a way as to forfeit His own specific identity. Once again, however, the entire New Testament seems to bear witness to the contrary. The essential key to understanding the significance of the verse is to understand the nature of redemption as specified, for example, in Matthew 19:28: "And Jesus said unto them, Verily I say unto you, That ye which have followed me, in the regeneration when the Son of man shall sit in the throne of his glory, ye also shall sit upon twelve thrones, judging the twelve tribes of Israel."

"Regeneration" (*palingenesia*) is used in two different ways in the New Testament. In Titus 3:5 it is clearly used of personal regeneration, but in Matthew 19:28 it is just as clearly used for cosmic regeneration. Not only does this suggest a remarkable in tervention of God in the cosmic order of the millennial era, but also it indicates that the effects of the cross of Christ and His redemptive activity must eventually shelter every aspect of creation which was tarnished by the fall. Accordingly, the full redemptive work of Christ is not complete until the earth no longer brings forth thorns and thistles but rather is restored to its original productivity (Amos 9:13). Consequently, the millennial reign of Christ on the earth is actually the final act in the redemptive drama, since the redemptive drama called for the incarnation and the voluntary act of Christ in becoming a man who willingly obeyed to perfection the law of the Father in order to be able to carry the guilt of the race on His innocent shoulders.

Since the millennial reign is the last portion of the redemptive plan of God, Jesus, though He is the glorified and exalted Messiah, is nevertheless still acting so as to identify Himself with a race He came to save. As such, He continues to exhibit as the perfect man perfect obedience to the will of God the Father. By the same token, when the kingdom era comes to an end, the Son presents the kingdom to the Father and subjects Himself willingly to the Father as the God-man's last redemptive and intercessory act relating to the present earth. At that point in time it can be said that God is all in all.

This last expression is not indication of a loss of identity of any members of the trinity but rather is a statement reflecting the full experience of all three members of the trinity for every believer in that age. At the present, for example, Jesus is "preparing a place" for us (John 14:2), and we do not see Him. We do experience the moving power of the Holy Spirit in our lives, but in that day when all earthly manifestation of the kingdom has been turned over to the Father, the entire body of Christ will know God in a sense beyond what is possible here.

15:29 This verse overshadows most of the verses of the book as the one which most interpreters would assess to be the most difficult. However, the present author would like to suggest that the verse, when properly understood, provides understanding of an important link between baptism and eschatology or the study of the last days. The difficulty of the verse revolves around the strange expression "baptism for the dead."

Paul, in part, was clear enough in returning to an argument for the resurrection and saying, "if the dead do not rise, then what use is there for those who are being baptized for the dead to act out what they are doing?" We note here that whatever else the verse may mean it is a clear indication, as is Romans 6, that baptism is definitely associated with a proclamation of resurrection. Historically, it depicts the burial and resurrection of Christ for our justification. Eschatologically it points inexorably to the day when we face death, while promising that for the believer there will be a resurrection. Any form of baptism that fails to convey these two important pictures has not grasped the real significance of baptism. Affusion or sprinkling may be sufficient for the conscience of some, but only immersion will faithfully tell the story which should be conveyed in genuine New Testament baptism.

Possible interpretations concerning what is meant by "baptism for the dead" are as follows:

(1) "Baptism for the dead" refers to the practice of baptizing new Christians over the graves of those who have given their lives for the cause of Christ.

(2) "Baptism for the dead" refers to the practice of surrogate baptism in which relatives, deeply concerned about the eternal destinies of loved ones, have had themselves baptized in behalf of their departed loved ones. This view is one which has been picked up in our own era by the Mormons and extrapolated to the extent that many Mormons are baptized numerous times, frequently in behalf of relatives so far removed from them in their genealogical tables that they never even knew them.

(3) "Baptism for the dead" refers to the act of some who had been inclined toward Christianity but had refused baptism up until the death of a loved one who had been a Christian. The prayers and concerns of that departed loved one were sufficient to bring about conversion in the recalcitrant one who was then baptized, in a sense, for the sake of the loved one who had gone before.

The problem with views one and three is simply that there is no evidence for the existence of any such practices in the New

Testament church, nor would it seem probable that Paul would have mentioned such practices, had they existed, without in some fashion or another correcting them, especially in light of the careful correction given to other matters in the Corinthian epistle.

The second view, on the other hand, is totally unacceptable, since it is at two points in serious violation of the teachings of the New Testament in general. First, it supposes that baptism either saves or in some way contributes to salvation or at least that some merit is to be gained in behalf of departed loved ones through the water of baptism.

The New Testament could not be clearer in its affirmation that baptism has nothing to do with salvation. In Acts 10:47 concerning Cornelius's household, Peter said, "Can any man forbid water, that these should not be baptized, which have received the Holy Spirit as well as we?" It is clear that Peter was arguing that they should be baptized because they had received the Spirit; i.e., they had been saved.

Water baptism was never intended to have salvific significance but only to picture and proclaim the uniqueness of that internal salvation and regeneration which is effected by the Holy Spirit. In the second place, Hebrews 9:27 plainly says that "it is appointed unto men once to die, but after this the judgment." In other words, once physical death has occurred, there is no hope for making the eternal state of anyone either better or worse. Consequently, the passage could have no significance at all if theory number two were correct.

The problem with all of this is that if all three theories are eliminated, is there a fourth option? The riddle is solved by a careful analysis of the Greek pronoun *huper* and a reminder that the word *poiēsousin* is a future active indicative verb meaning "what shall they do in the future who are baptized with reference to the dead?" Clearly Paul was not talking about any baptism that had gone on in the past but about those that should yet be accomplished in the future. He was asking about the significance of such baptisms if there was, in fact, no resurrection from the dead. The Greek preposition *huper*, like most English prepositions, has considerable latitude of translation. When used with the accusative case, it may generally be translated "over," "above," or "beyond." When used with the genitive or ablative cases, it usually functions in a substitutionary sense and may be translated "in behalf of" or "instead of." It is an important preposition in understanding the substitutionary nature of the atonement.

However, A. T. Robertson notes that when used with the ablative, the word not infrequently carries the sense of "about" or "concerning." Examples provided by Robertson include 2 Corinthians 8:23, where Paul asked the Corinthians whether any of them wished to inquire "concerning" (*huper*) Titus, or again in 2 Thessalonians 2:1, where Paul spoke to the Thessalonians "by," i.e., "concerning" or "with reference to" (*huper*) the coming of the Lord.

Other examples are found in extra-biblical accounts in the papyri and in other New Testament passages (2 Cor. 7:14; Phil. 1:7; Rom. 9:27). Robertson also acknowledges that this is "perhaps" the significance of 1 Corinthians 15:29.[70] C. F. D. Moule acknowledges several cases of this use of *huper* also.[71]

The passage, therefore, should be translated "else what shall they be doing who are baptized with reference to the dead?" The significance of the verse is that baptism is always practiced with a view to the dead. It portrays death, burial, and resurrection. Paul's argument was designed to ask what possible significance baptism would have for those who in the future would become followers of Christ. Baptism is undergone with reference to the dead. It has to do with the picturing of their burial and resurrection. If there is, in fact, no resurrection, then the ordinance of baptism is the most superfluous of all New Testament practices, and the only sane option would be to follow the suggestion of some of the spiritualizers in the Reformation era who wished to eliminate the ordinances altogether.

Consequently, it can be seen that the verse has nothing to do with surrogate or proxy baptism—rather, it fits perfectly into the

[70]A. T. Robertson, *A Grammar of the Greek New Testament in the Light of Historical Research*, p. 632.

[71]C. F. D. Moule, *An Idiom Book of New Testament Greek*, p 65.

argument thus far developed, emphasizing the essential nature of the resurrection. Paul had argued already that for many reasons the resurrection was essential. This time he simply said that if the resurrection was not a fact, then baptism had no significance either.

15:30 Paul then moved to still another pragmatic argument. Not only had he asked about the significance of baptism, but he also asked, "Why is it that we stand in jeopardy every hour?" Paul's own experience had taught him well the sufferings that were the essential corollaries of the Christian faith—so much so that he had written "Yea, and all that will live godly in Christ Jesus shall suffer persecution" (2 Tim. 3:12). When Paul was a learned rabbi, he had the respect of the establishment and was able to function without fear of loss of life or punishment. However, becoming a follower of Christ placed his life in continual danger. The apostle thus asked the question, "Why, if there is no resurrection, would a man choose to follow a path in life that would automatically expose him to the danger of death at almost every turn?"

15:31 The word order in this verse is the reverse of the King James translation. Paul began by affirming "according to the day," or "day after day, I am dying." The reference acknowledges the inevitability of death and even focuses on the growing nearness of it. Paul used a strong expression to say that even though he died daily, he protested "by your rejoicing," a somewhat unusual expression making use of the word *kauchēsis*, which generally means "glorying" or "boasting." Paul may well have had in mind his glorying or boasting about the Corinthians. Even though they were problematic to him in some ways, still he rejoiced in the Corinthian church, and the very joy that he had in the Corinthians in Christ Jesus the Lord was a testimony to the certainty of the resurrection.

15:32 The reference to fighting with wild beasts at Ephesus is, on the surface, self-explanatory. However, expositors have been hesitant to take the words literally based upon the fact that Paul, as a Roman citizen, would not have been compelled to fight with wild beasts in the arena. In addition to that, some suggest that it is unlikely that he would have omitted such an incident in his list of confrontations in 2 Corinthians 11:23-27. Consequently, it seems more probable to most commentators that the wording here should be metaphorically understood.

Nevertheless, in keeping with the general approach of literal interpretation, unless there is something in the text to indicate otherwise, I prefer to take the description literally. There are instances recorded in which Roman aristocrats appeared in the arena and fought with wild beasts. As to Paul's failure to mention it in 2 Corinthians 11, there is no reason to assume that Paul would have mentioned all the difficulties that befell him. Furthermore, the Ephesian incident may not have been a one-on-one situation where Paul was alone in the arena against the wild beasts. Barring special intervention of God, Paul probably would not have survived such an encounter, since the general descriptions of Paul in the New Testament do not depict him as possessing physical qualities necessary to persevere in such an encounter. It is more probable that he was one among many in the arena and certainly stood a good chance of losing his life. However, in the graciousness of God he was preserved, though others may well have died when the beasts were unleashed. Paul was aware of the fact that that experience in Ephesus was the direct result of his work for Christ. If the dead did not rise, why should he subject his life to such danger? What possible advantage or profit was there in it? Instead, he should do as some suggested and eat and drink knowing that tomorrow one faced death. This last statement is an allusion to Isaiah 22:13 and 56:12.

15:33 The admonition of this verse is certainly applicable to the epicurean advice of the last phrase of verse 32. Whether Paul intended it as merely an answer to the advice that we ought to eat and drink since we die tomorrow or as advice relating to the entire subject under consideration in the chapter cannot be ascertained for sure. In any case, the apostle had repeated a proverb which was familiar to the ancient world. It occurred in Menander and was common currency in the Greek world. Some are troubled by Paul's adoption of such a proverb in the Scriptures since on the lips of Menander and other pagan poets, to say nothing of the man of the streets, its content could scarcely be described as inspired. However, it must be remembered that there is much truth in the world which may not have been given under direct inspiration. Certainly the Spirit of God could bring to Paul's mind an old proverb which was not only true but was also uniquely applicable to the particular problem under consideration. If so, what was merely a poignant phrase in the mouth of the orator became the inspired word of God through the pen of Paul.

The Corinthians were urged not to be "deceived" (*planaō*, meaning "to wander about"). Eventually its nominal form was used to describe the heavenly bodies, giving us our word "planet." Ancient astronomers noticed the mobility of many heavenly bodies and observed that they had no apparent fixity and that their courses could be altered. They were spoken of, therefore, as "heavenly wanderers," influenced by no one knows what. The Corinthians were urged not to wander away under various influences but to remain steadfast. Particularly were they told that evil communications were likely to corrupt good manners. While *homileō*, the word from which we derive "homiletics," the study of preaching or communications, does mean "communications," it also originally covered the whole company with which one communicated. In this particular context, as in the old proverb, the word would be better translated "company." The phrase, therefore, warns that evil company will corrupt "good manners" (*ēthos*, the word from which we derive "ethics"). This word is defined by such ideas as "place of customary resort," "a haunt," or "a settled habit of mind and manners." The latter sense is primarily the way it is used in this verse. The warning is that evil company will corrupt good habits of mind and manners.

15:34 "Awake to righteousness" (*eknēphō*, meaning "to act out of sobriety rather than drunkenness") is the flip side of the exhortation "be not deceived" (v. 33). The Corinthians were urged to act out of sobriety in a righteous way and to avoid sin. These instructions were given because some of the Corinthians did not have the knowledge of God. Paul underscored the seriousness of this charge by indicating that he spoke this to the shame of the Corinthians.

4. *Untaintability of the Resurrection* (15:35–49)

The untaintability of the resurrection was Paul's next consideration. He examined the nature of the resurrected body (vv. 35–41), the glory of the resurrected body (vv. 42–44), and the image of the resurrected body (vv. 45–49).

15:35 Despite the warning in verse 33 concerning questionable company, Paul knew that someone was still going to say, "How are the dead raised up, and with what kind of body do they come?" The first query seeks to ascertain by what force and in what manner the resurrection is effected; while the second question seeks to examine precisely what kind of body will be present. The second question is frequently voiced in evangelical circles, especially from those who have lost infant children or suffered the loss of loved ones in some accident particularly destructive to the physical anatomy.

15:36 Paul's answer reveals a certain amount of irritation with those who would voice such queries from a perspective of basic unbelief. The King James Version "thou" is not present in the text. Paul simply said, "fools" (*aphrōn*, the word for "mind" prefixed with the alpha privative and meaning literally "mindless ones"). The reason for such a sharp judgment is given in the easily observable data that follows: "That which you sow is not made alive until first of all it dies." The expression "quickened" (*zōopoieō*) in the King James Version speaks of life being produced by some external agent—in this case by God.

The general analogy Paul had in mind is that of sowing seed in the field. Although the analogy may at first seem irrelevant to the resurrection, more profound consideration will show that it is most reasonable. The Corinthian critics knew well enough that upon death the body began to decompose. They were also cognizant that decomposition continued to the point that at most only bones, teeth, and skull remained. Consequently, they wondered how anything could ever be made of such a state of decomposition. Paul's answer was that they had already observed a similar phenomenon in nature, partially at their own hand.

15:37 The analogy Paul employed was then given still greater specificity. The body which the Corinthians placed in the ground in the sowing of the seed was not same body that emerged later as grain. There can be no question that the seed sown had a definite organic relationship with the stalk of wheat produced; yet the two were quite different indeed. In fact, Paul was beginning to call attention to a rather stark contrast that would be further developed (vv. 42–44). "Bare" (*gumnos* or "naked") grain is sown. Rather unimpressive, a dried up, unlikely looking, unproductive seed totally lacking the verdure and vitality of the plant which shall emerge is placed in the ground. This seed may be wheat or some other grain.

15:38 However, God gives to every seed sown in the ground its own body according to His own pleasure. In our own era the ability of the human family even to begin to explain how enormous plants may develop from such unlikely beginnings has only begun with the development of genetic investigation. Even with the progress that has been made, there are still multitudes of mysteries bound up in how so slight a kernel can give rise to such a beautiful and helpful plant. All of it belongs to the planning and purpose of God, and He has acted as it has pleased Him (*ēthelēsen*, literally meaning "as he willed"). The analogy is once again especially apropos. While the Corinthians might have been unable to explain the precise connection between the body which is buried and the one which God raises up, God nonetheless has the power to raise the body just as He accomplishes such raising up every time a grain of wheat is planted. Even more significantly, just as God gives to the seed planted a remarkable body, so God will fashion, as He wishes, remarkable bodies for the believers He raises up. Furthermore, there is variety, since from every seed there is produced a distinct kind of body.

15:39 This latter point is now illustrated in two ways. First, it is noted that all flesh (*sarx*) is not the same kind of flesh; rather one is the flesh of men, another is the flesh of "beasts" (*ktēnos*, which primarily refers to the cattle, donkeys, and other beasts of burden), a third is that of fish, and a fourth is the flesh of birds.

The basic pattern for the development of these various biological species is the same. Actually, this verse constitutes a powerful anti-evolutionary avowal. While Paul recognized that the biological pattern for men, beasts, fish, and birds may have much in common, he nevertheless argued that there is a precise difference. They are different in plan, origin, and destiny. While there may be mutations and changes that are called evolutionary in the sense of microevolution, the possibility of macroevolution, i.e., major changes which link all forms of life together, is unimaginable and impossible.

15:40 A second example is employed with reference to heavenly and earthly bodies. As modern astronomy has discovered, celestial and terrestrial bodies have commonalities just as do the bodies of the biological kingdom. However, those bodies are also very different. The unproductive barren surface of the moon is decisively distinct from the verdancy of the Amazon rain forest with its multiplicity of rivers, and yet there is a wonderful glory associated with the moon just as there is a glory associated with the jungles of the Amazon.

"Celestial" (*epouranios*) derives from *ouranos*, meaning "heaven," and, prefixed with the preposition *epi*, it means "upon the heavens." The same approach is made to "earthly" or terrestrial bodies (*epigeios*, utilizing *gē* or "earth" with the preposition *epi* and meaning "upon the earth").

Further exploration of the solar system has revealed that no two bodies are exactly alike. Indeed, there is a wonderful lack of uniformity. On the other hand, it may well be true that since verse 41 concerns itself primarily with cosmic bodies relating to the physical universe, the heavenly or celestial bodies of this verse may refer to glorified and angelic bodies, while the terrestrial or earthly bodies refer to the physical body inhabited by the soul at the present time. If so, this verse is naturally building upon the foundation of verse 39, which has demonstrated that there are differences in the kind of flesh. This latter interpretation is advantageous in that it shows that there is actual substance, in some sense of that word, in the glorified body. One remembers that Mary Magdalene had to be told by Jesus, "Stop clinging to me" (John 20:17 author's translation). This post-resurrection appearance of Jesus demonstrates that His physical body had sufficient substance to enable Mary Magdalene to lay hold upon it. Furthermore, in one of His appearances to the disciples, He ate a fish and a piece of honeycomb, demonstrating the ability of the glorified body to interrelate with the atomic structure of other substances. Therefore, Paul's analogy that the spiritual or glorified body is another kind of flesh—namely, a heavenly expression of the body—would be very logical.

15:41 No doubt exists concerning the subject of this verse. The discussion here centers upon the glory of the sun, the moon, and the stars. There are few places where the significance of the word "glory" (*doxa*) can be any more clearly observed than there. One readily observes the luminosity of the sun, moon, and stars. This glowing radiance does not constitute the entire essence of the sun, moon, or stars, but it does belong properly to them and is that means by which we observe the presence of those heavenly bodies. By the same token, the Bible speaks the glory of God as the quality that properly belongs to God and by which He manifests Himself in the world even though it does not fully reveal His essence.

This verse anticipates the further development of the argument in the succeeding verses to the extent that it argues for a different kind of glory attached to the various observable cosmic bodies. So the resurrected body will have a glory all its own.

15:42 This connection is now clearly affirmed. Just as there are different kinds of bodies, each with its own glory, so also is the resurrection of the dead. Four avowals are made regarding the nature of this body. First, it is sown in corruption but raised in incorruption. "Corruption" (*phthora*) is often used to describe moral as well as physical inability and corruption. Both may be intended in the verse, but primarily the emphasis is upon the corruptibility of the physical body. "Sowing" probably refers to the burial of the body in keeping with the seed analogy which has already been employed so that once the body is dead, it is buried, already having begun its decomposition. However, what is raised from the grave is incapable of corruption, being no longer subject to decadence.

15:43 The second antithesis proposed is that the body is sown in "dishonor" (*atimia*), a word frequently used to describe loss of citizenship and, hence, humiliation. The physical body may be placed in the grave with much care and tenderness amid the accolades of admirers, but there is the necessity of disposing of the body. It is no longer fit for society and, hence, is in dishonor. The miracle is that its resurrection is in such glory that association with it is sought and cherished by all in heaven.

The third affirmation is that the body is buried in "weakness" (*astheneia*), normally employed to describe the accompanying inability associated with injury or illness. Here that illness or injury has taken its full toll and the lifeless body must be buried since it has no ability to continue to function. But the inability of the body to function at death is transformed in the resurrection into a dynamic body which knows no weakness and few limitations. "Power" (*dunamis*) refers to the energy or dynamic associated with a perpetually living body.

15:44 The final declaration concerning the body is that it is placed in the ground a "natural" (*psuchikos*) body. Some have attempted to argue a trichotomous view of the nature of man based on this particular verse. The idea in that thinking is that here "natural" (*psuchikos*) is used in contradistinction to the "spiritual" (*pneumatikos*) body that is raised. But if the trichotomous view of man is true, it must be established on the basis of other passages. As has already been demonstrated, the word "sown" refers to the burial of the dead body. The reference to that dead body as a *natural* body in no sense of the word argues for a distinction between a man's soul and spirit. If so, the reference here to a *natural* body would mean that the soul also was capable of death—a position untenable even among trichotomists. Far better in this particular place is the understanding that the King James Version translators had of *psuchikos*, simply translating it "natural body." They might also have translated "physical body" in contradistinction to the *pneumatikos*, the *sōma* or spiritual body that is raised up. Thus, the discussion here is not over the internal makeup of man but over the fact of two different kinds of bodies.

As Paul concluded in the last phrase of the verse, there is a natural body. Someday there will also be a spiritual body. Admittedly, the terminology "spiritual body" is something of an anomaly. The two words "spirit" and "body" were almost inevitably viewed as mutually exclusive in the Greek mind. However, Paul was affirming that there is, in fact, an entity that is authentic and observable, yet it exists in an incorruptible, glorified state that can only be described as "spiritual."

15:45 An appeal is now made to Genesis 2:7 where it is affirmed that when the Lord God breathed into Adam the breath of life, "man became a living soul." Typical of Paul's argumentation is a return to the support base of Scripture. Once again the familiar expression *gegraptai* emphasizes the permanent and immutable nature of Scripture as emphasized in the Greek perfect tense, literally, "it stands written" that the first man, Adam, was made a living soul.

In Hebrew, the word "soul" is *nephesh*, here translated, as in the Septuagint, by the Greek *psuchē*. Once again, however, there was no intent on the writer's part to enumerate the aspects of the makeup of a man. The contrast was simply between Adam, who was made a living soul, and the last Adam, i.e., Jesus, who was made a living spirit. Once again, "made living" is *zōopoieō*, meaning "to make alive."

15:46 The necessary order of these events, both in the life of Jesus and in our own lives, was reemphasized by Paul in calling attention to the fact that one does not begin with what is spiritual. The natural appears first and gives way afterward to the spiritual body. This state of affairs is true not merely with regard to the body but even with regard to the spiritual experience of a man born into this life. He is born a natural man but must experience the regenerating activity of the Holy Spirit if he is to become a spiritual man.

15:47 The contrast between the first and second Adam continues in the observation that the first man, or Adam, "is of the earth, earthy." However, it is interesting to note that the words "earth" and "earthy" are not the same in Greek. "Earthy" (*choikos*) is derived from *chous*, meaning "earth dug out and heaped up," "loose earth," or even just "dust." In fact, one might well render the verse, "The first man, Adam, is of the earth, dusty; whereas the second man is the Lord from heaven." The first Adam was merely fashioned from the dust of the ground, but the second man, the Lord from heaven, is raised from the dead with a heavenly body.

15:48 This contrast between the earthy and the heavenly is now pressed in verses 48 and 49. The first affirmation refers once again to Adam and his earthiness. Just as Adam was earthy, so all men in his image are earthy. However, the heavenly or spiritual body that was the possession of Jesus in the resurrection also becomes the property of the redeemed upon their own resurrection.

15:49 This hope is spelled out with great clarity in this verse in the statement that just as man has "borne the image of the earthy," so we will also "bear the image of the heavenly." The usual word for "bear" is *pherō*. However, a most intensive form of the verb *phoreō* is employed in this particular text, indicating continuity of action and demonstrating, according to Leon Morris, a habitual state.[72] The aorist tense is used in contrast with the future tense of the same verb. The aorist tense indicates that the former prospect—that of bearing the image of the earthy or of Adam—will eventually pass and give way to a new permanent image—namely, that of the heavenly. "Image" (*eikōn*) gives us our English word "icon," which usually refers to an idol or a lifeless reproduction of some kind. However, the Greek word means "image," "representation," or "likeness," but may, and usually does, include these ideas in a living expression rather than a lifeless one. Literally, then, the verse stresses that just as we have been a reproduction of Adam in our earthy bodies, so our heavenly body will be a reproduction of the glorified body of Jesus.

5. Unimpeachability of the Resurrection (15:50–58)

The final section of this treatise on the resurrection examines the unimpeachability of the resurrection. The resurrection is of such finality that it is not a subject to change in any way. Paul examined the habitation of the body (v. 50), the hope of Christ's

---

[72]Morris, *First Corinthians*, p. 230.

coming (vv. 51–57), and the heart of man's labor (v. 58).

15:50 The concluding section of the chapter is actually devoted to a discussion of the first question Paul had anticipated from the Corinthian critics. In verse 35 there are two questions: (1) How are the dead raised up, and (2) what kind of a body will they have? In a sense, he answered the second question first. Then he moved to a discussion of how this process would be accomplished.

First, there is the indication that the flesh and blood of the earthy body cannot inherit the kingdom of God, just as under no circumstances can corruption inherit incorruption. There are severe limitations associated with the physical body, such as decadence and mortality, which ensued once man was excluded from the life-giving tree of life. Paul's purpose in this declaration was to emphasize that there must be substantive change before man is granted access to the kingdom of God.

Earlier it was mentioned that the expression "kingdom of God" is one with varied meanings. Sometimes it means the reign of God in the hearts of men. Clearly that cannot be the significance here, since even though the kingdom of God is heavenly in nature, there is a sense in which the kingdom of God does exist within the hearts of fleshly men. By the same token "kingdom" cannot refer to the kingdom age or the millennium, since we know that the millennium will be inhabited in part by men living in their physical lifetime. The "kingdom of God," then, must refer to the eternal state or heavenly kingdom. In our present physical state, we are not capable of inhabiting such a kingdom. The question remains: how does the change come about?

15:51 In order to explicate the change, Paul showed the Corinthians a mystery. "I show" (*legō*) means "I say to you a mystery" or "I show you by means of statement." "Mystery" (*mustērion*) does not refer in the Scriptures to a mystery in the sense of unraveling a criminal plot but rather to an understanding which has been given by direct revelation of God. Inevitably, it is an understanding which lies beyond the calculations of the unaided human mind. It refers to something that could not have been deduced by the combined powers of all human intellects. If it were known, it would have to be a part of special revelation. Paul, therefore, affirmed that the following statement had come to him by just such a revelation.

The revelation was that while many will die, "we shall not all sleep," a euphemistic expression indicating that not all will die. However, all (referring to all true believers) will be "changed" (*allassō*, a verb meaning "to alter" or "to transform"). In Acts 14 it is translated "change," referring to the customs some said Jesus was attempting to alter. Again, in Romans 1:23 the word reflects what man did in changing the glory of God into the image of corruptible man. In other words, a major alteration is in view here. The passive voice indicates that some external force—namely, God—is acting upon those being changed.

15:52 All of this shall happen "in a moment, in the twinkling of an eye, at the last trump." "Moment" is *atomos*, from which we get our word "atom." At the time of the writing of the New Testament, no one had discovered how to split an atom, and it was therefore considered to be the smallest particle of matter. Accordingly, its use here is to indicate a moment so short and quick as to be absolutely indivisible. Further, the quickness of the event is described as in the blinking (*rhipē*) of the eye. The word may mean "blinking" or, as the King James Version has translated, "twinkling of an eye," an even quicker reaction, referring apparently to that incalculably fast flash of recognition sometimes observable to the physical eye. Whatever the case, it is apparent that Paul was emphasizing an act so instantaneous as to be almost, if not altogether, unobservable. All this shall occur at the last trump.

The sounding of trumpets in Judaism has had a long association with festive and/or triumphant events. The *shopharim* or rams' horns were sounded in chorus, heralding the action of God in crumbling the walls of Jericho. The Feast of Trumpets (*rosh hashana*) was the first day of the seventh or sabbatical month in the Jewish calendar. To usher in and consecrate that sabbatical month, the trumpets were heard in chorus throughout the land. References to this feast of trumpets are found in Leviticus 23:23–25, Numbers 10:10, and 29:1–6. Ushering in the sacred sabbath month is, therefore, typical of the ushering in of the ultimate sabbath of rest for the believer. The anticipated last trumpet sound was predicted by Jesus (Matt. 24:31), anticipated again by Paul (1 Thess. 4:16), and alluded to by John (Rev. 8:2). This trumpet call is the clarion mandate for the dead to rise, and upon its sounding two things take place in rapid sequence. First, the dead are raised incorruptible, and second, those who remain until that moment are instantaneously changed.

15:53 Paul explained that the necessity for this change is brought about because what is corruptible must put on incorruption, and what is mortal must be endued with what is not subject to death. "Put on" (*enduomai*) means "to clothe" or "to array." There is the hint of a favorable exchange to royal garmenture. Certainly that is the case in the shedding of the corruptible and the acquisition of a body that is not subject to decay and mortality. Both of these factors are critical in understanding the nature of the resurrected body. Not only is that body incapable of experiencing death, as our present physical bodies do, but it also knows no corruption and hence is free from any disease or pain. Doubtless this is the same body to which John referred when he spoke of "no more death, neither sorrow, nor crying, neither shall there be any more pain" (Rev. 21:4) because the former things will have passed away.

15:54 When this eternal state is finally ushered in and believers have received their glorified bodies, when the corruptible has clothed itself with incorruptibility and when what was subject to death has arrayed itself in indestuctibility, the word which has been inscripturated will be brought to pass. "Is written" is a major form change from Paul's usual pattern. Instead of the perfect passive tense of *graphō* (*gegreptai*), he used the prefect passive participle (*gegrammenos*). Once again, the perfect participial form not only indicates that something had previously been written but also emphasizes the perfect nature of that writing.

"Saying" translated the term *logos* or "word." The "word" which had been written would prove its fulfillment and applicability in that death will be "swallowed up" (*katapinō*, from *pinō*, meaning "to drink," and *kata*, meaning "down") in victory. Hence, "death shall be swallowed down in triumph." "Victory" (*nikos*, from which the American military has taken the name of its Nike missile) means "to conquer" or "to overcome." Death, then, is seen as being swallowed down in one triumphant overcoming victory.

15:55 The thought of Isaiah 25:8 and its marvelous promise wrung from the heart of Paul a taunting chant in the face of death. Literally, it may be translated, "Where are you, Death, the victor? Where are you, Death, the sting?" The words translated "death" and "grave" are actually both *thanatos*. Also, the order is reversed from what it is in the Greek New Testament.

The first question is, "Where is conquering death?" Obviously, it has been swallowed down. This terrifying enemy that so relentlessly pursues every human through the corridors of history itself has been vanquished from the field of battle.

The second question addresses death again in the figure of speech we call apostrophe, "Death, where is your sting?" "Sting" (*kentron*) refers to the sting of a hornet or the bite of a venomous serpent or the sting of a scorpion. Any of the above cause excruciating agony and pain. That same pyschological and often physical agony is the ominous threat of death, but the sting has been nullified and the serpent's bite rendered harmless by the conquering resurrection of Christ.

15:56 The sting of death is sin and the power of sin is the law. In declaring that "the strength of sin is the law," Paul was not thereby indicating that the law was sinful. In Romans 5 and 7, Paul affirmed the divine origin of the law and spoke of the commandment as being holy, just, and good. The problem was that men could not succeed in the keeping of the law—hence, the failure to keep the law made that good and holy commandment of God become the standard by which men were judged. In Romans 4:15 Paul noted, "the law worketh wrath: for where no law is, there is no transgression." The abysmal failure of man to meet the standard of perfection required by the law identifies man as transgressor and, therefore, as sinner. This is what Paul meant by the "strength of sin" existing in the law. The "strength of sin" refers to its power to inflict that numbing sting of death.

15:57 Both sin and death, however, have been nullified by the victory gained through the Lord Jesus Christ. As he concluded the lofty considerations of the resurrection, Paul could not help but express thanksgiving to God, who had freely given the triumphant experience of victory through the Lord Jesus Christ.

15:58 As a result of the promised glorification to come and the triumphant resurrection of Christ, it follows that there is impetus given for steadfastness and energetic labor for the Lord. Three activities were enjoined upon the Corinthians in light of the resurrection.

First, they were to remain "steadfast" (*hedraios*, derived from *hedra*, meaning "a seat"). Hence, the admonition was for the Corinthians to remain in a settled and constant posture, trusting in the grace of God. Further, they were to be "unmovable" (*ametakinētos*, a vivid term derived from *kineō*, meaning "to excite," "agitate," or "move rapidly around"). Prefixed to the word are (1) the preposition *meta*, meaning "again" or "with," and (2) the alpha privative which negates the whole statement. To be unmovable, then, means to be so steadfast as not to be subject to any outside agitation, excitement, or movement.

The first word, "steadfast," refers primarily to their own settled faith. The second word, "unmovable," refers to the lack of vulnerability to outside influences. Therefore, the Corinthians were to know precisely what the gospel was and what they believed, and then they were to remain impervious to the assaults of outside influences upon them.

Finally, they were to abound more and more in the work of the Lord. One cannot abound in the work of the Lord until he has reached that steadfast and unmovable posture which enables him to work from a position of strength. Once there, he will abound in the work of the Lord. This is to be done knowing that the labor of the Christian is never in vain in the Lord. "Vain" (*kenos*) means "empty." Though believers may frequently not see the immediate results of their labor and may even experience a feeling of futility, Paul assured the Corinthians that even here confident faith must prevail. The promise from God is that "my word...shall not return unto me void, but it shall accomplish that which I please" (Is. 55:11).

The Open Door

1. A Door for Collection (16:1-4)
2. A Door for Conflict (16:5-12)
3. A Door for Consensus (16:13-20)
4. A Door for Communion (16:21-24)

The final chapter of 1 Corinthians consists of the usual exhortations, announced agenda, and concluding personal observations. The insights into the life of the first-century church make such sections invaluable. While those interested in theological complexities may find such chapters less compelling, historians and those who want a clear picture of the activities of the first-century congregation will do well to observe them carefully.

1. A Door for Collection (16:1-4)

The poor saints in Jerusalem constituted the first order of business. Paul first discussed an offering for the saints (vv. 1-2) and then an official for Jerusalem (vv. 3-4).

16:1 "Collection" (*logeia*) is one of several terms used by Paul to describe the collection, which was obviously a matter of major concern. In verse 3, the same collection is called a "grace" (*charis*). Then it is described as a *koinōnia* or a "sharing" (2 Cor.

9:13) or a *diakonia* or "ministry" (2 Cor. 8:4). In 2 Corinthians 8:20 Paul labeled the same collection *hadrotēs*, meaning "an abundance," which probably reflected confidence that what was given would be an abundance.

In 2 Corinthians 9:5 the collection is called *eulogia* or "a good communication"; while 2 Corinthians 9:12 represents the offering as "liturgy" (*leitourgia*), referring to an act of worship. In Acts 24:17 *eleēmosunē*, meaning "merciful expression," is employed, and in the same passage *prosphoras*, meaning "that which is brought forward as a gift," is also used to describe an offering.

In this passage the word *logeia* basically means "communications." From these varied expressions, all designed to describe the generosity of those who would give such an offering, a rather remarkable theology of giving can be constructed. Out of the merciful expressions of hearts bound together in common commitment, motivated by the grace of Christ, a good communication is provided in abundance as an act of worship and service brought forward in a public expression of participation. Perfunctory giving out of mere habit or demand of law, therefore, is excluded in favor of a consecrated act of willing participation in the work of the kingdom of God.

This collection for the saints, destined for assistance to the impoverished Jerusalem saints, is obviously the same one to which other passages allude. The precise nature of the poverty experienced in Jerusalem is not entirely clear. It has been argued by some that the saints in Jerusalem were suffering as a result of their early experiment in community of goods. According to many, this program had quickly exhausted the resources of the church in Jerusalem and left them floundering and without adequate compensatory potentials. However, it is equally possible that by the time this offering was being gathered, the church in Jerusalem had been clearly identified as an offending sect excluded from the concerns of the Judaistic community. As a result, hard times may have descended, such as loss of employment and even confiscation of goods and properties. Perhaps it was a combination of all of these things or even other matters with which we are not familiar. In any case, the collection was an assurance that those who were followers of Christ were not deprived of the necessities of life. Paul was including the Corinthians in a mandate already given to the churches of Galatia concerning this collection.

16:2 The expression "the first day of the week" is important for two reasons. First, it indicates the plan for the accumulation of the generous offering to be prepared at Corinth. On that particular day, Sunday, every person was to lay up in his treasury to the extent that God had given him prosperity. This was to be done apparently on a regular basis on the first day of the week, so that by the time Paul got there a considerable offering would have been accumulated, and there would be no necessity for him to be personally involved in securing such funds.

The phrase "in store" is *thēsaurizō*, which is transliterated into English as "thesaurus." A thesaurus is a treasury. Chrysostom and other commentators were convinced that the reference was to something that should be done at home. However, if this were simply to be kept at home, it is difficult to see how Paul, upon his arrival, could avoid the necessity of involving himself in the acquisition of what had been saved at home. Consequently, it is better to understand that the Corinthian church had already developed a common treasury for the church. This would be in keeping, of course, with the methodology of Jesus, who appointed one of the apostolic band to handle the financial aspects of the ministry.

An amount to be placed in this treasury was not specified. Rather, it was assumed that the prosperity that God gave would be the guide. Clearly, the apostle desired everyone to participate in the offering, and he expected those who experienced the greatest material prosperity to participate to a greater extent than those who had less.

The second crucial observation concerning the expression "the first day of the week" is that this passage provides the first insight into an alteration in the day of worship. Much of the liturgy of the synagogues was maintained by the early church. There is evidence that for awhile the church continued its services on the Jewish Sabbath, primarily on Friday evening after sundown. Other indications would point to almost daily meetings of the early church, particularly in Jerusalem. However, by the time of the writing 1 Corinthians, distinctions between Judaism and the faith of Jesus Christ were becoming more apparent and solidified. To honor and celebrate the resurrection of the Lord, the Christians further precipitated this clear division by beginning to worship on Sunday, the first day of the week. The first indication of this regular practice is provided here.

16:3 When Paul made his promised visit to Corinth, he was going to send to Jerusalem the Corinthian "liberality" (*charis*) with those approved by the church through letters. In this statement Paul provided us with a second insight into the life of the early church. Not only did they now meet on the first day of the week in honor of the Lord's resurrection, but also the church was basically constituted as a democratic society. No mention was made of elders involved in selection of men to go to Jerusalem, much less of Paul's making such a selection. Rather, it is stated that the church as a whole would make judgment concerning who would go and testify to that judgment with letters commending them to the church in Jerusalem. These in turn would convey the generosity of the Corinthians to Jerusalem.

16:4 "If it be meet" translates the expression *ean de axion*. Most commentators indicate that *axios*, meaning "worthy," suggests that if the Corinthian offering were sufficiently generous, Paul himself would accompany its delivery to Jerusalem. On the other hand, if it were unsubstantial it might not be worth his while to go. Such interpretations are scarcely worthy of a man of such unselfish proclivities as Paul. More likely *axios* is used in the sense of "good" or "suitable." The meaning then becomes "if it is good or suitable that I go also, then those appointed by the church will accompany me." The record seems to indicate, however, that mature judgment suggested Paul not go to Jerusalem at this time.

2. A Door for Conflict (16:5–12)

The early church had learned to live with conflict. A door for further conflict was certainly open to Paul. In the second section he wrote of approaching Corinth (vv. 5–7), then alluded to adversaries at Ephesus (vv. 8–9), and concluded with the charge of assisting Timothy (vv. 10–12).

16:5 Paul's desire to pass through Macedonia is expressed with some determination. He was determined to come to the province of Achaia only when he finally had opportunity to pass through Macedonia. Robertson and Plummer suggest that *dierchomai*, meaning "to journey through," has become almost a technical term for a missionary tour or evangelistic journey.[73]

16:6 Paul suggested that he might remain at Corinth for a greater length of time than he would linger elsewhere in Macedonia. "Abide" (*parameno*) literally means "to remain beside." Paul might have intended to linger for a more lengthy period in Corinth for several reasons. The very problems which had arisen in the church reflected the need for his special attention in this church. However, that rather negative purpose may have been augmented by the fact that the church at Corinth for all its problems was the most successful of the early Christian efforts in Macedonia. The very fact that it was strong with the potential for being the hub of missionary expansion for all Greece may also have influenced Paul's desire to linger in Corinth. Then, too, the verse expresses a meteorological reason of an extended stay in Corinth. The winter months made traveling, especially maritime travel, precarious. Robertson and Plummer indicate that after September 14, navigation was considered dangerous, and after November 11 it ceased altogether until around March 5.[74]

These factors account for Paul's determination to spend a period of time in Corinth, after which he anticipated that the Corinthians would take him along in his journey. "Bring along" (*propempo*) literally means "to send before" or "to accompany." There were two possible ways to accompany someone. One's physical presence would be one of these, but in the inability to be physically present, one might also send provisions and, therefore, be-

---

[73]Robertson and Plummer, *First Corinthians*, p. 387.

[74]Robertson and Plummer, *First Corinthians*, p. 388.

come a participant in the journey. It is this second sense in which Paul spoke of the Corinthians as "bringing" him along on his journey wherever he would go. This is a particularly interesting phrase, since Paul had made so much in the book of having labored in Corinth without reliance in any way upon monetary support from the Corinthian Christians themselves. It seems, however, that at this point he was not only willing to accept the offering for the saints in Jerusalem but also willing to be assisted in his missionary journeys by the relatively prosperous saints in Corinth. This is, however, in keeping with what Paul had already argued in 9:7–18.

16:7 An immediate journey of Paul to Corinth was not possible at the present time. However, he hoped to remain with them for awhile when he did come, if the Lord permitted. "Trust" (*elpizō*) literally means "to hope." It was Paul's eager desire to be able to visit among the Corinthians for an extended time. Even this hope was conditioned, as always, upon the will of the Lord. The statement is a wholesome reminder that our fondest ambitions and our most determined plans are always to be subject to the express will and purpose of God. Care is always to be taken that there is not confusion between what constitutes our plan and purpose and what is the actual will of God.

16:8 The plans of the apostle called for him to remain at Ephesus until after Pentecost. The purpose of this was not to celebrate that Jewish feast of Pentecost but was prescribed, first of all, by Paul's preference for travel in the early spring and, second, by the opportunities that had presented themselves in Ephesus.

16:9 Specifically, these opportunities had to do with the opening of a great door in Ephesus. "Opened" (*aneōgen*), perfect tense of *anoigō*, indicates that the door had been opened and remained open. It is described as a great (*megalē*) door, which apparently was viewed by Paul as particularly open to his own leadership. "Effectual" (*energēs*) gives us our English word "energetic" and may be translated "effective" or even "active." On the other hand, almost in passing, Paul noted that there were many adversaries. The statement was not made as though great reflection was required. Rather, it is as though Paul simply knew that where the gospel of Christ was effectively experienced, Satan must be at work. Therefore, the door was wonderfully open, but Satan was woefully active.

16:10 Timothy had been sent to Macedonia and in all probability would come to Corinth. However, Paul was concerned that his coming be without fear (*aphobōs*, a word which might also be rendered "without intimidation"). The reference is an indication of the fact that Timothy's constitution may not have been as strong as Paul's and that in the past he had perhaps experienced some intimidation. Furthermore, Paul knew that since Timothy was his own emissary, he might face some of the wrath that would normally be directed toward the apostle himself. Consequently, the Corinthians were charged to understand that Timothy was involved in the work of the Lord just as was Paul.

16:11 Furthermore, no man was to "despise" (which literally means "to subject him to contempt or scorn") Timothy. To the contrary, he was to be conducted forth in peace, an expression that signals a warm reception and an eager participation in his ministry. The invocation of peace pressed upon the Corinthians with regard to Timothy was a further reminder that they were to receive him and conduct him on his way without rancor or dissension. "Peace" (*eirēnē*) gives us our word "irenic" and always indicates a settled circumstance in which there is absence of open strife.

16:12 Corinthian devotion to Apollos was the occasion for an earnest request on the part of Paul that Apollos pay a visit to the brethren in Corinth. The expression "greatly desired" is *parakaleō*, which is elsewhere translated "to exhort" and indicates on the part of Paul an intense lobbying with Apollos, based perhaps on the theory that since the eloquent young orator already had a considerable following, his presence might very well bring healing. The very fact that Paul so desired Apollos to make the pilgrimage to Corinth is indication that Paul knew that he had nothing to do with the Apollos party or with the schism which existed in the church.

Still another insight into the life of the church is discernible in this verse. Although Paul pressured Apollos to return to Corinth, Apollos steadfastly resisted Paul's admonition. Here is persuasive evidence that even though apostolic authority was certainly a powerful influence among the New Testament congregations, that authority definitely had its limits. The will of Apollos was not to come to the Corinthians at that time. The verse, as it is translated in the King James Version, suggests that it was not convenient for Apollos to come at that time. The word rendered "convenient," however, is *eukaireō*. A better translation would be "appropriate time" or even "propitious time." *Kairos* differs from *chronos*, which usually recounts succession of time. The significance of *kairos* is more often that of a chosen or special time. In this particular case the prefix *eu*, which means "good" or "well," has been added. One might even translate the phrase "at the right time," indicating that Apollos would come to Corinth when the Spirit of the Lord induced him to go. There is no information about Apollos' specific activities at that moment. In fact, it seems not to be so much the press of whatever he was doing at the moment as it was a conviction in his heart that it was not the appropriate time to go.

3. A Door for Consensus (16:13-20)

In the third section of the concluding chapter the apostle began by discussing the reign of love (vv. 13–14), proceeded to an examination of the righteousness of submission (vv. 15–18), and concluded with an analysis of the refreshment of fellowship (vv. 19–20).

16:13 Verses 13 and 14 encompass five succinct mandates. The four in verse 13 have a distinctly military overtone. Paul often viewed the work of the Christian in terms of military conquest on a spiritual level rather than a physical one. The first exhortation is to watchfulness. The term refers to attentiveness and vigilance. The specific object of this watchfulness is not declared, but since spiritual warfare apparently was herein envisioned, it seems probable that the watchfulness enjoined upon the Corinthians was an awareness of the approach of the enemy. In the face of that enemy, the Corinthians were also asked to stand fast or resolutely in the faith.

The interesting King James Version phrase "quit you like men" is a translation of one word, *andrizō*, which literally means "act like men" or perhaps better in this case "behave in the midst of the fray like men and not like cowards or youths." The final mandate, "be strong," is a rather mild translation of the verb *krataioō*, which literally means "to subdue" or "to vanquish." The sense of the word is not so much passive strength as it is aggressive onslaught. An offensive maneuver rather than a defensive one is envisioned. The first two mandates of the verse are defensive in nature. The Corinthians were to watch and to stand fast in the faith. The last two are activist principles that are offensive in nature. They were to enter the conflict like men, and they were to conquer or vanquish the enemy.

16:14 Unfortunately, efforts to accomplish the commands of verse 13 frequently precipitate behavior patterns that are less than charitable. Therefore, Paul reminded the Corinthians that it was essential that even the Christian's warfare be motivated by godliness. One might be watchful, stand fast in the faith, approach the conflict like men, and pursue the enemy, and do it all without love. The whole point of 1 Corinthians 13 is to warn against the impropriety of the exercise of spiritual virtues in the absence of love. Paul returned to this theme, insisting that everything be done with love.

16:15 Stephanas and his house were the subjects of the request begun in this verse and concluded in verse 16. The command actually occurs in verse 16, while verse 15 simply identifies the household of Stephanas as to its importance. *Stephanas* (Greek) is literally "victor's crown" and is transliterated into English as "Stephen." This household is identified as the first fruits of the ministry in Achaia. Others may have found the Lord chronologically prior to the conversion of Stephanas, but the household of Stephanas was the first full house to believe, and its members certainly were among Paul's earliest converts in Achaia. Not only were they of significance as the first fruits of Achaia, but they also had proven themselves through having "addicted themselves to the ministry of the saints." "Addicted" (*etaxan*, aorist of the verb *tassō*), has as its essential meaning "to place in order for battle" or "to appoint to any service whether of military or civil significance." Sometimes the word is used of the assessment of taxes. However, the King James Version's translation "addicted" is relatively rare. It is translated "addict" only once in the New Testament, and in the other eight uses it always means "to set" or "to appoint." Therefore, the vividness of the King James Version translation, while appealing, probably needs to give way to the translation, "they have appointed themselves to the ministry of the saints." "Ministry" (*diakonia*), as indicated earlier, is a term describing a slave who waited upon tables or who served essentially as a butler. The ministry to which they had appointed themselves was one of service rather than rule.

16:16 Nevertheless, this service to which they had appointed themselves was one which should have caused the Corinthians to submit themselves to Stephanas and his house. In fact, there is a deliberate play on words contrasting *tassō* of verse 15 with *hupotassō* of verse 16. While Stephanas had appointed himself to a ministry of service rather than ruling, the Corinthians were to appoint themselves under his leadership. The verb *hupotassō*, combining *tassō*, meaning "to order," with the preposition *hupo*, meaning "under" is, therefore, "to station oneself in rank beneath another." The Corinthians were instructed to submit themselves to Stephanas and to all others who worked together with Paul and to labor diligently.

16:17 Gratitude is expressed for the coming of Stephanas, Fortunatus, and Achaicus. Fortunatus and Achaicus are unidentifiable beyond the obvious fact that they were among the brethren from Corinth. Apparently they should not be identified as belonging to the household of Stephanas but rather were brethren who perhaps were sent as couriers of the letters from Corinth, seeking Paul's answer to the questions addressed earlier in the book. However, they had made an additional contribution. They had supplied to Paul what was lacking on the part of the Corinthians. Again, there is no indication of rebuke in these words. Furthermore, it is not certain whether Paul referred to the fact that, though the Corinthians could not come to Paul at that time, their emissaries had been an adequate representation, or whether the emphasis is upon the benevolent activities of the three ambassadors who may have brought financial or other material assistance to the apostle. In some way or another the three had proven to be of real assistance to him and were thus commended as having supplied what the Corinthians themselves were not able to supply at the moment.

16:18 A hint as to the primary nature of their ministry to Paul is provided in the statement that Stephanas, Achaicus, and Fortunatus "have refreshed my spirit." "Refreshed" (*anapauō*) basically means "to give rest again." When one has labored copiously and experiences bodily fatigue, the rest he then experiences results in a refreshed and invigorated state. The ministry of these three Corinthian emissaries to Paul was that of invigorating his spirit. Therefore, the Corinthians were asked to acknowledge this unique ministry that apparently was characteristic of these three men.

16:19 Acknowledgments were not made. The letter had been written from Ephesus, which was across the Aegean Sea from Corinth and was geographically in Asia. By the time of the writing of this letter, there evidently were a number of Asian congregations in the vicinity of Ephesus. Such would be, among others, Smyrna and Pergamos, to name the ones nearest at hand. Perhaps these are included in the salutation. "To greet" (*aspazomai*) meant more than just a verbal greeting in the ancient world. Some expression of genuine affection was involved in the word. This is indicated further by the holy kiss of verse 20. Of course, it was impossible for the churches in Asia actually to dramatize their affection for the Corinthians, but the very word employed carried that precise connotation and is far stronger than a mere verbal greeting.

Aquila and Priscilla (actually the short form *Priska* is used here) saluted the Corinthians, among whom they had labored diligently, as recorded by Luke in Acts 18. This husband-wife team, especially prominent as teachers in the early church, had a significant influence upon the ministry of Apollos. Aquila and Priscilla were joined in their greeting by the church that was in their house. Two important insights may be observed in this simple phrase. First, most of the churches were still meeting in the homes of the people at the time of the writing of the Corinthian letters. Aquila and Priscilla had continued to be at least moderately successful in their commercial endeavors. Hence, they were able to dwell in a home sufficient in size to encompass a church family also. One notes again the use of "the church" to describe the local assembly that met in their home.

The second observation is that this verse may hint that more than one congregation functioned in some of the cities. It seems unlikely, if a great door of opportunity had been open to Paul in Ephesus, that the home of Aquila and Priscilla would be adequate in size to house such a burgeoning congregation. Possibly in each city there was only one church, which met in several different locations on a regular basis and came together as a whole only occasionally. However, the language found here and elsewhere tends to indicate the greater likelihood that rather early in the larger cities, more than one congregation of believers came to exist.

16:20 The fact that all the brethren brought greetings to the Corinthians seems to distinguish these brethren from those who were meeting in the home of Aquila and Priscilla. This might provide further evidence of the presence of more than one church in Corinth. Not only were greetings extended from the believers in Ephesus, but also the Corinthians were to greet one another in an affectionate way. This way is described as a kiss of holiness. The custom apparently was observed by men kissing the cheeks of men and women kissing the cheeks of women. In most cultures the kiss has been a unique expression of affection and brotherhood. As such, it indicates a special form of familiarity and empathy. The Corinthians were asked, therefore, to be demonstrative in their expression of love for one another.

4. A Door for Communion (16:21–24)

The closing phrases of the book speak of the necessity of loving the Lord (vv. 21–22) and the saints (vv. 23–24).

16:21 First Corinthians was written with the assistance of an amanuensis or secretary. However, when Paul came to the concluding paragraph, he indicated that he had not dictated this but written it with his own hand in order to authenticate the message as genuinely his. Paul's handwriting apparently was recognizable to those who had previously observed it. At least a portion of this was due to the fact that he obviously wrote with larger letters than would be customary among ancient calligraphers (Gal. 6:11). Some have supposed that this was due to poor eyesight, possibly his thorn in the flesh, which may have resulted from the blinding light and subsequent blindness afflicting Paul as a result of his Damascus Road encounter with the resurrected Lord. This, of course, is all speculation, but it is clear that Paul's greeting to them was written with his own hand.

16:22 A period should definitely occur between the Greek expression "Anathema" and the Aramaic expression "Maranatha." "Anathema" corresponds to the Hebrew term *cherem* and refers to that which is set aside for destruction. "Maranatha" is a combination of three Aramaic words: *Mar*, meaning "Lord," *an*, indicating "our," and *atha*, which may be translated either "has come" or, perhaps, "will come." The expression may even be understood as a benedictory prayer translated "Our Lord is coming." Early Christian vocabulary developed certain ways of identifying other believers readily and also of expressing the fundamentals of the faith in a succinct way. The early Christian confession of faith, *Iēsous Kurios*, meaning "Jesus is Lord," was a common greeting which may often have been answered antiphonally with the phrase *maran atha*, meaning "Yes, and our Lord shall come."

The verse calls for division of humanity based upon love for the Lord Jesus Christ. If men do not love the Lord, they are ultimately to be set aside for destruction. This does not constitute a command for any sort of action on the part of the church with regard to those who do not love the Lord. It is merely an observation of the state that exists. Those who do not love the Lord will be set aside for destruction. This is to be noted especially in light of the fact that the Lord is coming.

16:23 The customary conclusion expressing an ardent prayer that the grace of the Lord Jesus Christ would be with the Corinthians was offered. Bound up in it was the recognition that whatever good was accomplished in Corinth would be done as a result of the grace of the Lord.

16:24 Especially appropriate is the concluding sentence in light of the fact that the message of the first Corinthian letter is confrontational in nature. Much of it must have been unpleasant for at least a portion of the Corinthian church. Therefore, it is altogether appropriate that Paul would conclude with an earnest expression of his own love. This love is made possible in the Lord Jesus Christ. "Amen," of Hebrew etymology and meaning "to affirm something to be true," is a fitting conclusion to the letter, since it is a mark of reaffirmation of the truth, not only of the immediately preceding statement but also of the entire message of the book.

B I B L I O G R A P H Y

Selected References on First Corinthians

Alford, Henry. *The Greek Testament with a Critically Revised Text, a Digest of Various Readings, Marginal References to Verbal and Idiomatic Usage, Prolegomena, and a Critical and Exegetical Commentary.* Volume III. Chicago: Moody, 1958.

Barclay, William. *Letters to the Corinthians.* Philadelphia: Westminster, 1960.

Beet, Joseph Agar. *A Commentary on St. Paul's Epistles to the Corinthians.* London: Hodder and Stoughton, 1892.

Bengel, John Albert. *New Testament Commentary.* Vol. 2. Grand Rapids: Kregel, 1981.

Calvin, John. *Commentary on the Epistles of Paul the Apostle to the Corinthians.* Volume I. Grand Rapids: Baker, 1979.

Colet, John. *An Exposition of St. Paul's First Epistle to the Corinthians.* London: Gregg, 1874.

Conzelmann, Hans. *A Commentary on the First Epistle to the Corinthians.* Philadelphia: Fortress, 1975.

Edwards, Thomas Charles. *A Commentary on the First Epistle to the Corinthians.* Minneapolis: Klock & Klock Christian, 1979.

Ellicott, Charles John. *Commentary on the Whole Bible.* Volume VII. Grand Rapids: Zondervan, 1981.

Godet, Frederic Louis. *Commentary on First Corinthians.* Grand Rapids: Kregel, 1979.

Gromacki, Robert G. *Called to be Saints: An Exposition of First Corinthians.* Grand Rapids: Baker, 1981.

Grosheide, F. W. *Commentary on the First Epistle to the Corinthians.* Grand Rapids: Wm. B. Eerdmans, 1964.

Hodge, Charles. *Corinthians I and II.* Edinburgh: The Banner of Truth Trust, 1978.

Hovey, Alvah, ed. *An American Commentary on the New Testament:* Volume V. *Commentary on the Epistles to the Corinthians* by E. P. Gould. Philadelphia: The American Baptist Publication Society, 1887.

Ironside, H. A. *Addresses on the First Epistle to the Corinthians.* New York: Loizeaux Bros., 1981.

Jones, J. D. *An Exposition of First Corinthians 13*. Minneapolis: Klock & Klock Christian, 1925.

Lang, J. P. *Commentary on the Holy Scriptures*. Volume 10. Grand Rapids: Zondervan, 1960.

Lenski, R. C. H. *The Interpretation of First and Second Corinthians*. Minneapolis: Augsburg, 1966.

Morgan, G. Campbell. *The Corinthian Letters of Paul: An Exposition of First and Second Corinthians*. New York: Fleming H. Revell, 1946.

Morris, Leon. *The First Epistle of Paul to the Corinthians* in the *Tyndale New Testament Commentaries*. Grand Rapids: Wm. B. Eerdmans, 1980.

Parry, R. St. John. *The First Epistle of Paul the Apostle to the Corinthians*. London: Cambridge University, 1957.

Robertson, Archibald, and Plummer, Alfred. *A Critical and Exegetical Commentary on the First Epistle of St. Paul to the Corinthians* in the *International Critical Commentary*. Edinburgh: T. & T. Clark, 1978.

Schaff, Philip, ed. *A Select Library of the Nicene and Post-Nicene Fathers of the Christian Chruch*. Volume XII. *Homilies on the Epistles of Paul to the Corinthians* by Saint Chrysostom. Grand Rapids: Wm. B. Eerdmans, 1969.

Smedes, Lewis B. *Love Within Limits: A Realist's View of I Corinthians 13*. Grand Rapids: Wm. B. Eerdmans, 1978.

Stanley, Arthur Penrhyn. *The Epistles of St. Paul to the Corinthians with Critical Notes and Dissertations*. Minneapolis: Klock & Klock Christian, 1981.

Thrall, Margaret E. *First and Second Corinthians* in *The Cambridge Bible Commentary on the New English Bible*. London: Cambridge University, 1965.

Zodhiates, Spiros. *Conquering the Fear of Death: An Exposition of First Corinthians 15 Based upon the Original Greek Text*. Grand Rapids: Wm. B. Eerdmans, 1970.

————— . *Getting the Most out of Life: An Exposition of First Corinthians 3*. Ridgefield, NJ: AMG, 1976.

————— . *A Revolutionary Mystery: An Exposition of 1 Corinthians 2:1–16*. Ridgefield, NJ: AMG, 1974.

————— . *A Richer Life for You in Christ: An Exposition of 1*

Corinthians 1 Based on the Greek Text. Ridgefield, NJ: AMG, 1972.

_____ . *To Love Is to Live: An Exposition of 1 Corinthians 13, Based upon the Original Greek Text*. Grand Rapids: Wm. B. Eerdmans, 1967.

_____ . *Tongues? A Study of the Biblical Record from the Greek Text*. Ridgefield, NJ: AMG, 1974.

_____ . *You and Public Opinion*. Ridgefield, NJ: AMG, 1977.

Other Works Consulted

Archer, Gleason, *Encyclopedia of Bible Difficulties*. Grand Rapids: Zondervan, 1982.

Blaiklock, E. M. *Cities of the New Testament*. Westwood, NJ: Fleming H. Revell, 1965.

Buswell, James Oliver. *A Systematic Theology of the Christian Religion*. Grand Rapids: Zondervan, 1962.

Criswell, W. A. *The Holy Spirit in Today's World*. Grand Rapids: Zondervan, 1966.

Criswell Study Bible. Nashville: Thomas Nelson, 1979.

Dandy, Herbert. *The Mishnah Translated from the Hebrew with Introduction and Brief Explanatory Notes*. Oxford: Clarendon, 1933.

Foh, Susan T. *Women and the Word of God: A Response to Biblical Feminism*. Grand Rapids: Baker, 1979.

Cryson, Roger. *The Ministry of Women in the Early Church*. Collegeville, MN: Liturgical, 1976.

Kaniel, Michael. *The Art of World Religions: Judaism*. Poole, Great Britain: Blandford, 1979.

Kittel, Friedrich, ed. *Theological Dictionary of the New Testament*. Volumes II, III, VI, VII. Grand Rapids: Wm. B. Eerdmans, 1967.

Knight, George W., III. *The New Testament Teaching on the Role Relationship of Men and Women*. Grand Rapids: Baker, 1977.

Liddell, Henry George, and Robert Scott. *A Greek-English Lexicon*. Oxford: Clarendon, 1966.

Lightfoot, John. *A Commentary on the New Testament from the Talmud and Hebraica*. Volume 4. Grand Rapids: Baker, 1979.

Morris, Leon. *The Apostolic Preaching of the Cross*. Grand Rapids: Wm. B. Eerdmans, 1965.

Moule, C. F. D. *An Idiom-Book of New Testament Greek*. London: Cambridge University, 1975.

Nygren, Anders. *Agape and Eros*. Philadelphia: Westminster, 1953.

Oden, Thomas C. *Agenda for Theology: Recovering Christian Roots*. San Francisco: Harper & Row, 1979.

Patterson, Paige. *A Pilgrim Priesthood: An Exposition of First Peter*. Nashville: Thomas Nelson, 1982.

Robertson, A. T. *A Grammar of the Greek New Testament in the Light of Historical Research*. Nashville: Broadman, 1934.

Ryrie, Charles Caldwell. *The Role of Women in the Church*. Chicago: Moody, 1970.

Scanzoni, Letha and Nancy Hardesty. *All We're Meant to Be*. Waco: Word, 1974.

Trench, Richard C. *Synonyms of the New Testament*. Grand Rapids: Wm. B. Eerdmans, 1975.